Helen Piper is Sen[illegible] the University of Bristol, where she h[illegible] undergraduate and postgraduate program[illegible] sible for numerous published journal art[illegible] and other genres. Previously, Helen Pip[illegible] as a theatrical agent and held a number of senior management positions at BBC Worldwide and for the Entertainment Group at BBC Television.

Popular Television Genres

General Editor: James Chapman

Television is the dominant mass-entertainment medium of the modern age. Yet, while popular genres in film have received much attention, their television equivalents have remained relatively unknown and unexplored. *Popular Television Genres* explores the lineages and taxonomies of fictional television worldwide. Written by experts in the field, each book in the series focuses on a particular genre or cycle of popular television. The approach is methodologically broad, balancing the textual analysis of narrative with the need to place popular television in its cultural and historical contexts, as well as analysing its critical and popular reception. Intended for use on television and media studies courses, *Popular Television Genres* provides informed and accessible reading for scholars, students and general readers alike.

Titles:

American Science Fiction TV: Star Trek, Stargate and Beyond
Jan Johnson-Smith

Beyond Dixon of Dock Green: Early British TV Series
Susan Sydney-Smith

Beyond the Killing: Contemporary Danish Television Drama
Tobias Hochscherf and Heidi Philipsen

British Science Fiction Television: A Hitchhiker's Guide
John R. Cook and Peter Wright (Eds.)

Saints and Avengers: British Adventure Series of the 1960s
James Chapman

The TV Detective: Voices of Dissent in Contemporary Television
Helen Piper

Up the Creek: Twenty Years of Teen TV
Hannah Ellison

THE TV DETECTIVE

VOICES OF DISSENT IN CONTEMPORARY TELEVISION

HELEN PIPER

I.B. TAURIS
LONDON · NEW YORK

Published in 2015 by
I.B.Tauris & Co. Ltd
London • New York
www.ibtauris.com

Popular Television Genres

ISBN: 978 1 78076 294 4 HB
978 1 78076 295 1 PB
eISBN: 978 1 85773 572 0

A full CIP record for this book is available from the British Library
A full CIP record is available from the Library of Congress

Library of Congress Catalog Card Number: available

Typeset by Newgen Publishers, Chennai
Printed and bound by CPI Group (UK) Ltd, Croydon, CR0 4YY

MIX
Paper from responsible sources
FSC www.fsc.org FSC® C013604

Contents

	List of Figures	vi
	Acknowledgements	vii
	Introduction	1
Chapter One	Broadcasting the Detective, 1992–2012	4
Chapter Two	Engaging with the Detective Character	23
Chapter Three	Residual Voices: *A Touch of Frost* and *Lewis*	44
Chapter Four	Ambivalent Voices: Moral Allegiance in *Prime Suspect* and *Cracker*	66
Chapter Five	The Reactionary Voice: *Life on Mars* and 'The Gene Genie'	87
Chapter Six	Emergent Voices I: *Wallander* and *Vera*	107
Chapter Seven	Emergent Voices II: *Luther*, *Scott & Bailey* and *Line of Duty*	122
Chapter Eight	The Resonance of the Detective	136
	Notes	156
	Bibliography	173
	Index	186

List of Figures

Figure 2.1	*Vera* 'Hidden Depths' (2011)	37
Figure 2.2	*Vera* 'Hidden Depths' (2011)	38
Figure 3.1	*A Touch of Frost* 'Held in Trust' (2003)	51
Figure 3.2	*Lewis* 'Wild Justice' (2011)	58
Figure 3.3	*Lewis* 'Wild Justice' (2011)	59
Figure 5.1	*Life on Mars* series 2, episode 8 (2007)	100
Figure 5.2	*Ashes to Ashes* series 1, episode 1 (2008)	104
Figure 5.3	*Ashes to Ashes* series 1, episode 1 (2008)	105
Figure 6.1	*Wallander* 'Faceless Killers' (2010)	112
Figure 6.2	*Vera* 'Hidden Depths' (2011)	118
Figure 7.1	*Luther* series 2, episode 4 (2012)	129
Figure 7.2	*Scott & Bailey* series 1, episode 6 (2011)	132

Acknowledgements

For some years now I have been able to incorporate crime series into my teaching of television drama, so I should begin by thanking a near generation of undergraduate and MA students for all the lively class debates. Thanks also to my colleagues at the University of Bristol, not least Peter Milner for so patiently answering all my random technical questions, Alex Clayton, Katja Krebs, Angela Piccini, and Kristian Moen for their support and advice, and Sarah Street for her helpful feedback on Chapter 4. Some short sections of Chapters 2 and 4 were previously published as part of an article in *Screen*, so a belated thank you to Karen Lury for her editorial input on this earlier piece. I am also particularly indebted to Esther May Campbell for taking the time to share with me her experience of working on *Wallander*, and to Anna Coatman for her editorial support.

Researching and teaching a subject on which everyone already has an opinion is one of the mixed blessings of television studies, but I have also been genuinely privileged in this instance to write on a topic about which so many of my friends and family have been interested. I am especially grateful to those who took the time to watch television with me, particular Ava, who witnessed more Oxford murders than can possibly be healthy for a child of her age, and my mother, for suffering again several old episodes when, inevitably, she had 'seen this already'. This book has been a while in coming but thanks finally to Diane, and to Colin, Katherine, and all the other fortysomethings who so willingly enthused about *Life on Mars* at the school gate, who may now be reassured that reminiscing about flares, Wagon Wheels and Party Seven need not be time wasted.

Introduction

Of all the fictional characters that populate British television there are few as frequently encountered yet as richly varied as the police detective. Investigation, a structure that permits endless permutation, may be a common enough premise in all narrative art forms, but it is the episodic possibilities that a regular caseload can provide that has made the policeman's lot so perfectly suited to broadcasting. This study explores an influential raft of British crime series from 1992 to 2012 for which a particular type of returning protagonist is the common denominator. Such figures may be defined as investigators working (however nominally) alongside a police team, and thus quite different in class and constitution to the well-heeled amateur sleuth of the 'heritage whodunnit'. Officially licensed to detect and remedy injustice, they are yet at one crucial ethical remove from the state, often in regular conflict with authority themselves. If this sounds in some ways predictable, the creations themselves are not: indeed they have distinctive personae, instantly recognisable to many by name. For these reasons the ambition of this study will be both particular and general, designed to interrogate specific questions of form, aesthetics and idiosyncratic personality, but within a conceptual frame that foregrounds their shared social, cultural and market significance.

The emphasis on Britain is strategic rather than parochial, recognising that television crime fiction has a distinctively national flavour. Acts of crime, like day-to-day policing, are territorial in form, although 'crime' (as an abstraction) may also be considered to be emblematic of broader malaise, a litmus test of social morality. A premise here is that fictive investigations may therefore be understood as microcosmic, extending the question 'what went wrong?' beyond the text and inviting audiences to reflect more broadly on the social world around them. Such a mode of reflection may be national in its particular inflection yet still cross-cultural in its potential, and the conceptual and critical perspective developed here will also lend itself to application in other local and national contexts. It is sometimes said that good stories might travel but they always come from somewhere, and in the words of the late television writer, Alan Plater, we may yet hope that 'the proper decent future for world television should be based on a very simple notion that I should tell you the stories from my backyard, and you should tell me the stories from yours'.[1] Whereas the focus here is on story forms told and received within one particular national 'backyard', it may be extended to others of comparable experience.

This book is one in a series about popular television genres, a means of classification I recognise in turn as broad, fluid and cultural, made meaningful by the presence of 'family resemblances' amongst texts. Although, as Jason Mittell has argued, '[t]he members of any given category do not create, define, or constitute the category itself',[2] past practice does routinely inform the strategies of creation, commissioning and production that bring ideas into being. Such assumptions of similarity are actively explored in Chapters 1, 2 and 8, which together elaborate a common historical and theoretical context for understanding the contemporary detective series and its significance. More particularly, Chapter 1 addresses the specific shifts and transformations of British television broadcasting since 1992, *apropos* the popular drama series as a cultural commodity. As it is a form specific to modern broadcasting, the police detective series deserves to be considered in its field of practice rather than glossed within a much-rehearsed genealogy of crime fiction. Chapter 2 takes up a critical-theoretical perspective, and interrogates some of the issues for academic television studies that are raised by the privileging of a common character type, such as whether it is viable to conceptualise television detectives as 'heroes' or to anticipate moral and emotional viewer responses from the programmes as texts. Thereafter a number of the shows already encountered will be explored in detail. Chapters 3, 4 and 5 focus on key series that collectively span the 20-year period, namely *A Touch of Frost*, *Lewis*, *Prime Suspect*, *Cracker* and *Life on Mars*. Chapters 6 and 7 continue this approach, this time providing comparative critiques of shows as similar and different to one another as *Wallander* and *Vera*, *Luther* and *Scott & Bailey*, that have been selected to demonstrate aesthetic directions and the emergence of new 'voices', concluding with reference to the emblematic example of *Line of Duty*. Ultimately, Chapter 8 returns us to more general issues by reflecting on the broader cultural significance of the TV detective series in the context of contemporary discourses about place, nation, crime, policing and deviance.

Finally, I should add that, concerned as I might be about a broadcasting environment that discourages creative risk, I attach no particular cultural value to generic self-distinction. Simply valorising novelty over repetition makes for a rather limited set of critical criteria, but self-evidently, as Creeber notes, '[i]f all detective stories were identical then the genre would soon become redundant'.[3] Whereas one aim of this book is to attend to the artistic strategies of these often critically undervalued series, this is always with a mind to their potential use, exchange *and* cultural value. Television is always repetitious in its forms, and it is through reiteration as well as surprise that a detective 'voice' might catch attention, work through anxieties, challenge social orthodoxies and – with surprising frequency – articulate profound dissatisfaction with the world around us.

1

Broadcasting the Detective, 1992–2012

For scholars, broadcast television has always been a moving object. At first it was the programmes that seemed to defy: live, unrecoverable, ephemeral, seemingly undeserving of the close attention that film was seen to warrant. Today it is the apparatus that eludes the pause button; politically and economically complex markets, ever multiplying channels, platforms and delivery systems, rapidly shifting modes of participation and engagement. Aware that this could all amount to a research object no longer simply in transit but approaching oblivion, the broader academic field of television studies has lately taken a reflexive, even solipsistic turn, mourning its own loss of radicalism as a discipline,[1] struggling with the obligation to maintain a political-theoretical agenda in a 'post-television' era[2] and generally acknowledging the need to change tactics – perhaps, as Charlotte Brunsdon suggests, to reinscribe the medium 'diachronically, within a series of histories' rather than continuing the early attempt to 'characterize its specificity'.[3] If television will not stay still long enough for us to puzzle over what 'it' *is*, we must look backwards and contextualise its cycles of perpetual motion.

I too shall adopt a diachronic approach and begin by relating a number of key developments since 1992 which have been significant to the most recent generation of British television detective series. Amongst other concerns, this chapter will address the exchange value of crime drama, as construed through the strategies of the television personnel who are described by Georgina Born as:

> [A] category of specifically media intellectuals whose task is to mediate the generic dynamics that bridge the past, present and future of media output. Their skill is in the art of judging how to progress a set of generic

> possibilities in given conditions, and how to balance the enhancement of the entertainment, pleasure and education of the audience.[4]

Understanding editorial decisions of the past will require a degree of imaginative recovery on the part of the reader, who must bear in mind that they may have been following a logic that has since shifted on its axis. Investment and commissioning choices were made in an atmosphere of tortuous uncertainty about the 'digital future', when it was not clear which game may be 'safe' to play. In such a context it is indicative that although, as Derek Johnson argues, the tripartite relationships between industry, viewer and text may have been entirely 'reshaped' by multiplatform broadcasting,[5] the market status of the detective series has remained surprisingly constant.

It is tempting, with hindsight, to assume that a continuous phase of intense development has followed a teleological trajectory, and so see as somehow inevitable its market failures or newly adopted technological norms. However, active choices are always made (and not made); a determinist history of technological innovation – in which causality is attributed to such possibilities as new digital spectrum, production methods and interactive capabilities – is only one available interpretation of the past twenty years. One viewer's riches is another's 'choice fatigue'[6] and, as I have argued elsewhere, for all the excitement around new modes of participation, audiences have also been characterised by nostalgia, anxiety and regret for a diminishing national culture of shared viewing.[7] 'Progress' is not an ideologically neutral concept, and many of the developments experienced in the television industry have also to be understood as consequences of deregulation, incipient power struggles, political attacks on creaking institutions, falls from domestic dominance and the globalising growth of the 'super-independent' and multinational.

Amidst such turbulence, it is worth recalling Roger Silverstone's pithy dictum that 'traditions may change but tradition remains'.[8] For BBC1 and ITV, as Britain's oldest television channels, the constant challenge is to reinvent tradition and balance familiarity with novelty in order to maintain large, cross-demographic, returning audiences. Typically, they might decant the proverbial new wine: a replacement set, 'shiny floor' or judge for the talent panel show, the resurrection of a forgotten format, a new role for a well-known actor or the introduction of a newcomer to an established serial ensemble. It is precisely such carefully metered innovations that enable them to maintain stability without stagnation, and infer continuity. The detective was, and remains, a key weapon in the programming armoury deployed in an adversarial, once duopolistic, struggle measured by ratings. As ITV and the BBC are still responsible for virtually all original British TV crime drama production, they will enjoy a privileged place in this account.

The Detective in the 'Era of Availability'

The 'era of availability' and 'era of plenty' are terms suggested by John Ellis in *Seeing Things* to characterise the second and third stages of broadcasting, once the 'era of scarcity' ended in the mid-to-late twentieth century.[9] Although loosely historical, they are suggestive of the residual and emergent phenomena of periods that overlap, and cannot be given clear start and end dates. Indeed, the two decades of industry development addressed here may actually be summed up as the progressive, if sometimes halting, arrival of 'plenty'. During this time two series that exercised a continuing hold on both broadcasters as market models were *Inspector Morse* (Zenith/Central for ITV 1987–2000) and *A Touch of Frost* (Yorkshire for ITV 1992–2010), and I will first introduce both as touchstones for this account.

Already an established series by 1992, *Inspector Morse* maintained its presence on British television up to and beyond the death of its central character in 2000. Unsurprisingly, the series has received a degree of academic critical attention directed at its balance of conservative with radical elements, noting its ability to succeed commercially 'without completely espousing the political ethos of its time',[10] and implied hostility towards 'the increasingly formalized nature of police bureaucracy'.[11] It is the series's reputation, summed up by Lyn Thomas as 'synonymous both with quality and mass popularity',[12] that is most relevant here, as quixotic aspirations for something similar have continued to inform the commissioning of new drama over two decades, *Morse* being an example to which both the BBC and ITV have constantly aspired, 'a form of television fiction which has become the goal of all channel controllers'.[13] Even though its measured pace and feature-length format were initially rejected by commissioners, in the mid to late 1980s Central Television had considerable leverage and guaranteed access to ITV peak-time, enabling it to take what was then regarded as a gamble. Ongoing vindication of the risk was quickly and readily to be found in the ratings success and financial returns that *Inspector Morse* brought to corporate ITV, not least by winning six BAFTAs (including Best Drama Series, 1992 and 1993) and being sold by Central Television to over 200 countries, securing them a Queen's Award for Export in the late 1980s.

Running contemporaneously, and appearing to track the changes of the last twenty years, is *A Touch of Frost* (1992–2010), a series that ran for a remarkable 18 years. Although it never quite attained the prestige associated with *Morse*, *A Touch of Frost* was also celebrated, not least with the populist National Television Award for Drama (2003), the BAFTA Lew Grade Audience Award (1999, 2000) and the BAFTA for Best Drama Series in 1995. Crucially, the series was a solid ratings 'banker' for the duration of its life, a prime example of those reliably performing dramas described in *Broadcast* as 'the backbone of ITV schedules'.[14] Although I will analyse *A Touch of Frost* more fully in Chapter 3, it may be useful to pause here for a snapshot of British television in the week of its debut in December 1992, and thereby to consider the aspirations of the industry with which it may have been invested.

As many readers will remember, in 1992 there were four UK terrestrial channels (ITV, BBC1, BBC2 and Channel 4/S4C) as well as digital satellite television services that had been launched in 1989 and were by then available in 2.3 million homes, either via satellite dish or by cable. *A Touch of Frost* was scheduled on ITV as three feature-length weekly editions, initially at 8.15pm on a Sunday night, picking up the strong inheritance of a one-hour episode of another long-running crime series, *The Ruth Rendell Mysteries* (ITV 1987–2000). Terrestrial opposition was lacklustre: the first episode of *Frost* had to contend only with a series on the art of comedy on BBC2, poetry and American football on Channel 4, and an episode of American import *Perry Mason* on BBC1. A glance at the rest of the week reveals the BBC's systematic weakness in reliable quality popular drama and how, being locked in to the *Nine o'Clock News* and a set of unexciting 9.30pm shows, it was able to offer little resistance to ITV's strong peak-time schedule. The latter is evident from the weekly data: in the week commencing 7 December the average viewer watched ITV for 11.5 hours and the channel averaged some 41 per cent of the total available audience, comfortably exceeding the BBC1 average of 33 per cent.[15] The very first episode of *A Touch of Frost* made it to number 20 of the top terrestrial programmes for 1992 with 16.8 million viewers, narrowly beating the most watched episode of *Inspector Morse* from the same year.[16]

ITV is recorded as having broadcast an average of 31 hours per week of 'Plays, Series and Serials' in 1992, compared to the BBC's equivalent average of only 7.65 hours of (non-acquired) drama.[17] Popular quality drama was clearly central to ITV's ratings supremacy and its post-*Morse* strategy of investment was crucial to its ability to sustain its performance. In 1996 the newly appointed Controller of BBC1 attributed the evident appeal of ITV drama to its emphasis on 'action, pace and everydayness', in contrast to BBC1 which, he supposed, had a rather more worthy reputation for being 'uplifting, reliable and disciplined'.[18] ITV success with police shows as diverse as *Inspector Morse*, *The Bill* (Thames/ITV 1984–2010) and latterly, with *Cracker* (Granada/ITV 1993–2006), was diagnosed pithily by Michael Jackson as the product of creative risk-taking combined with a relentless address to the everyday. It is significant that even by the mid-1990s the challenges for the BBC and ITV were still being discussed in metaphors of binary combat. If nothing else, the game then was simpler, and involved fewer players. In 1992 the first ever web browser had its first public demonstration, so it is reasonable to suppose that few viewers would have anticipated the full potential of the internet, let alone have been ready to adjust their viewing practices. Similarly, although television executives had the sense to be anxious about the future, 'other viewing' (as non-terrestrial services were summarised by BARB) then accounted for but a small proportion (5.6 per cent) of the audience overall. Knowing now how consumer technologies were poised to develop and proliferate, we might register the week of *Frost*'s launch – the ratings for which were broadly consistent with the annual averages for each channel – as the high before the inevitable fall.

Beyond the bald statistical data of the ratings, viewing habits in the early 1990s are unusually well-surveyed and documented thanks to a BFI tracking study that required 500 participants to keep a viewing diary over a five-year period (1991 to 1996).[19] David Gauntlett and Annette Hill's analysis of the research concludes that, although daily household routines varied, most were 'structured by a clearly organised schedule' or timetable in which television provided 'fixed marker points',[20] coinciding perhaps with a routine break (such as eating an evening meal) or because a particular programme provided a regular, anticipated pleasure. Although many households had more than one television set and some 36 per cent of adults had one bedroom TV, most viewing still took place in a shared space where it could be 'the centre of collective attention' by which families were 'drawn together, and sometimes divided in argument'.[21] Planned viewing rather than spontaneous channel hopping was common, although scrutiny of listings was most practised by those for whom television was more important as a leisure activity, either because they spent a lot of time in the home and relied upon it heavily, or because they were very selective about which programmes to invest with their time and attention. Student viewing, unsurprisingly, tended to be less premeditated and was often secondary to other forms of leisure.

Mid and late evening were the times when television received most attention, with expectations highest for the peak-time schedule, and if this was found unsatisfactory then it was at this time that households were most likely to choose a pre-recorded programme instead. In this sense, home video recording was considered by the authors to be more socially significant than new delivery systems such as cable and satellite TV.[22] By 1992, nearly 70 per cent of TV households were also VCR households,[23] but it was still possible to reference broadcast television as 'the inflexible party in the TV–viewer relationship' around which 'people's everyday activities are shifted, elongated or cut short to accommodate the programmes that they want to watch'.[24] Nevertheless the radical possibilities of the VCR for increasingly active time-shifting should not be under-estimated, and Gauntlett and Hill observed that those viewers for whom it was important to see particular programmes were effectively being 'cut free' from the fixed schedules. Creativity was attached to the integration of new technology 'into the unique texture and circumstances of their own life',[25] whether that was simply recording a programme that would otherwise be missed, rescheduling daytime or late night programmes to watch during the evening, watching a long programme in chunks or actively archiving programmes for posterity.

Interesting, with hindsight, is the speculation in which some participants engaged regarding the future of television technologies, with one respondent expressing a desire that TV should become 'more like a library' from which she could call up programmes of choice whenever she wanted. Another middle-aged male diarist noted the accelerating pace of change, even during the course of the study:

> In the near future our experience of television will be totally fragmented. At the beginning of these surveys [1991] technological innovation in TV was mainly concerned with video, satellite and the prospect of cable TV. Now [1996] we have such innovations as virtual reality and computers with TV quality screens. In the future – who knows, perhaps 3D, holograms and screens hung on the wall like pictures.[26]

If impending transformations in viewing practices were considered futuristic by viewers, they were also regarded with trepidation by terrestrial broadcasters, uncertain as to how consumers would take to them. The future secondary potential of the detective series was not yet fully realised, the TV sell-through market then dominated by comedy and sports compilations. However, the 90- or 120-minute feature length format was to prove very much in the detective series's favour, and ideally suited to the now ubiquitous DVD boxed set. Moreover, as a consequence of deregulation in the late 1980s, many European commercial broadcasters had attempted to reduce costs by acquiring blocks of feature films and reorganising peak-time schedules around 90–120-minute slots, prompting Roberto Pace to advise an industry audience in 1993 that 'the television movie as a format is one of the most saleable, the most presentable, the most successful ... formats in television'.[27] Whilst this could have damaged sales of conventional episodic shorter format series such as *Casualty* (BBC 1986–), it created an additional and lucrative market for the feature-length, episodic series. European producers were later to return to the one-hour format, but often in a more serialised form, to enable episodes to be packaged together to fill feature-length slots on a weekly basis.

In spite of growing distribution markets, broadcasting talk in the 1990s was often still fixated with domestic position-taking. For the two main terrestrial channels, further anxieties revolved around how to spread a commissioning budget over increasing hours and channel opportunities, and cope with the rising costs of drama production. In response to the challenge, the ITV companies maintained their investment in new high-end drama, a strategy vindicated by achieving 18 of the ratings-driven 'Top 20 Original TV Drama Productions' of 1993, a list that included six crime dramas.[28] Such investment was not unnoticed by the BBC, whose own channel commissioning budgets were later to be rebalanced by across the board 'cheese paring' designed to free up funds from routine output for prestige drama. Institutional confidence was at a historically low ebb, indeed John Birt was later to admit to realising, on arrival as Deputy Director General in 1987, that 'the organisation I joined had come very close to a nervous breakdown'.[29] The years in which Birt was Director General (1992–2000) were perceived by many as perpetual structural revolution, beginning with 'Producer Choice' and the reorganisation of the television service in 1993 into programme genre 'Groups', the most mighty of which were News, Entertainment and Drama. Charles Denton was appointed as the new Head of Drama, having been brought in from Zenith, the production company that made *Inspector Morse*. Denton's brief was allegedly to bang heads together, break up petty fiefdoms and develop an audience-oriented culture in the service of channel controllers' needs, prompting his early and public declaration: 'we are in direct competition with ITV for the mainstream popular audience'.[30] In spite of his initiatives, Denton was to leave in 1996, after yet more Birtist structural reorganisation (which separated BBC Production from BBC Broadcasting), under the cloud of the hugely expensive and high-profile ratings disaster *Rhodes* (BBC 1996).

Georgina Born's anthropological research into decision-making within BBC television was conducted during the mid to late 1990s, and testifies to the growing culture of managerialism and loss of autonomy for creative personnel. In one telling diary entry dated 1996, Born documents a presentation of audience research given to a sceptical gathering of Drama Group staff:

> She speaks of viewers' categorisation of drama into types: action, realistic, plot-centred, easy watching, calm, soapy, psychological, far fetched, demanding or cosy. Granada's *Cracker* and *Prime Suspect* have set the benchmark for demanding dramas. Under the heading 'What Makes a Good Drama?' she lists viewers' ingredients for success: good characters, involving storylines, believability, a good plot, it 'makes you think or doesn't make you think', stimulating emotions (tragedy, excitement, mystery or humour) or an interesting location or setting.[31]

The event was typical of many such crudely executed attempts by BBC senior management to persuade practitioners (with an intimate understanding of television aesthetics) to be more responsive to whatever sense audiences were able make of what 'worked'. As the balance shifted from the creative producer towards the market, the ideal of viewer satisfaction was used to justify the centralisation of commissioning responsibilities, and the replacement of certain editorial freedoms with a purchasing authority vested in the channel controllers rather than the Group heads.

Although there were some good reasons for the redistribution of power, including BBC1's undeniably poor record in popular drama, the poverty of insight in agenda-driven audience research was unlikely to ease the institutional tensions between a growing cohort of managerial strategists and editorial/production personnel. Born notes that the 'troubling' conflation of product sales techniques with public service ideals did at least subject such ideals to 'collective deliberation'. Audience research could be used fruitfully in some instances but also 'punitively to batten down and curtail the particular and expansive imaginative engagement required by good programme-making', the problem being 'that they were wielded by the new layers of management intent on justifying their existence and augmenting their influence and powers within the organisation'.[32] It represented a strategic reversal of Reith's famously paternalistic ethos,[33] and for neither the first nor last time the rhetoric of giving the public 'what they want' would be the means to a political end.

The drive to make production staff more responsive to the market did not bear immediate fruit, although the ratings performance of BBC1 was subsequently to decline at a far slower rate than that of ITV, and in 2001 the channel that had once enjoyed an absolute monopoly was able to reclaim itself as the country's most watched channel for the first time since ITV surpassed it in 1956. Critical and popular BBC drama successes of the 1990s included a raft of high-profile period and literary adaptations such as *Pride and Prejudice* (1995) and *Wives and Daughters* (1999). The reinvention of the classic serial chimed nicely with those public service values of which the BBC felt most secure, but the institution was more reluctant when it came to crime fiction. A notable exception was *Dalziel and Pascoe* (BBC 1996–2007), a series loosely adapted from the Yorkshire-set novels by Reginald Hill, and starring Warren Clarke and Colin Buchanan as the titular CID characters. Buchanan later claimed that when first approached for the role, he had thought it 'the worst idea in the world to make another detective series',[34] an indication of the wariness about a form supposed to proliferate indiscriminately on ITV. Such doubts were implicit also in the insistence that *Dalziel and Pascoe* would be not so much an episodic series as a strand in which, so its associate producer Nick Pitt claimed, 'each film would be highly authored and different from the one before'.[35] It is an ambition laden with literary-critical prejudice but a clear attempt to square generic popular appeal with aesthetic ambition.

Such tensions were particularly pronounced during the 1990s, when the BBC seemed to be constantly on the wrong foot, or as Born puts it, '[l]owbrow, highbrow; damned if it does and damned if it doesn't'.[36] Lack of 'reach' would undermine the principle of a universal licence fee, but blatant intrusions into ITV territory would be seized upon by those vociferously opposed to its market-based reforms. Amongst others, the Writers' Guild was a frequent critic of centralised commissioning and in 1998 joined forces with Equity to call for the government to examine 'the failure of TV corporations to invest in genuinely original drama'.[37] Similarly, in 1999 the self-styled Campaign for Quality Television (CQTV) published a report undertaken for them by the University of Westminster, emotively titled *A Shrinking Iceberg Travelling South*.[38] The report flagged key trends in television drama over the previous decade, such as the decline of the single play, proliferation of soap operas and series, and a more welcome increase in home-grown programming from the mass entertainment channels.

Most pertinent here is what the CQTV report identified as growing 'pressure for predictable hits, renewable series, recognised stars and "drama reassurance"',[39] and its declaration that '[p]olice/detective stories are now easily the most common dramatic themes across all channels except BBC2'.[40] Besides its unqualified citation of views from disgruntled practitioners as evidence of declining quality, the researchers' reliance on a limited set of fortnightly indicators produced some anomalous and inaccurate conclusions, such as the allegation that 'costume drama on the BBC has dropped dramatically',[41] after a decade in which, for others, it had seemed to reach saturation point. Nevertheless, it is an emblematic instance of counter-position-taking by a dedicated pressure group, and chimed with widely held practitioner perceptions. Ironically, some six months prior to publication the BBC had already raised the flag, with Alan Yentob declaring publicly that 'today, in television, to be popular is good, but it isn't good enough'.[42]

The Detective in the 'Era of Plenty'

By the turn of the millennium, the police/crime series had settled into its role as a mainstay of British schedules, with Mark Lawson likening the form to 'the postman in the Father Brown mystery, quite unnoticed as it goes about its work'.[43] Also in 2000, Inspector Morse himself met an untimely end from a heart attack ('The Remorseful Day'), a closure greeted as the end of an era by commentators, including Barry Cox of Channel 4, who opined:

> If one programme demonstrated the supreme achievement of ITV over the past 15 years, it was *Inspector Morse*. No other channel has offered a comparable standard of sustained, intelligent, serious and popular storytelling... We should be grateful that ITV still has David Jason and *A Touch of Frost*, which has the quality of Morse if not the glamour. We may not see their like again.[44]

'The Remorseful Day' attracted over half the available audience with its 13.6 million viewers which, whilst cause for ITV celebration, distracted from how ratings of the detective genre were beginning to disappoint. The pace of this was still gradual: over the preceding decade the proliferation of broadcast channels and other forms of distribution had led to an unprecedented demand for television content, but the industry was 'rushing towards an emerging era of plenty whilst the majority of viewers are still coming to terms with the era of availability'.[45] This same period has also since been loosely categorised as 'TV3' by Robin Nelson and others, defined by a distinctive 'conflation of influences (cultural, technological, industrial, social, aesthetic) with particular implications for TV drama forms and their production, distribution and reception under new circumstances'.[46] In the context of my particular concerns, the salient trends that Nelson charts are the increasing commercialisation and internationalisation of formerly national broadcasting organisations, markets and delivery systems, accompanied by an emphasis on 'high-end' quality product, marked by an enhanced visual style, a tendency sometimes crudely referred to as 'cinematic'.

The aesthetic development of television drama is usually more evolutionary than revolutionary, although, as Creeber argues, it has undergone 'a profound shift from the word-based aesthetic of the medium's formative years to an increasing emphasis on the "look" of a show and its overall visual spectacle'.[47] Such emphasis is facilitated by new technological norms that became commonplace after the millennium (a high-definition image, widescreen filming ratio, sophisticated post-production techniques of colour-grading) and resulted in new generic trends that I will address in later chapters, such as the use of landscape as spectacle. Jermyn notes of the early 2000s that '[w]ithin crime drama, the signifiers of realism had opened up to incorporate a "glossier" look and more "hi-tech" finish' and she cites the sixth and penultimate *Prime Suspect* in 2003 as an example of how the series revised its earlier dependency on 'a fly-on-the-wall documentary style to instead mount a thoroughly polished aesthetic, drawing on contemporary cinematographic effects'.[48] For a returning series to survive against new competitors it must keep pace with shifting generic conventions even if, as the example of *A Touch of Frost* will later suggest, a growing reliance on visual signifiers of quality may be accompanied by a retreat from moral complexity.

Less visibly, the deregulation of national television infrastructures in TV3 has facilitated the substitution of consumerism, choice and individual gratification for the collective, public-interest values of the past. The practitioner and pressure groups who sought to oppose the commodification of television drama in the early stages of TV3 argued that a ratings culture would lead ultimately to risk aversion, homogeneity, reassurance and predictability. However, Nelson's diagnosis of TV3 suggests that the opposite can also occur by shifting the balance of power away from distribution systems and enhancing the value of content:

> Thus there is a case for saying that the TV3 environment gravitates towards distinctive, 'quality TV' product in contrast with the formerly in-built industrial disposition towards mediocrity in former eras. The

> American networks and British terrestrial channels are forced to compete both in terms of audience strategy and to produce that 'quality' product the economically desirable audience segments are coming to expect.[49]

There are inherent complications here to which Nelson is not oblivious. Ideals of 'quality' are not reducible to a slick visual style: they are contestable and may be culturally specific. Moreover, small local and national producers may lack the funds and infrastructure to provide sufficiently high-value product and although, given the choice, most audiences tend to prefer 'home-grown content', it is nevertheless cheaper to import foreign product than to produce original drama from scratch. However, although Nelson recognises the potential dangers of a polarising market, he ultimately rejects the likelihood that 'high-end' drama will dilute the overall pot of available funding.[50] If we might take the specific case of the detective series as an emblematic form in TV3, the implication would be that its survival has largely been achieved through a set of generic developments that have been co-extensive with the trends Nelson identifies, not least budget inflation, increasingly high production values, sophisticated visual aesthetics and the sort of narrative complexity with proven appeal to 'blue chip' viewers. However, I propose neither to develop nor contest such a quality argument here: many of the series discussed in this book are long-running and overlap with one another and, in spite of growing aesthetic sophistication, there has been no simple progression within the genre from 'least objectionable programming' to 'high-end'. The detective form was already one in which talent, resources and aesthetic aspirations had been invested and a 'cinematic' visual style is no guarantor of enhanced cultural value.

What is clear in any event is that for British terrestrial broadcasters, the experience of TV3 has been one of progressively diminishing authority. Most obviously, the audience share of the once mighty ITV is now a fraction of what it was previously. From 1992 to 2002 it dropped from an annual average of 41 per cent down to 24.1 per cent, and by 2011 it had dropped to just 16 per cent. In the week commencing 10 December 2012, 20 years after the launch of *A Touch of Frost*, ITV garnered an average share of just 12.9 per cent. The share of BBC1 has followed a similarly downward trend, although it has been less severe, losing fewer of its viewers to non-terrestrial channels, and averaging 21 per cent in the same week.[51] Significantly, the collective performance of non-terrestrial 'others' shot up from 5 per cent in 1992 to 44.8 per cent in 2011, after which the performance of digital channels ceased to be aggregated by BARB. Although these data may now seem charged with inevitability, it is worth remembering the commercial uncertainties that attended the launch and early years of satellite broadcasting, a story that was played out again, not least with the collapse of ONdigital in 2002, and the subsequent formation of the Freeview consortium, which launched later the same year.

Consumer take-up of new services had been quite slow during the 1990s, particularly compared to other technological innovations in broadcasting, such as the take-up of colour television from 1968 onwards, and of video recording equipment (VCR) in the 1980s. Indeed, analysis conducted for the Royal Television Society at the end of the 1990s led to the conclusion that '[m]ultichannel services, for all their trumpeting about freedom to choose and boundless variety, have undershot even Teletext'.[52] Confirming consumer reluctance in October 1999, Chris Smith (then Heritage Secretary of State) elaborated the Labour government's plans to switch off analogue altogether, telling the RTS Cambridge Convention: 'The big dream is digital television, the bigger challenge is that it's a dream which 94% of viewers – your customers – do not yet share'.[53] Smith claimed moving from analogue to digital was a 'technical detail': the success of the digital revolution would depend upon the range and quality of 'new and better and more services at an affordable price'. Crucially, the plans he announced also included changes to the regulatory regime and the removal of so-called 'barriers to investment and expansion'.

Thus the success of digital was by no mean an inevitable endgame of consumer demand, but had to be secured by the Labour government's phased switch off of the analogue spectrum, a decision given the final go-ahead by Tessa Jowell in 2005, and which took place between 2007 and 2012. During 2007/8 the number of television homes able to receive digital (via cable/satellite or DTT) crossed the crucial 20 million mark, bringing free-to-air access to potentially hundreds of channels, a reasonable number of which were available via Freeview (although exactly how many a household might receive still depends upon its proximity to transmitters). In addition to the corresponding decline in the ITV1 and BBC1 audience, this growing roster of new digital channels also began to erode the previously stable shares of BBC2 and Channel 4, the traditional alternatives to the mainstream entertainment channels, making the latter also part of the collateral damage of digitalisation.[54] Of course, with switchover complete, the very opposition between terrestrial and digital becomes anachronistic as the five terrestrial channels, like all the others, are now only available digitally. Moreover, a number of so-called 'other' channels are already run by the BBC and ITV themselves, with repeats of ITV detective series providing the mainstay of ITV3, a channel that in 2012 was averaging a 2.5 per cent share of the total audience, making it one of the most successful of all the 'new' digital channels, a performance often equivalent to that of all the Sky Sports channels combined.

Increasing distribution opportunities have allowed the market for imported programming to grow significantly, perhaps bringing to recognition high-end police detective shows from other countries that may once never have found a home on British terrestrial television. For example, following its success in 2010 in broadcasting *The Killing* (Denmark, 2007–), BBC4 later showed

Inspector Montalbano (Italy, 1999–) and *Spiral* (France, 2005–) in the same Saturday evening slot. A few lesser-known American series also found a place in British schedules, including *Dexter* (2006–), some series of which have been screened by FX, and *Rizzoli & Isles* (2010–) acquired for the UK pay-TV channel, Alibi. Although digitalisation has clearly fuelled the number and volume of acquisitions (particularly of those shows which have an evident cross-cultural appeal), there is also a possibility that the circulation of detective programming around Europe has stimulated the demand for indigenous production of police and crime series in individual countries, quite aside from those changed format productions of British series that have been licensed and made in other territories.[55] Joost De Bruin notes that Dutch police series were virtually unknown prior to 1995 but the Netherlands has since produced successful series such as *Baantjer* (1995–2006) and *Spangen* (1999–2004) which repeatedly work though Dutch experiences of racism and multiculturalism.[56] From the mid to late 2000s 'Scandi-crime' became an international publishing, film and television phenomenon, the influence of which was evidenced by English-language versions of successful shows such as *Wallander* (UK, BBC 2008–) and *The Killing* (US, AMC 2011–). Although quality American drama series as varied as *The Sopranos* (1999–2007) and *The Wire* (2002–8), have also offered an aspirational aesthetic model since the 1990s, a very different set of national anxieties makes the influence of American television on the detective series a complex question, and one to which I shall eventually return in Chapter 8.

For both broadcasters and producers, the intensifying competition brought by digitalisation accompanied an increasing imperative to trade as sizeable entities in international markets already dominated by multinational media corporations. One obvious consequence of this was the amalgamation of what was once a loosely 'federal' organisation of ITV regional franchise holders. The takeover of Tyne Tees Television by Yorkshire Television in 1992 had been the first of a progression of mergers that subsequently took place between regional ITV companies and led ultimately (after complex trading and rule changes) to a single, unified ITV plc in 2004 when the final two giants, Granada and Carlton, joined forces. There have been various attempts by other corporations to buy ITV since then, including the contested acquisition of a 17.9 per cent stake by BskyB in 2006. Although filming for ITV drama series clearly takes place in any number of regional locations, the post-merger surplus of regional studio and post-production facilities has since been rationalised into ITV Studios, which now has only two main bases in London and Manchester.

The market in drama production has inevitably been transformed by similar pressures to those shaping broadcasting. Independent production had been set in train during the 1980s by the arrival of the first publisher-broadcaster in Channel 4 and stimulated by regulatory quotas for the BBC and ITV. During the 1990s a number of larger independents acquired more leverage within commercially significant genres such as drama and entertainment, often by virtue of their relationships with key talent, although it was really the digital boom that facilitated the emergence of what were soon to be described as 'super-indies'. After the Communications Act of 2003, independent producers became entitled to retain ownership of programme rights, thus allowing them to build up a roster of assets and free them from the patronage of broadcasters and the financial dependency of the fully funded commission, although with this came the need to self-fund ongoing development and organisational overheads. A number of independent drama production companies, such as Red Productions, Left Bank Pictures, Kudos Productions and Tiger Aspect, continued to develop strong 'quality brand' identities around successful drama rosters, although by 2012 most of these had been gobbled up in a frenzy of acquisition by media organisations such as Shine Group, Shed Media, Endemol and All3Media, leaving others to shelter under looser affiliations and umbrella networks.

Neither the proliferating broadcasting sector nor the emergence of an increasingly autonomous production sector has yielded an increase in the volume of UK-originated drama series. The critical mass of the British television drama production industry has relied upon continued investment by BBC and ITV, investment that had been justified as strategic by the duopolistic contest between them, even if they were also responding to other developments, such as the critical ardour which greeted American quality TV imports. Statistics gathered for a recent OFCOM market report show that investment in originated output by the top five channels actually declined by £500million between 2005 and 2011.[57] The commercial troubles attending ITV in the wake of its plummeting audience share and advertising revenues have been a particular matter for political and regulatory concern, and since being required to restore the *News at Ten*,[58] the broadcaster has made repeated demands of successive governments, notably for the relaxation of its public service obligations, the repeal of the contract rights renewal protection for advertisers and for legislative changes allowing product placement in programming. It also made radical efforts to regenerate its drama slate: series that did not perform as well as expected were cancelled quickly, others, such as *Wire in the Blood* (ITV 2002–8), were not renewed as costs began to exceed likely returns. In 2006, declaring that its departing chief executive had made ITV 'unwatchable' and 'like a bargain basement', the ITV controller of drama devised an autumn season around the revival of two of its once most prestigious series, *Cracker* and *Prime Suspect*.[59] Although critically admired, *Prime Suspect: The Final Act* was greeted with some despondency, one reviewer even using the very same phrase Cox had used to lament the death of Morse, when he too mourned, 'we shall not see her like again'.[60] A cycle of prime-time crime born in a period of near duopoly and commercial confidence seemed to be coming to a close, with little of comparable impact to replace it.

The example of *Foyle's War* (ITV 2002–) is also particularly apt in such a context. This series had originally been commissioned following an ITV call for *Inspector Morse* replacements in 2000, perhaps because its World War II setting suggested an equivalently heritage appeal. Although the new series did not attract the instant success of *Morse*, it enjoyed an approving consensus amongst reviewers for the intelligent, quiet 'understatement' of its star (Michael Kitchen), whose performance was described by Jonathan Meades as 'an unalloyed display of high art', albeit within 'the depressingly banal confines of yet another detective series'.[61] Nevertheless, in 2007, *Foyle's War* was cancelled before the sixth series had been aired, only to be recommissioned a few months later by Peter Fincham when he took over as ITV director of programmes. Although the new series was greeted somewhat hysterically by the *Daily Mail* as a vindication of people power, the likelihood was rather that Fincham had already recognised the folly of expecting a drama series to do more than deliver solid audience ratings of around 7 million (as *Foyle* had consistently done), and the continuing need for the channel to identify itself with prestigious drama series.

However, prestige alone was not going to reverse ITV's downward trajectory. In May 2009, after the axing of *The South Bank Show* (ITV 1978–2010) Melvyn Bragg warned that lack of action would 'kill off' the broadcaster, arguing that it had experienced 'crunch after crunch after crunch' whilst the government 'dithered' over the lifting of financial restrictions.[62] Profits continued to plunge, and in the same year Michael Grade announced an overall cut in its production budget, and 'an adjustment of the mix' away from drama to mid-week entertainment shows, complaining once again that current levels of investment in original drama were unsustainable.[63] For those series that did survive, budget constraints were often the price that had to be paid, as lowered advertising prices and ratings expectations meant that the cost-to-financial-return ratio had shifted dangerously. Interviewed in 2010 regarding the forthcoming finale of *A Touch of Frost*, David Jason noted the steady decline in programme budgets over the years in which he had played the leading role: 'We started out with lots of well-paid extras in the background of the police station, for example, and ended up with two guys from the lighting department doubling up as police officers in costumes that didn't fit.'[64] The final episode attracted an audience of 7.2 million, a relative success in spite of being less than half what it had once achieved: evidence, if it were needed, of the reduced profitability of even the most popular British dramas.

For the regular terrestrial viewer, however, the near continuous terrestrial presence of a series such as *A Touch of Frost* across two decades helped to provide a veneer of stability that masked the fundamental shifts in the power base and dynamics of British broadcasting. For such a viewer, change has not come in the content, budget, ratings or even forms of drama output so much as in the manner of its reception. By 2012, the widespread availability of sophisticated digital recording devices, 'plus 1' and selection channels, iplayers, YouTube, file-sharing websites, portable tablets and smart TVs had all massively extended the time-shifting, ease and customisation first offered by the VCR in the 1980s, and the rhythmic routine of weekly series viewing looked destined to decline, if not disappear altogether. Equally significant is the change in the nature and mode of engagement precipitated by on-line chat rooms and interactive discursive formats. Coming in the context of transformed work and leisure, the opportunities for participation brought by the rise of social media have profoundly altered the nature and tone of discourses that surround drama texts, turning television more generally into an increasingly mobile 'party turn' whose pre-eminent function may simply be to provide the characters and incidents that fuel gossip and on-line discourse.[65]

Although consumerism may have been discursively 'naturalised' as a self-evident 'end to the history' of a commercial/public service dichotomy, the full implications of these changing modes of consumption and performance have yet to play out. In the era of plenty, having ever kept an awkward balance between paternalistic public service and commercial interests, British broadcasting increasingly abdicated cultural responsibility to the marketplace. The transformation did not go unnoticed by commentators such as Will Hutton for the *Guardian*, who warned repeatedly of hostility to BBC values, a reluctance of New Labour 'to confront private business interests' in broadcasting[66] and again, some years later, of the threat to creativity posed by an increasingly large and economically powerfully independent production sector that would soon become 'the industry playmakers'.[67]

Elsewhere, the mood was with new free-market advocates, such as Elisabeth Murdoch, with much to gain from repositioning television as just another commodity industry for which 'the combination of choice and competition guarantees that the cream will rise to the top'.[68] Although Nelson's previously cited argument bears a superficial resemblance to this in its claim that competition in TV3 provides incentives to produce quality, he nevertheless maintains that, in many national contexts, the continuation of regulatory frameworks for broadcasting is essential to 'ensure the maintenance of diversity and to meet local needs'.[69] The ideology of consumer satisfaction is, in this formulation, still compatible with an infrastructure which supports rival ideals of collective interest, and in which the publicly funded BBC maintains a significant market share. Indeed, the folly of the absolutist free-market view had become clear, even to OFCOM, by the time they completed their second Public Service Broadcasting Review, the final statement of which notes that:

> despite two decades of multi-channel broadcasting, investment in high quality UK content other than in sport is overwhelmingly by the current public service broadcasters. There remain several areas vital to the delivery of public purposes where purely commercial players are unlikely to invest significantly in content for television or other digital platforms, because the returns are too low and the commercial risk is too great.[70]

Although the 1990s 'fantasy of the market as an anti-elitist machine'[71] seemed to have evaporated, so too had the appetite to raise more public money and the political will to challenge private interests.

OFCOM's final recommendations were to preserve key public service institutions (the BBC and Channel 4) whilst freeing up other advertiser-funded providers (notably ITV) from their public service obligations. The main priority was to ensure a supply of public service *content* by whatever means, although the options for the provision of funding to providers other than the BBC and Channel 4 were restricted, even in the more radical of OFCOM's proposals, to the provision of children's programming, news and local television. Certainly, by then no one was petitioning the government to intervene on behalf of 'genuinely original drama', and in spite of OFCOM's warnings about funding, the incoming coalition government announced a freeze of the BBC licence fee for six years from 2010, equivalent to a cut of 16 per cent in real terms. At the beginning of 2012 Lord Patten, Chairman of the BBC Trust, called again for the BBC to clarify its philosophy, but could offer only a fairly familiar, tautological diagnosis of its value as an institution that is essentially good because it matters, and that matters because it is good. Emphasising its continuing importance as a national purveyor of quality entertainment, ideas and ambition, he admitted: 'to do any of these things, the BBC needs to be at the top of its game'.[72]

The particular bind for both BBC1 and ITV in the foreseeable future is that the need to maintain peak share in a transformed market has affected the ability and inclination of either to take the sort of radical, expensive programming risks that are nonetheless necessary to survive in a polarising market. In this context the critical approbation reserved for high-concept American shows has been rather difficult for some British producers to swallow, partly because these high-volume imports are produced and distributed to a scale unmatched by routine domestic production, and partly because in ratings terms they are actually less popular than UK dramas. As the Controller of BBC1 observed in 2009, powerful edgy series such as *Criminal Justice* (BBC 2008–9) or *Five Days* (BBC 2007–10) had received ten times the UK audiences of *The Wire* but generated hardly any critical attention, even though 'the creative challenge involved in creating a show that appeals to 9 million viewers – and does so day in, day out – is far greater than in creating an edgy show for a niche audience'.[73] British advertiser-funded programmes are produced according to an entirely different economic logic to most high-end American series. Given the significantly smaller size of the domestic market, a UK channel along the lines of the subscription model adopted by American premium provider HBO (with an estimated 30 million US subscribers in 2012) would never be able to match the level of investment in UK drama that has historically and routinely been made by ITV. However, the production values and on-screen spend evident in American quality television has raised expectations for British-made drama output, resulting in the sort of budget deficits that will need be met by investment from co-producers and distributors, likely to demand in turn a more internationally appealing product.

In such a tough market, the lure of the detective is contradictory. On the one hand, it is popular with viewers and advertisers, a relatively successful British export that still satisfies the requirement (for example, expressed by OFCOM's consulted audiences) to preserve quality 'UK content' on free-to-air national television, not least as an 'expression of common cultural identity'.[74] On the other hand, contrary to reputation, no drama is 'safe': innovation is risky, but repetition and proliferation makes crime genres vulnerable to cries of saturation. By 2011, Danny Cohen, the new Controller of BBC1, declared there to be simply 'too much crime' and 'too many male detectives',[75] and ITV similarly described its own mix as 'too skewed towards crime and detectives'.[76] The following year, however, ITV once again rolled out a slate of detective drama that included a second series each of *Vera* and *Scott & Bailey*, a sixth of *Lewis*, and even renewed the once-axed *Foyle's War* by commissioning three new feature-length films set in peacetime. It also threw its corporate weight behind *Endeavour* (ITV 2012–), the very title of which was a clue for fans of *Inspector Morse*, who would immediately recognise the detective's long withheld forename. Made and broadcast initially as a one-off special, this was billed as a 'prequel' purporting to tell the story of where it all began for DC Morse in 1965. It was written and devised by Russell Lewis who, like others in the production team, had been creatively involved with both *Lewis* and *Inspector Morse*, and was full of loving in-jokes for fans, even a small role for John Thaw's daughter Abigail as a local newspaper reporter who asks the young policeman 'haven't I seen you somewhere before?' A reportedly 'enthusiastic' response to *Endeavour* prompted ITV to quickly green-light a series of four episodes for transmission in 2013, promising to introduce new characters and re-establish some 'old favourites, all of whom are destined to have a massive impact on the future inspector's life'.[77]

In spite of such affection, the tone of ITV public relations makes it increasingly difficult to continue to regard 'Morse' as a 'character' in any meaningful cultural sense. In this chapter I have repeatedly referred to *Inspector Morse* as a model for its successors, although such estimation influence pales before the hubris demonstrated by ITV Studios in their 2012 MIPTV sales catalogue, which bundles together *Endeavour*, *Lewis* and all 33 original episodes of *Inspector Morse* as, variously, 'The Morse Legacy', 'legend' and 'phenomenal global franchise'.[78] More than just 'sales speak', the distance between 'model' and 'franchise' is revealing in the different creative possibilities the concepts seem to respectively open or close. Until now, the creative variety of TV crime fiction suggests that narratives of investigation, although not indefatigable, have been sufficiently flexible to address a considerably broader set of concerns than anticipated by the dismissively homogeneous category of 'police/detective fiction' used by Barnett and Seymour.[79] Since the late 1980s the genre has radically diversified, with texts such as *Foyle's War*, *Garrow's Law* (BBC 2009–11), *City of Vice* (Channel 4 2008), *Life on Mars* (BBC 2006–7),and *Ashes to Ashes* (BBC 2008–10) moving into the lost genres cited in the CQTV report, such as 'wartime', 'other historical' fiction and 'science fiction'. If such innovations have been obliged to negotiate pre-existing holes in the schedule, then it has nevertheless been possible that 'those parameters become the creative opportunity' for producers such as Gub Neal, whose proposal of *Cracker* was also prompted by an ITV call for a 'Morse replacement'.[80] What remains now to be seen (and I leave this as an open, if apparently rhetorical, question) is whether the visual, thematic and ideological continuities required for the creation and distribution of a 'worldwide franchise' will allow a similar scope for creative diversification and generic growth, whilst maintaining a commitment to UK content, no matter how dynamic the market in its gravitation towards 'quality' product.

2

Engaging with the Detective Character

Where the post-*Morse* cycle of TV detective series differs most noticeably from its predecessors is in its increased preference for 'centred biography',[1] by which a central figure is afforded considerable narrative interest and visual privilege. Although the ensemble police series continued to grace schedules until 2010 in *The Bill*, and briefly in *City Central* (BBC 1998–2000), elsewhere it had largely morphed into 'biographical' background, either in the guise of a supporting team or the extended uniformed force for which the detective has occasional use. By foregrounding individual characterisation and performance over other formal, stylistic and ideological strategies, contemporary TV detective narratives make the engagement between viewer and protagonist the key to the form's pleasures and meanings, and especially deserving of academic attention. That said, the theorisation of character and engagement is fraught with conceptual complications that the general reader may wish to defer, although they will be worked through here as a critical framework for the case studies that immediately follow this chapter.

An immediate problem is presented by simply recognising a particular type of protagonist as definitive. Although it might seem an obvious category and clearly crucial to the emotional and moral investment of the viewer, 'character' has not received much critical attention in television scholarship; and is seldom used as either means or rubric to classify texts. In screen and literary theory the concept seems to be everywhere yet also nowhere, neglected first by the declining dominance of literary humanism and its expectation of psychologically complex creations, capable of transcending the conventions that inform them, and neglected again since the heyday of structuralism when fictional characters were theorised explicitly, albeit reductively, as serving finite functions in 'spheres of action'.[2] Shifting paradigms have thus left screen characters to be attended to only in the pursuit of other concerns, at best considered 'unsatisfactorily novelistic',[3] conflated with star performance or reduced to a mere layer of ideological 'displacing', 'individualising' and 're-binding'.[4] Standing out as a more recent exception to this in film theory is Murray Smith's work on the cinematic character and emotion that he sees as filling 'the void' between structuralist and humanist conceptions[5] and which I shall draw upon later.

Dramatic Form and Function

Television drama's complex flexi-narratives tend to work best within a series or serial structure, with a discrete topography and a large cast that works as an ensemble rather than clustering around a single protagonist or classic hero. The apparent exception to this is such central characters who, as Raymond Williams once noted, are actually 'palpable devices to explore something that is more interesting than themselves',[6] chief amongst equals being the detective or other professional (often a doctor or pathologist) in a largely investigative role which provides the interface through which the narrative is commonly apprehended.

As the agents in a narrative of investigation, it is the reasoning and logic of the investigator that determines the broader narrative meta-logic of causality and emplotment, and it is often their privileged insight into other characters that determines how the narrative enigma is unravelled. This is actually a highly specialised narrative function that might be best understood as a form of mediation, for as Williams noted, they are a 'device' or lens through which we might contemplate broader social tensions and interpersonal conflicts. It is only through their privileged perspective that the television viewer is in a position to know and closely observe the forms of excessive criminal behaviour that are under investigation, and it is the detectives' insight and professional expertise that mediates the representation of all other characters. As suggested by the journalist, Sarah Crompton, 'they make order out of chaos on our behalf; they bring moral certainty to the messiness of life'.[7] In this sense, their 'voice' (a term I use figuratively) may be seen to correspond to the text's 'metalanguage', a concept Colin MacCabe explains, by analogy to the novel, to refer to the narrative discourse that is privileged with the truth.[8] Although MacCabe's broader argument is in many respects problematic and somewhat dated, it does usefully highlight the hierarchical ranking of character discourses within the order of the narrative, and the extent to which these are regulated in terms of their credibility, judgement and moral justification. Like the metalanguage of the novel, screen discourse may visually regulate the 'object languages' of the characters, declaring its own privileged hold on the truth. However, although the detective's judgment may occasionally be undermined by the camera's visual revelation ('seeing is believing'), such instances are rare and trust is always later restored. It is precisely because the police series, as Jonathan Bignell observes, 'necessarily addresses the meanings of seeing and knowing',[9] that the detective's mediation can neither be neutral nor (consistently) unreliable.

Realism, Myth and Heroism

The proximity to criminal activity that allows the police detective to mediate is uniquely bound up with his or her licence to act, specifically to redress or prevent wrongdoing. Although a common plot device in the police-detective series is for the detective to be in some way restrained by circumstances or authority, rendered (temporarily) unable to act, it is the overcoming of this obstacle that will tend to drive the episodic storyline. This is generically crucial because the formal and stylistic tropes favoured by TV crime series create an expectation of intervention, as Kirsten Moana Thompson suggests: 'Ultimately the character of the detective is a fantasy response to the anxiety provoked by crime's transgression, restoring social order and moral certainty by solving the crime'.[10]

A witty, if overblown, demonstration of this essentially utopian impulse is provided by a crucial action sequence that comes towards the end of the first episode of *Ashes to Ashes* (the sequel to *Life on Mars* and a new vehicle for its character DCI Gene Hunt). In the course of a drug-trafficking investigation, various members of Hunt's police squad find themselves stranded at a critical and dangerous moment on a dock by the River Thames near the City of London. With exquisitely eleventh-hour timing, Hunt himself appears at the helm of a speedboat, flanked by his two loyal sidekicks, Chris and Ray. The three men stand proud, sporting large dark sunglasses as the boat speeds to the rescue, framed by the iconic landmark of Tower Bridge under which it passes. With typically elevated significance for the music of the time (the early 1980s), the entire rescue is played out to The Stranglers hit 'No More Heroes'. Clearly, and in a knowing, self-reflexive nod to his unofficial fan base and unlikely cult status, Hunt is back and back on form, oozing his customary anachronistic glamour.

The humour of the sequence quite obviously plays with audience expectations regarding the usually better disguised *deus ex machina* of the episodic detective series, and parodies the heroic purpose of all police detectives, namely to intervene, prevent and redress social and moral transgressions. For all the irony and scepticism aroused by the very idea of a 'hero' in the current age, there is still pleasure and reassurance to be had from engaging in the 'how': the imaginative operations by which beneficial agency may be exercised to achieve rescue, resolution or retribution. Particularly distinctive to the contemporary detective series is the narrative emphasis on the *obstacles* to police action, and questions of power and method are repeatedly worked through, alongside themes of trust and judicial authority. Both *Life on Mars* and *Ashes to Ashes* demonstrate this repeatedly, persistently counter-posing conflicting styles of policing, and questioning Hunt's abuse of his own authority at the same time as it creates a narrative desire for his intervention.

Whereas the detective's heroic agency may or may not be equivocal, it will always coexist in structural tension with the character's need to mediate. Most series reconcile these two functions, interweaving personal and professional storylines, shifting interest backwards and forwards within a single episode, deflecting attention to and through the detective character. The mediation function means these characters cannot be reduced to simple archetypes and have no obvious classical counterparts. Indeed, as Susan Sydney-Smith shows in her history of the genre, the British institutional police television series did not develop from either a fabulist or a theatrical tradition, but grew out of the story-documentary, a product of postwar experimentation with broadcast form.[11] Something of documentary's concern to record actuality persists in the contemporary detective series, not least through its inter-textual trade with other televisual representations of crime, including news and current affairs programming and public appeals such as *Crimewatch* (BBC 1984–). At a deeper level, the police series can offer analysis (and imply a diagnosis) of the diegetic social world in which criminality is seen to operate (see Chapter 8).

Consistent with its loose and historic association with the truth claims of documentary, British television crime fiction tends to stay within the stylistic, dramatic norms of social realism, a tradition that typically displays a heightened awareness of social problems and, as Marion Jordan suggests, requires 'that the settings should commonplace and recognisable ... that the time should be "the present"; that the style should be such as to suggest an unmediated, unprejudiced and complete view of reality'.[12] Although since the mid-1990s there have been examples of an imaginative negotiation of these strict realist conventions, even the more innovative series – such *Life on Mars* – continue to work (or play) with the stylistic conventions of social realism, rather than rejecting them altogether. A potential problem here is sometimes referred to as generic 'conventionalism', a tendency for all genres to claim a direct relationship to the 'real' social world when they are actually referencing the iconic, apparently 'realist' conventions of the genre itself. For Paul Cobley, the problem then is not so much the aesthetic limitations of realism *per se*, but the recessive claims of originality that contemporary crime fiction makes by re-adhering to an 'increasingly conservative ideal of "realism"' as the reference point for the genre's own claims of innovation'.[13] His suggestion is that the contemporary crime series simply rehearses the critical gambits long since identified by Roman Jakobson,[14] by revealing an authorial intention that the representation should be 'true to life', have a narrative focus on inessential detail and gravitate towards mild 'rule-breaking (implying that the text has managed to escape the genre ...)'.[15] From this Cobley concludes that 'claims to realism – and by association, "objectivity" and artistic status – are insidious and harbour little explanatory power', as they amount to little more than an appeal to doxa. Innovation, he argues, 'is forced by a changing doxa', meaning that 'assertions about which literary-artistic forms are necessary to be "closer to life" are neither here nor there' and hinder a richer understanding of 'the features of crime fiction with which readers' expectations engage'.[16] Similarly, one might suggest that, although contemporary crime drama continues to stylistically and thematically reinforce its connection to the actual world, the accuracy of this connection is less relevant than the challenge it may (or may not) make to ways of thinking *about* actuality, including crime events themselves.

Thus, although the realist paradigm continues to find favour with journalistic critics still wont to celebrate the 'unemotional' and 'anti-escapist' as imitative of a higher order of realism, it is only by decentring this set of concerns that we come a little closer to understanding the pleasures and expressive possibility of the detective form. To this end, we could challenge the common-sense divide that appears to separate so-called realism from either melodrama or myth. As the literary critic Northrop Frye once noted:

> In myth we see the structural principles of literature isolated; in realism we see the same structural principles (not similar ones) fitting into a context of plausibility ... The presence of a mythical structure in realistic fiction, however, poses certain technical problems for making it plausible, and the devices used in solving these problems may be given the general name of displacement.[17]

Although the structure may be the same, the displacements effected by realist modes can make metaphoric significance incidental rather than explicit, an art of 'implicit simile' as opposed to the 'implicit metaphorical identity' of myth. Such a distinction is useful, and implies that metaphorical meaning may still be on offer, even in the most doggedly referential realist text, but interpreting it will nevertheless be something of an act of recovery, a restoration of a symbolic dimension that is not necessarily obvious to the naïve gaze even though it may enrich subconscious meanings. John Izod's Jungian approach also (re)claims myth as a psychological possibility, leading him to suggest that texts have different degrees of symbolic register from the clearly 'visionary' down, but even in instances where there appears to be no symbolic material, analysis might be enriched by an understanding of how it 'allegorically draws upon established mythological themes'.[18] Thus, rather than being regarded as mutually exclusive, the mythic and realist dimensions of textual signification can be theorised as potentially complementary. It is interesting that Christine Gledhill should make a similar argument, albeit about *melodrama* rather than myth, when she observes that many mainstream texts operate in both realist and melodramatic modes with a 'dual constitution' that enables them 'to work both on a symbolic imaginary level internal to fictional production and on a "realist" level, referring to the socio-historical world outside the text'.[19] By extension, the detective character may also be interpreted at two levels: as a hero in (mythological) function, perhaps within a melodramatic structure of emotional rise and fall; yet at the same time remain plausible, commonly mortal, and directly *relevant* to the perceived actuality of the contemporary world.

Individuated Typicality and Modernity

Raymond Williams notes that the proliferation of the detective story 'dates from that critical period of transition in the 1890s, which literary historians see as the emergence of Modernism but which cultural historians are bound to see as the stabilisation of modern middle-class forms'.[20] Integral to the genre was the positioning of an individual protagonist such as Edgar Allen Poe's seminal creation Dupin (a dysfunctional yet brilliant amateur investigator), in response to a society that is similarly, but excessively, dysfunctional, as indicated by its criminal transgressions. That which is celebrated in *Lady Audley's Secret* as the 'wonderful chain forged by the science of the detective officer'[21] was developed, in part, as a remedy to the ills of modernity.

A staple of popular literature ever since, the British amateur detective story was not at first a great success on television, particularly in its more conservative manifestations during the 1950s, and crime fiction only came into its own with procedurally realist institutional series such as *Z Cars* (BBC 1962–78), which managed 'to convey some of the stale but tense atmosphere of everyday work'.[22] The post-1950s shift from aristocratic amateur to police employee is perhaps revealing, and coincided with a period in which domestic and workplace environments increasingly provided the routine settings for British television drama.[23] Today, notwithstanding the successful reinvention of the gifted amateur as 'geek' in a series such as *Sherlock* (BBC 2010–), it is the salaried police detective who continues to dominate British schedules, thus making the investigator subordinate to the logic of 'ordinary' working life, and giving a rationale for their romantic failures. The conflict between public and private life is pivotal for the genre.

Certainly, evidence of the detective's private dysfunction is readily available. Spouses fall like ninepins: between Morse's death and his own reinvention as inspector, Lewis's wife is killed in a hit and run incident making him, like Inspector Foyle, a widower. Jack Frost's wife dies in the very first episode of *A Touch of Frost*, although as he later tells her sister, 'it wasn't much of a marriage anyway' ('Not with Kindness'). DCI John Luther is estranged from his wife, of whose murder he later finds himself accused, and Kurt Wallander is divorced, rather unhappily, before his narrative begins. In common with the protagonist of *Vera*, DCI Jane Tennison (*Prime Suspect*) is childless, never married and demonstrably unable to maintain a relationship alongside the pressures of work; and in *Cracker*, Fitz's relationship with his wife Judith breaks down repeatedly, not least because of his compulsive addictions and an affair with a police colleague. Most recently, the serialised storylines of *Scott & Bailey* have been dominated by the need for its titular characters to maintain professional standards in the face of numerous personal and domestic crises, many of which revolve around their inability to get or stay married. Clearly, the absence of a romantic partner deprives the fictional detective of an on-screen intimate confidant(e), and so makes these characters more available to the intimate representations of the viewer. However, the detective's inability to reconcile private loyalty with public duty may additionally imply a more historically significant critique of public service and the contemporary workplace.

Such a possibility returns us to a key critical question, once held dear in Marxist theory, which is whether broad historical and social events might be depicted or understood through the represented experience of an individual. The answer provided by Georg Lukács for the realist novel lay in the challenge of typicality:

> The 'centre' figure need not represent an 'average man' but is rather the product of a particular social and personal environment. The problem is to find a central figure in whose life all the important extremes in the world of the novel converge and around whom a complete world with all its vital contradictions can be organized.[24]

A character's potential cultural significance may thus reside in its potential to embody the 'vital contradictions' specific to a particular historical moment. Lukács's ideal of typicality is best understood as a response to the crisis of individualism suggested by the new bourgeois tragic hero that appeared on stage at the turn of the twentieth century. Previously, he had argued that in pre-industrial societies the inner conflicts of the individual had not been considered sufficiently problematic because 'life itself was individualistic, not men', but now the paradox had emerged that, being conceived simultaneously as agent of his own personality and product of his own environment, man must constantly 'find himself'.[25] In post-modernity, this essentially modernist paradox of 'finding' the vital self has morphed into ideas of the destabilised or decentred self, endlessly reinvented and in constant flux. Thus identity remains an existential preoccupation, albeit one more likely to be understood as actively constituted *through* performance and action rather than expressed by them. Even if we accept Dyer's argument that Lukács fails to properly explain 'how this articulation of history/society through the individual character works, how one knows it when one sees it',[26] Lukács's ideal of typicality nevertheless offers insight into the broader cultural significance the figure of the TV detective can sometimes achieve. The broader social resonance of the detective series, along with its insistence on questions of authority, public/private identity, morality/legality, implies a clear lineage between the paradox of self-realisation identified by Lukács and the existential crises in which television detectives are increasingly embroiled. Perhaps, rather than simply telling of a TV 'love affair with the eccentric and the individualist',[27] the lonely detective is indeed an effective recalibration of the crisis of bourgeois individualism, or what Lukács celebrates as 'everyman': a central figure who embodies contradictions of agency/constraint, and around whom the modernist contradictions of public and private are inflected and replayed repeatedly.

Unlike many cinematic variants, the television detective is rarely a complete loner, at least not back at the station where his or her individualism is typically couched 'within the context of the supportive team'.[28] However, the stress of investigation and political/institutional pressures upon it means the team is often divided in conflict, with the most significant tensions occurring between the detective and a senior authority figure. The latter are often managerial prototypes, generally of unsound judgement, and unsympathetic to the practical problems caused by the procedures they insist upon. The faintly ridiculous figure of Superintendent Mullett, Inspector Frost's immediate superior, is a paradigmatic example of this, the embodiment of politicised managerial authority with no instinct for front-line decision-making. Such a trope is echoed, interestingly, in the hospital/medical genre, most notably in series such as *Cardiac Arrest* (BBC 1994–6), and *Bodies* (BBC 2004–6), which dramatise the consequences of a remote NHS management whose priorities are public relations, cost-cutting and the suffocation of 'whistle-blowers'. In such environments, personal happiness and moral convictions become problematic. Again, Lukács's observations appear to be still relevant, not least that:

> Modern life liberates man from many old constraints and it causes him to feel each bond between men (since these are no longer organic) as a bondage. But in turn, man comes to be enclasped by an entire chain of abstract bondages, which are yet more complicated.[29]

The detective's inability to sustain a stable private life or an intimate relationship is a manifestation of how, in the contemporary public or working world, personal ties can be experienced as an inorganic, imposed 'bondage'. Indeed, the tension between bond and duty is often mapped on to a whole set of narrative oppositions, and may be made manifest in series structures through techniques of parallel montage that contrast the unravelling of the detective's private life with demonstrations of professional competence. Additionally, these may suggest an affiliation between the detective and perpetrator (*Cracker*) or victim (*Prime Suspect*, *Vera*) that puts them at odds with the institution for which they work. For a series to 'compromise' the professional neutrality of the detective's judgement in this way, it is crucial that their actions be contained within a structure designed to support and demonstrate the 'truth' of their moral viewpoint. Such structures prompt in turn particular modes of engagement from the viewer, and it is these that I shall explore in the next section.

Between Text and Viewer

It is an elemental paradox of mimesis that whereas fictional screen characters are textual constructions and not real people (in that they do not exist independently of their audio-visual narrative representation), they are nevertheless interpreted by real viewers through comparative reference to actual empirical subjects. Television characters are generally received as dynamic social beings, albeit hypothetical ones, they are not commonly perceived by viewers as functional composites of generic traits, not least because 'we assume that these traits correspond to analogical ones we find in persons in the real world'.[30] As Sonia Livingstone's psychological studies reveal, viewers are attracted by character and are themselves active in its *construction*, being responsible for their own representations which draw upon common sense, personal experience and other contextual sources.[31] This makes the process of engagement unpredictable, and it also means that a viewer assessment of, say, the morality of a character may be quite distinct from a judgement as to their sociability or potency, and the relative significance of each type of assessment may vary from text to text. Thus, in lay terms, whereas viewers may be positioned to share a character's perspective, they still may not 'like' that character, although the converse is equally true, as they could find their sympathies elicited by a character whose behaviour they would normally find morally reprehensible. The character of Gene Hunt will later be seen as a paradigmatic case of these very contradictions, which in turn make it difficult to locate the exclusive source of a character's 'meaning' in either text or viewing subject.

The analysis of television fiction is always, then, operating in an unstable space. To what extent is a character's meaning determined through performance, fixed by the construction of the text (via script, *misé-en-scene*, cinematography or editing), or contingent on its appeal to extra-textual ideologies, social likes and dislikes, and subjective to the viewer? As Livingstone notes, it is 'an impossible ideal' for a researcher to distinguish between the elements of characterisation that are available in a text and those which a viewer may construct using their 'repertoire of social knowledge'.[32] However, recognising the social dimension between viewer and actor/character is crucial, if only to counterbalance lingering Formalist assumptions about narrative predictability, such as Umberto Eco's claim that the detective story produces 'redundancy: pretending to rouse the reader it in fact reconfirms him in a sort of imaginative laziness and creates escape by narrating not the Unknown, but the Already Known'.[33]

By ignoring the manifold unpredictability that attends character engagement, such a view evacuates the politics attending television and its impact, theories of which tend to cluster midway between one polar extreme, which conceives of a 'dominant text' as a repository of immanent meaning holding audiences in thrall, and its opposite, which advances the possibility of a 'dominant audience', positioned as autonomous receivers, creating meanings that may be quite arbitrary to those apparently suggested by the text.[34] Across the spectrum of theories addressing the relations between TV and audience, it has become conventional to distinguish the actual and variable *social audience* of broadcast television from the theorised *television spectator* or *textual viewer* addressed by the medium or implied by a given programme. Clearly the two are not mutually exclusive, although the fluidity between spectatorship and social consumption has often been avoided in theoretical work which falls into one of two camps, that which addresses the text as a determining object (which 'reconfirms' the reader), or that which investigates the (socially situated) activity of audiences.

One difficulty for the cultural theorist or the textual critic attempting to use research produced by either camp is that each has tended to conceive of the viewing subject as somehow 'fixed' by whichever set of determining forces is under scrutiny. Thus a textual approach might infer a spectator locked into a fixed viewing position, whilst audience research tends to position an object of investigation that can be known and classified by age, class, gender and race and thus, as Brian Massumi puts it, already 'boxed into its site on the culture map'.[35] Massumi associates this with a theoretical reluctance to conceptualise movement or *possibility* (and therefore change), and he insists on the distinction between 'the field of emergence' (from whence, say, text or viewer might come) and the 'positionings' that may emerge from it. It is precisely the *interaction* between the individual and the collective that is 'socially determined – and renegotiated by each and every cultural act'.[36] Moreover, 'conditions of emergence change. Emergence emerges. Changing changes.'[37] Identities are not fixed outside of viewing, indeed, identities may be arrived at *through* viewing.

Thus, to reiterate, although the significance of the television text has tended to be contested by the broader theorisation of the social subject, both fields of enquiry have at times fallen into the same trap of seeking to regard the objects of their analysis as static rather than understanding the interaction of the two as a *constant* dynamic of no fixed points. If, as Massumi argues, the challenge for cultural studies is to think in terms of ontogenesis rather than ontology, then a parallel challenge for textual approaches might be to embrace the text *as a form of potential* and to conceptualise its audiences as emergent, and also indeed, as 'possible'. Textual analysis does not simply need to interpret the meaning of the text but also needs to address the processes of engagement that it can invite, the common emotional responses it elicits, and the particular moral worldview towards which it orientates the spectator. This does not to return us to a spectator who is 'interpellated' by a text, but rather to a text that might yet be scrutinised for the ways in which it orientates, offers pleasure, invites ethical judgement and generally opens up a range of possibility.

Such a range is also, always, governed by relative norms, or as Terry Eagleton once noted of literature:

> The claim that we can make a literary text mean whatever we like is [in] one sense quite justified. What after all is there to stop us? There is literally no end to the number of contexts we might invent for its words in order to make them signify differently. In another sense, the idea is a simple fantasy bred in the minds of those who have spent too long in the classroom. For such texts belong to language as a whole, have intricate relations to other linguistic practices, however much they might also subvert and violate them; and language is not in fact something we are free to do what we like with.[38]

One might make a similar argument regarding the linguistic practices of the television text, with its audio-visual codes, generic conventions and collectivising cross-demographic address to a heterogeneous audience. Meaning-making – like all acts of communication – will be variable but the range of possibility is more likely to be clustered than scattered, and it is to such activity that I shall now turn.

Television Spectatorship

A key focus of attention in the following chapters will be the precise ways in which individual detective programmes invite the viewer to exercise particular forms of moral judgement. Such judgements lie at the heart of the text–spectator dynamic, raising questions as to how the viewer might establish the veracity of a detective's interpretation (how do we 'know' when the television detective's instinct is 'right' in any given instance?), or be inclined to approve or tolerate behaviour that may otherwise be considered unethical. Given that detectives are always, emphatically fallible, why is their *moral* verdict on a perpetrator likely to be trusted? These questions are important because they relate to the persuasive properties of the text *and* to its likely interpretation: a character can only become liked or trusted through a system of structural privilege, performance *and* reception.

Tellingly, one available model of the functions of the literary hero developed by Hans Jauss[39] reworks an earlier proto-structuralist theory developed by Frye, yet decisively shifts the emphasis from how a hero is constructed by the text to a system of classification according to how the hero might be *received*. Jauss describes his five categories of function as 'interactional patterns of aesthetic identification with the hero', and maps these on to a spectrum that ranges from participation to distanced aesthetic reflection, describing the levels in turn as 'associative', 'admiring', 'sympathetic', 'cathartic' and 'ironic' modes of identification.[40] Following this logic, responses to the TV television detective (as an aesthetic subject bound up in its own public/private crisis) are most likely to fall within the 'cathartic' category, the spectator having been placed 'in the position of the suffering or hard-pressed hero' in order 'to bring about for him an inner liberation which is supposed to facilitate the free use of his judgement rather than the adoption of specific patterns of activity'.[41] Here what had originated (in Frye's earlier work) as an attempt to delineate different constructions of hero, has instead moved towards a presentation of 'norms of reception'[42] according to levels of empathy and identification. The hero is now being classified according to assumed affect, rather than purely within the terms of its own construction, although the schema is largely unsupported by psychological theory and is, as John Frow notes, 'remarkably unsuspicious of the "imaginary"'.[43] Because there is an almost inevitable gravitation in such schema towards the imaginative activity of the viewer, it is this that must be addressed, specifically as it has been configured in theories of spectatorship which take cognitive science as their legitimising framework.

Cognitive approaches have not greatly influenced the development of television studies, which has rather neglected the hypothetical spectator, although there have been attempts to theorise viewing as a general practice. Rhona Jackson, for example, has produced a hybrid model of 'the skilled viewer' of television that marries the 'Uses and Gratifications' model of mass media theory with an application of Fish's model of the 'informed reader'.[44] Such models are useful in grounding assumptions about audiences, and in recognising the range of skills and competencies that viewers bring to bear, although they are less useful for the critic who is looking to explore *how* a particular audio-visual or dramatic strategy might elicit a particular viewing response to a given character, the very question that psychoanalytic film theory has addressed through the concept of 'identification'. Identification has been particularly problematic for screen analysis, often used to refer to a whole spectrum of engagements from an abstract emotional sense of empathy with a character subject position, to star–fan relationships, of which it can imply 'that members of the audience, in imagination, want to fuse identities with that of the star'.[45] As Noel Carroll has argued, however much the notion of character-identification might be qualified by the critics who use it, its 'core-meanings ... really seem to require that I feel at one with or identical to another',[46] an assumption he entirely rejects.

By contrast, Murray Smith's work is designed to retain some of the possibilities that can be implied by 'identification' whilst proposing more precise categories of response, and so refining an understanding of the 'evaluative attitudes which underlie emotions',[47] notably empathy, sympathy and antipathy. Smith borrows Richard Wollheim's distinction between 'central imagining' and 'acentral imagining' which roughly maps onto the difference between empathy (sharing the emotions of another) and sympathy (which requires a positive attitude to another's feelings). Acentral assimilation by a spectator means they will understand *why* a protagonist is feeling or responding in a certain way without actually sharing his/her mental state, although there may be times when imaginative sympathy may, nevertheless, give rise to real empathetic emotions. In his acceptance of empathy, Smith distances himself from Carroll, for whom fictive engagement must be an exclusively acentral process, and who ruled out the active sharing of a character's emotions by the spectator. Smith argues that a form of 'central imagining' may indeed be experienced during viewers, and that such a possibility is even implicit in Carroll's acknowledgement that spectators may occasionally engage in 'a form of imaginative "simulation" of the mental states of characters'.[48] Clearly Smith's is a relatively complex model that, crucially, allows for 'plurality' in the complex range of alliances a spectator may form with more than one character during the course of a single narrative, as well as emphatically recognising 'the imaginative activity of the viewer'.[49]

With such a model, it is also possible to see that empathy, sympathy and simulation apropos a fictional character may inform a viewer's constantly emerging identity and the trajectory they may 'back-form' retrospectively for its emergence. Emphasising that imaginative engagement is a complex activity by a viewing subject, rather than the exclusively 'central' imagining of the private self, also makes it possible to conceive of emotions aroused in a subject simply by the *thought* of something. It means in short that, in spite of being a different gender, age and nationality, I could be understood to share something of the intense emotional trajectory experienced by a character such as Kurt Wallander, even though I may also have no direct participation in his predicament and am able to maintain an otherwise appropriate detachment from his narrative agency. Moreover, it even allows that my own understanding of self may be subsequently informed and shaped by the emotional encounter.

Murray Smith's theoretical model further involves the identification of a text's 'structure of sympathy', which comprises three levels often conflated under the notion of 'identification', namely: 'recognition', 'alignment' and 'allegiance',[50] all of which are crucial to emotional engagement. 'Recognition' is the process by which a spectator 'constructs' or apprehends various textual traits as 'a character'. This is mimetic in that the traits typically cohere 'around the body, as an individuated human agent',[51] and in this form are assumed to correspond to analogical ones found in persons in the real world. The spectator apprehends the agent as both 'individuated' and 'continuous', both of which enable a consequential process in which the same individual may be recognised or 're-identified' in different contexts and at different times. Secondly, 'alignment' is the process by which spectators are positioned *vis-à-vis* characters both spatially and also according to how knowledge is distributed (for example, between the spectator and the protagonist) which may grant a degree of 'subjective access' (for example, to a character's thoughts and feelings). In articulating the concept of alignment, Smith cites David Bordwell's notion of 'detective narration' derived in turn from the classical Hollywood 'noir' film, the narration of which was restricted in scope to only that seen and known by the protagonist, but Smith prefers to describe this as a particular pattern of alignment in which 'we are exclusively attached to the protagonist, and we have access to most of what she is thinking and feeling' as there is no limit to the other patterns of alignment and shared knowledge that would also be possible.[52] Given the extent to which television detective narratives deviate from early cinematic models, Smith's would seem the more useful and flexible critical concept, not least because few such attachments are exclusive.

Smith also substitutes the notion of 'optical alignment' for the cinematic concept of point of view (POV), which usefully separates the technique of simply showing what a character can see from the possibility of a more extensive shared psychological perspective with the protagonist. He argues that POV is an expressive limitation because

> the more a film attempts to render in a literal fashion the subjectivity of a character through the adoption of optical POV, the more it surrenders the power to evoke the full range of a character's mental states, through the powerful mechanism of facial expression.[53]

In practice, POV is rarely used in television drama to achieve alignment with the detective character, unless to indicate his or her altered state of mind – after a blow to the head, perhaps, or in the case of Sam Tyler in *Life on Mars*, to communicate his bewilderment at the visible transformation of the world around him

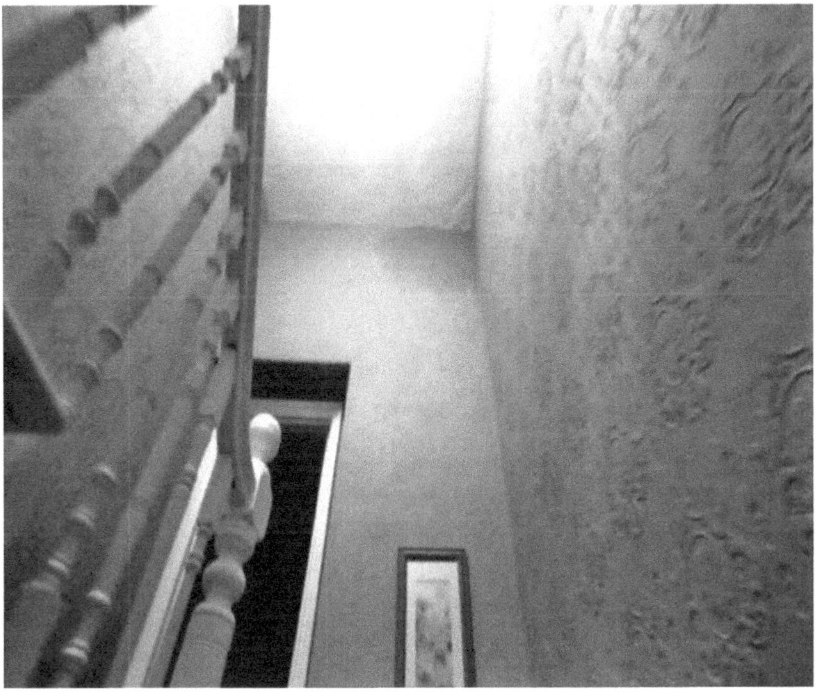

Figure 2.1 *Vera* – 'Hidden Depths' (2011)

when he has gone back in time. In fact, optical alignment, if used at all, tends to be reserved for a less recognised subject position, such as the hunter (a murderer) or the hunted (a victim) rather than the protagonist, so generating fear (and empathy with fear) rather than 'identification' with character. A case in point would be the fast-moving handheld camera work at the beginning of the first episode of *Vera* (2011), as it prowls a house, approaching young sleeping figures in their teenage bedrooms, inferring a menacing intent (see Figures 2.1 and 2.2). Optical alignment in a given sequence is thus highly variable in its function, but a pattern of allegiance with a central character may begin to emerge through repeated access with them (spatial alignment). Conventionally, camera direction in police-detective drama emphatically privileges the facial gesture of the detective, often allowing them 'the last word' by returning to a close-up on his or her face after an interrogation or exchange, so giving an indication of how preceding discourses should be interpreted. The indulged face of the detective is thus a visual, stylistic reinforcement of his or her expressed 'voice'.

Typically the spectator may *see* more than the detective, often being a privileged observer of events leading up to a murder, but will *know* less, so the face

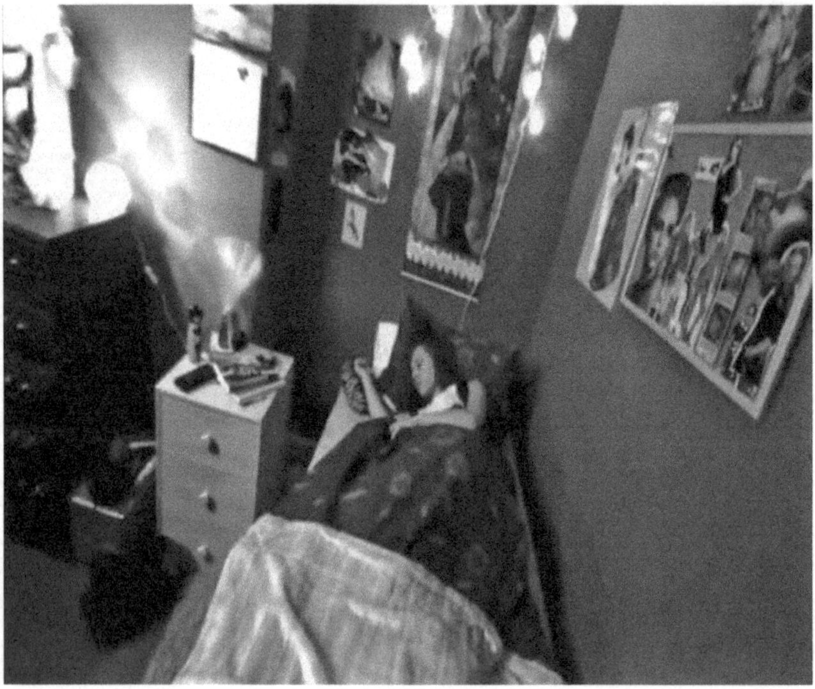

Figure 2.2 *Vera* – 'Hidden Depths' (2011)

can also act as a cue to align with the detective's informed understanding of the case (not least by enacting the moment when 'the penny drops'). The viewer is also denied access to the gradual process of reasoning referred to by the detective as 'instinct' (often in contrast to procedure) until an effective deduction can be made, in turn vindicating the trust so far invested in the detective. Trust will already have been aroused by various expressive norms, including access to the character's uncontrolled and private expression. This is what Smith calls the 'Expressive Truth Schema' as it is linked in turn to various cultural beliefs about truth and transparency.[54] Again, performance is crucial here, as it can infer a layer of equivocation or dissent that may otherwise not be evident. Indeed, John Caughie has argued that by sustaining an 'aesthetic of detail', acting can present a small rebellion within an increasingly commodified culture,[55] and it is often through performance that the repetitive can be made singular and sometimes elevated beyond the clear functionality of the discourse.

For the returning TV detective, we might also note that trust will be cumulative, reinforced by repetition over time, and crucial to 'allegiance', the third of

Smith's concepts which refers to the moral evaluation of a character by the spectator. Allegiance can have both cognitive and affective dimensions and is best 'conceived of as a dynamic phenomenon which develops across the text',[56] or in the case of a television series or serial, across successive texts. Crucially, although detectives may appeal to the pre-existing moral value system of the viewer (by tapping deliberately into prevailing social attitudes towards certain types of offences, such as child sex crime), some suspension of personal values is necessary in order to engage with the internal system or 'moral structure' of the text. Character is one of the foremost mechanisms of communicating moral orientation because persons are placed into 'positions of relative desirability' with one another, allowing the formation of 'preferential and hierarchized sympathies and antipathies towards the various characters'.[57] It will be seen repeatedly that it is the rather complicated assemblage of the TV detective series – including the oppositional or complementary relationships that senior police investigators may have with their 'bag men', superiors and nemeses – which provides the relational framework that enables the articulation of a morally complex 'voice'. Dynamic character relations provide a hypothetical moral order in which expedience can justify what may be objectively unjustifiable in actuality. This is clearly crucial for maintaining the viewer's allegiance whenever the detective may be breaking the rules in a way the viewer might otherwise condemn. It also means that TV police series are able to infer moral propositions that are not necessarily reducible to the received values of a dominant ideology.

By virtue of his structural emphasis on acentrality, Smith's three processes of recognition, alignment and allegiance are effectively states of emotional hypothesis and thus more intellectually qualified than could be assumed by the premise of 'sutured identification' in film theory (which implied, *ergo*, that there could be no position or pleasure outside the realist continuity characteristics of classic narrative). 'Allegiance' is crucial to understanding how the detective may fulfil all three of the functions suggested earlier – namely mediation, heroic agency and individuated typicality – but can operate slightly different for each. Whereas sympathy facilitates trust, it is nevertheless quite separate from the fantasy of hope invested in the detective's professional agency, and although both ethical judgement and emotion are elicited from the viewer, they are not necessarily elided.

Television Engagement: Time and Seriality

It is hoped that Murray Smith's model of cognitive engagement might offer insight into the possibilities of engagement between TV viewer and detective character, and that there is no need for this to come at the expense of studies of the social audience, nor should it belittle 'the fantastic spectrum of emotions experienced by readers and viewers in each and every textual engagement'.[58] For my purposes in this volume, the question arises as to how best to adapt Smith's schema, for although the feature-length quality detective format might bear visual similarities to the cinematic film there are key differences of form and reception that also have to be worked through, most obviously the temporal implications of seriality and repetition. Over the past two decades, British broadcast terrestrial television has provided a consistently mixed menu, a range of programming at particular, often predictable, times to appeal to the routines, weekly and daily rhythms, and likely preferences of self-selected audiences. Although new viewing practices and time-shift opportunities continually now threaten to circumvent broadcast television's ordered schedules altogether it is still, as yet, an activity that is both routinised and routinising.

The routine and ritualistic aspects of television consumption make demands upon its forms: narratives are extended over consecutive nights, repeated and developed weekly, and return annually with reassuring regularity. The viewer who works their way through a series via a DVD boxed set will often recreate these temporal rituals. It is the central characters that guarantee familiarity, and underwrite the quality of the police-detective series over time, particularly if production is intermittent. The temporal dimensions of series and serials thus have profound implications for an already intimate relationship between viewer and television that privileges performance and character as its locus of engagement. Complex characters will elicit complex emotional responses from viewing subjects, but for returning formats the process is constantly enriched by each renewal, leading to a distinctive mode of engagement defined by duration and informed by the interplay of familiarity/surprise, predictability/unpredictability, that characterise in turn the sequential structures of detection narratives.

One problem with adapting cognitive models of emotional engagement for television drama is that they are tied to the cues of the particular text in hand. In order to acknowledge successive re-engagements it is imperative to further extend Smith's concept of 'recognition'. Individuation will make a character distinctive, reidentification will recognise the same character in different contexts at different times, and together they constitute 'recognition of that character'.[59] However, this still falls somewhat short of accounting for the *depth* of emotions triggered by the opportunity to observe the return of an enigmatic figure with whom a viewer may have developed a growing and deepening cognitive allegiance that absorbs but transcends the contingent moral alliances invited by a single text. Reidentification will be enriched by successive encounters because each will evoke memories of previous engagement with the same character, whilst continuing to tantalise with the prospect of new knowledge, hitherto withheld. The revival of a series sometime after its heyday – as with both *Prime Suspect* and *Cracker* in 2006 – is particularly likely to prompt viewer memories of aesthetic pleasures past, and anticipation for their ritual repetition, all of which may be bound up with the immediate recognition of a returning character.

The affective possibilities of anticipated re-engagement are not necessarily limited to pre-existing, self-identifying 'fans' of any series, as the nature of the text–viewer relationship at the point of reception accommodates those who may not classify themselves as committed at all. The point, perhaps, is that whereas participatory modes of fan engagement publicly *perform* emotional attachment and debate meaning, a similar intensity and quality of engagement may nevertheless characterise the viewing experiences of so-called 'mainstream' viewers who would not self-identify as fans, nor choose to participate in forms of demonstrative engagement or engage with on-line communities. Designating intense and serial engagement as a fan practice returns us to thinking of viewing in the context of a social audience, rather than viewing as a durational cognitive activity. One theoretical possibility for bridging the divide is offered by Massumi's concept of 'topology', which for Karen Lury suggests itself as a way for criticism to insist 'upon the engagement between the autobiography of the viewer (which is their history, their knowledge, their place) with the various and specific spatial qualities and duration of the programme'.[60] Duration, she notes, is particularly key here to intensity, a particular quality of viewer engagement over time that is not readily explained by textual emotional cues, not least because it is unpredictable and so much more self-reflexive, and presumably arises out of a greater investment of self that is always emergent, informing (as well as informed by) cultural praxis.

Emergence and possibility suggest a progressive dynamism that is somewhat at odds with the designation of series and serial forms as reiterative. For Eco, 'the same type of repetitive procedure can produce either excellence or banality',[61] and he argues that an aesthetics of series and serial forms is possible as an appreciation of 'the way in which the same story is worked over to appear to be different', from the experience of which the 'critical addressee is invited to pronounce a judgment on the best variation'.[62] However, Milly Buonanno has revived the case for television seriality as more profoundly 'elemental', suggesting that its value resides in how it is put 'at the service of the inextinguishable human desire for immortality'.[63] Although Ricoeur famously argued this of all narrative,[64] Buonanno hypothesises that serial forms in particular arise out of the need (exposed by individualism and secularism) to exorcise fears of inevitable death by helping us to defer, indeed 'to forget the transience of our existence'.[65] Germane here is her distinction between the different temporal regimes that characterise the series and the serial. The episodic series, with its typical reliance on the 'cumulative adventures of recurring heroes', accommodates 'autonomous and conclusive segments' and is typically a-chronological and cyclical. The serial, by contrast, includes unfinished segments, ordered by chronological continuity and in a strict interrelated sequence.

Although the formal distinctions between series and serial may be familiar, Buonanno emphasises the differences in worldview they produce: whereas the serial portrays a world that is 'evolutionary and metamorphic', the series represents 'an iterative world, preserved (relatively) from the metamorphic effect of time'.[66] Almost all contemporary detective series accommodate serial elements, although they are still episodic in form, even if a single story line may sometimes be stretched over two or three broadcast episodes. Limited progression in the protagonists' private lives may seem to occur, often in parallel to developments in the episodic plot, but such 'progress' usually conforms to a cyclical pattern. In *Cracker*, for example, Fitz's wife Judith leaves him then comes home, Fitz gives up gambling then starts again; one or other of them has an affair, leaves, and so on. In all cases, the worldview is evolutionary yet predictable, progressive but familiar.

This mix of series and serialisation thus presents a paradox of evolutionary yet cyclical logic, and the status or 'fate' of all the detective characters is crucial to what Buonanno describes boldly as the 'life-giving potential' of television seriality. Each form offers a different temporal subterfuge. Whereas 'delay and removal of the ending are the prerogative of the serial', the series is able to restore 'the mythical concept of cyclical time and – through the eternal return to the present – sets the suspension of time itself against its unstoppable flow'.[67] This means that character progression must be very limited, and any developments that threaten significant change, such as Frost's impending marriage or Fitz's move to Australia, will either be a means to terminate a long career or the narrative premise for renewal after a period of off-screen absence. More complex self-reflexive possibilities of closure are demonstrated by longer running narrative serial forms, but given that British detective dramas tend more to repetition than serialisation, their endings are either left open (perhaps for some future revival) or returned to where they began, focused on the life of the central character, for whom as Nancy Banks-Smith once quipped: '[h]istory suggests there are only two options: death or marriage'.[68] That said, the on-screen demise of Morse in 2000 is unusually absolute, a form of closure that reveals the instability of its iterative worldview. More commonly, episodic series simply cease, leaving the constancies of character in eternal suspension, ever in defiance of the march of time.

Predictable as the detective's personal fate may be, TV crime series are rich with visual and narrative binary oppositions that sometimes conform with what Eco dismisses as 'elementary wisdom, constructed and communicated by a simple play of light and shade',[69] but may also open up more nuanced and ambivalent interpretative possibilities for the viewer. These oppositions, even at their most predictable, foreground concerns of a markedly ethical and social nature, and exploring these as well as their common strategies will be one starting point from which the particular system of signification of an individual series will be explored. Questions of *alignment*, *recognition* and *allegiance* have been privileged in this chapter because they are helpful to the understanding of character as the locus of textual possibility, and I have introduced further critical concepts to account for the complexities of repetitive television viewing, such as *re-recognition*, *intensity*, *duration* and *trust*. I have also suggested that the symbolic dramatic functions of the contemporary detective might be usefully understood as *mediation*, *agency* and *individuated typicality*, all of which are intended to shed light on the commonalities between characters. Crucially, of course, dramatic construction becomes significant only as part of a broader system of cultural (and culturally contested) meaning, and these conceptual tools of analysis need to be exercised within a context that recognises the broader resonance the detective series may have for contemporary social audiences. The following case studies will draw upon a number of contextual concerns around place, space, crime, policing, deviance and dissent: considerations that I will further reflect upon in the final chapter.

3

Residual Voices: *A Touch of Frost* and *Lewis*

The industry model and generic influence of *Inspector Morse* will be a recurring refrain in this study, and particularly relevant to the two shows I will discuss in this chapter, albeit for different reasons. I shall begin by discussing *A Touch of Frost* (Yorkshire Television/ITV 1992–2010), a series already introduced to some extent in Chapter 1, of interest here for its articulation of a residual voice, hostile to both change and authority, and for a diegesis sharply differentiated from that of *Morse*. Later I shall consider in some detail the official sequel to *Morse* itself, namely *Lewis* (ITV 2006–13). In neither case will I attempt a sustained comparison to their predecessor beyond acknowledging their immediate debt.

Although production of *Frost* was often intermittent (there were only four isolated episodes from 2003 to the start of 2008) it was rarely off-screen altogether during its remarkable eighteen-year run, a sense of continuity often being provided by frequent repeats on ITV1 and later ITV3. However unlike *Lewis*, which was to maintain a fairly consistent 'house style' which accommodated routine changes of writer and director, *Frost* displays an unevenness of style and tone that makes these qualities difficult to typify. In other respects the series was relatively constant: most notably its use of place, its configuration of crime and modern society, and the performance of its titular character, Inspector Jack Frost (David Jason), who begins television life as an officer already approaching retirement, with a distinguished record, a bullet scar and a distinct lack of patience.

Frost and Middle England

In keeping with public taste for gritty realism during the recessionary gloom of the early 1990s, early outings of *A Touch of Frost* were muted, serious and presented an obvious visual opposition to the golden deep-focus cinematography and heritage locations of *Inspector Morse*. Whereas Morse could be seen cruising along country lanes in his precious vintage Jaguar, Frost (an unnervingly careless driver) might choose to be driven by a sergeant through the streets of Denton in his old blue Ford Sierra (later an equally tatty Volvo). The background glimpsed in these sequences amounts to a moving portrait of a rather drably indistinct sort of a place. Indeed, Frost's Denton is something of an 'everytown', a sprawling fictional district in a semi-specific Thames Valley location, with outlying suburbs and villages. Although the characters cite Swindon, Reading, Oxford and Bristol as regional reference points, the series was actually filmed some distance away in Leeds and the Wakefield district of Yorkshire.

The axis of anxiety and resolution of the series is directly linked to its visual representation of generic 'middle England'. The episode 'Hidden Truth' (2003) begins with a cautionary tranquil moment – a slow aerial pan of a mock Tudor estate, cutting to an old man washing his car 'again' in the driveway – that is violated when a rather ordinary-looking, clean-shaven assassin shoots a young woman at close range on the doorstep. The woman is presently revealed to be a police officer, there to guard a witness to an earlier violent assault. Later, when Frost relates to a colleague the story of the original crime, the attack is represented with black and white footage, before cutting back to a colour image of Jack at the front of the house, as he emphasises how it had all occurred 'right here, in the middle of leafy suburbia' (a phrase delivered with sarcastic stress on each syllable of the final word). The neighbourhood is certainly more affluent than Denton's usual streets and crime scenes, and Frost's presence anticipates local suburban reactions 'to the apparent withering of the order and security in which people have invested so much economic and emotional capital'.[1] The suggestion is that a brutal assault in a quiet suburb is not merely an event but a symptom of decline, although the slight tinge of sarcasm to Jack's delivery would seem to actively engage a viewer less privileged than the residents of this particular street.

More usually, fictional Denton boasts a consistently credible quota of grey characterless streets, corner shops and supermarkets, and testifies repeatedly to the banality of routine police work and everyday crime. Its spaces tend towards the generic: crimes occur frequently in domestic houses, urban alleyways and unidentifiable patches of woodland; typically, investigations entail visits to the river, the canal, railway tracks, public toilets, local farms, churches and factories. In the course of duty, Jack also visits local council estates such as the East Dean, which he describes as the 'crime academy of Denton' ('A Minority of One', 1994) as well as a few more particularised locations such as Denton Athletic Football Club ('Dead Male One', 1995; 'Held in Trust', 2005), Denton Quarry ('Close Encounters', 2003), and even a local pole-dancing club ('Dancing in the Dark', 2003). Denton has a university (featured in 'Deep Waters', 1996), but it is an appropriately red-brick municipal establishment and a far cry from the academic elite depicted by *Morse* and *Lewis*. If Frost is occasionally obliged to leave the featureless streets of working- and lower middle-class Denton, it is usually in pursuit of a suspect, as in the chase which culminates at a massive power station in 'Line of Fire' (1999–2000). Occasionally he is sent, reluctantly and at the instigation of his senior officer, Superintendent Mullett, into such class-coded spaces as the local golf club ('Keys to the Car', 1999) and cricket pavilion ('Fun Time for Swingers', 1996) of which Mullett is himself a member.

In line with its repertoire of everyday locations, Jack Frost's roster of cases extends beyond homicide and represents a broader range of routine CID work undertaken by a local constabulary. There are still a great many murders in Denton, often of a less than sensational variety, as in the case of the elderly husband who is battered to death by his frustrated wife ('No Other Love', 1997), but also a number of other cases, such as hit-and-run ('Conclusions', 1992; 'Private Lives', 1999; 'If Dogs Run Free', 2010), armed robbery ('No Refuge', 1995; 'Unknown Soldiers', 1996), pet shootings ('Line of Fire'), animal smuggling ('Endangered Species', 2006), domestic burglaries ('Widows and Orphans', 1994), predatory paedophilia ('No Other Love', 1997; 'Held in Trust') and a disproportionate number of abductions of infants and teenage girls. Crimes against children offer the moral clarity of an irrefutably blameless victim, which sharpens the delineation of Jack's ethical position, allowing him to make social judgements, to distinguish between the sympathetic and the reprehensible, the deserving and undeserving. In one episode he actively defends a single mother, who had been working from home as a prostitute but had nevertheless tried her best for her abducted child ('Care and Protection', 1992), but in another he condemns the feckless parents of Bobby Kirby ('Penny for the Guy', 1997) of whom he jests wryly, 'remember when kids grew up in families?' Jack's caustic sarcasm, like his suspicion, is usually justified but sometimes reliant on easy targets and dialogue that glosses over the moral complications. In the final part of 'If Dogs Run Free', a teenage boy hangs himself in guilt, after which Jack tells Mullett: 'I can't tell you how many years I've been watching terrible things happen to people's children, and they always blame themselves. And too many times they're right to ...' It is a clear allocation of responsibility to the boy's father, the bullying, patently hypocritical drug trafficker Gerry Burland (Adrian Dunbar), but in its moral certainty works to close off the interesting ethical ambiguity around the boy's own earlier crime against a schoolfriend.

Frost's own unhappy marriage was childless, and after his wife's death in the very first episode his domestic spaces are shown less frequently. His is just another, drab, suburban house with dated décor, cast in a palette of browns, dull greens and beige. Following his bereavement his sister-in-law occupies his house to 'look after' him, but he is a churlish recipient of her cooking, and when asked 'what kind of vegetables *do* you like?' he simply snaps 'grey ones'. By the end of the episode she has returned to America, leaving him in solitary peace, free to eat whilst sitting on the sofa. Usually he arrives home clutching a take-away only to be called out again, or pops in to grab a black bin liner full of washing to take to the launderette. In 'Paying the Price' (1996) his house burns down, and some three years later in 'Private Lives' (1999), he reveals to DS Sharpe that he has not yet acquired a new bed. Much later Jack takes in young DC Presley as a lodger ('Endangered Species'), but bans him from entertaining women if they are both at home, which of course means that it is Jack who ends up discomforted, obliged to sit in the car until Presley twitches the living room curtain to give the 'all clear'. In the final ever episode, Jack departs for the church on the day of his wedding, looks with satisfaction at the 'For Sale' sign outside, and is driven down his residential street for the last time. The shot is immediately juxtaposed with that of cattle grazing on an idyllic village green in front of the house of his fiancée, Christine (Phyllis Logan), creating the obvious promise of a more peaceful haven in retirement. Although the marriage does not actually take place, Jack later tells Christine that Denton police station had always been a 'refuge as well as a job' for him, a distraction from the shortcomings of his private life, adding: 'Now we've got a life to live, and we've an awful lot to cram in'. The final sequence centre-frames a rear view of the couple as they walk hand in hand down a tree-lined path, a clear visual contrast to the urban and suburban streets of Denton.

In the years prior to his farewell, Frost does indeed seem most at home in his office, cramped and perfunctory as it is. It is most frequently here that he eats, mends his shoes, avoids paperwork and shares banter with other officers. Although often unorthodox, Jack's professional commitment is never in any doubt, and in an episode directed by Roy Battersby ('Widows and Orphans') there is an exemplary sequence, shot in 'bird's eye' view from above sight lines, the camera angled sharply down on Jack's right profile. It is late evening, and he is at his desk, lit by an overhead light that illuminates surrounding files and paperwork. The light catches only the very tip of his profile as he reads out sections of witness statements to DS Maureen Lawson, who sits at an adjacent desk, her work also sharply lit amongst the shadows, this time by an angle-poise lamp. The camera remains static to record the sequence in one continuous grainy, sepia-tinged take until Jack stands, switches off the overhead light and leaves the frame. A similar bird's eye shot is used some years later for 'Hidden Truth' in a sequence that commences with Frost, Toolan and Reid framed collectively, slouched at their desks amongst piles of detritus, loose papers and empty take-away cartons. However, on this occasion the shot quickly cuts back to eye-level: it has been ages, Toolan sighs, since they did an 'all-nighter', cueing a more familiar single camera exchange of looks designed to frame Jack's face and privilege his reactions. It is in such stylistic shifts from series to series that the early endeavour to deploy a 'documentary gaze',[2] which situated the viewer as a concerned observer, gives way to a less equivocal and complex structure of alignment as the series keeps pace with the norms of ITV peak-time drama, and adopts an altogether glossier, colourful, high-definition aesthetic from the late 1990s onwards.

The creep away from stylistic austerity is gradual, and given some narrative justification in the episode 'Penny for the Guy' (1997) in which Denton Central police station has been given a facelift. It is a gift to Jack's caustic humour, especially the chintzy office décor ('who ever heard of a nick with carpets') and brightly coloured canteen where he has to ask for 'chipolatas with a side dish of French fries' rather than his customary sausage, chips and beans. This is a carefully pitched episode, one of four written by Malcolm Bradbury, the celebrated author and contributor to many detective series, including *Inspector Morse*. Typically for *A Touch of Frost*, this narrative blends a primary plot of abduction with a secondary sub-plot about a missing teenage girl which, in true Shakespearian mode, 'consists in a sympathetic counterpoint'[3] to the main plot. The sub-plot in this case is later revealed as a staged set-up, an act of vengeance by the girl on her father and stepmother that it takes Jack's nose for mischief to detect. Exposed for the familial debacle that it is, the case is left to dwindle, leaving the last 30 minutes or so for the resolution of the main crime, and an intense night-time rescue sequence in which Jack deploys a team of men against Mullett's advice, and wades along a riverbank to find an abducted boy, boxed into a damp wall but still alive. It is an act of understated heroism, most interesting for how it allows Jack to regain the moral advantage after a succession of controversial breaches of procedure. Earlier, he had recruited Tommy Dunstan, an alcoholic and disgraced former police officer, to conduct inside surveillance on a supermarket chain, resulting in information that he then uses to coerce the owner into dropping charges of shoplifting against Dunstan himself. He also smashes a car window belonging to a suspect (so as to bring him out of his house), and refuses to either tape his interrogation or allow it to be witnessed by a duty constable. When he becomes convinced that the kidnapper is actually Henry Finch, to all appearances a benign old man, Jack repeatedly harasses him, twice breaking into his house to conduct an unwarranted search.

In such episodes, Jack's disregard for police rules is not simply an affectation, but a narrative driver, the entire sequence of events is plotted on one or other side of the fine line that he walks, and allegiance is arrived at as a destination rather than secured from the outset. Although it remains a consistent trait, his disregard for procedure (for which he is reprimanded in court in 'Hidden Truth') is sometimes the only mild complication to an otherwise very clear set of oppositions, and is itself little more than an irritation with bureaucracy or Mullett's latest management idiocy. Certainly, it seems unwarranted for DS Annie Marsh to bid him farewell at the close of 'Dead End' (2008) by warning 'you still bend the rules Jack ... it will prove your undoing', when he had done nothing more controversial than enter a lift shaft to rescue an injured man. A dashing exploit for a 68-year-old actor, certainly, but a far cry from the edgy maverick Jason had played fifteen years earlier. The courageous willingness to resort to the unorthodox methods which once genuinely complicated his moral 'voice' was eventually to settle into a rather generalised disenchantment with the excessive strictures governing his working environment.

Moral Allegiance, Dissent and Performance

Unlike Morse, Jack Frost has no constant sidekick, but is accompanied by a succession of subordinates, a strategy that refreshed the situational premise of each episode. These partnerships were also used to enrich his own characterisation, allowing him to take up different moral perspectives and sometimes confound expectations. In 'Minority of One', he is paired with a black detective constable, Carl Tanner (Lennie James), an opportunity to air his contempt for political correctness (he tells Tanner he must be 'pig first, black second') yet still reaffirm his essential fairness. Indeed it is only his careful management of a case that prevents racial tensions from spilling over in a deprived community. Visiting the council flat where one of his informants died in a fire, and suspecting that her tip-offs were racially motivated, Jack descends into self-pity and blames himself for what he assumes to be an act of retribution. He is framed by a camera angled slightly below his eye-line initially recording his upward glance at Tanner to the right of the frame, but which remains steady as he drops his eyes and looks away, left frame, to indicate his introspection as he berates himself. Briefly, there is a cut to Tanner's reaction and protestation, before Jack continues, eyes left, as before: 'All I did was to use the poor little girl, like I use everyone, for the sake of the job.' After a brief exchange, Tanner chivvies the elder man out of his maudlin state, enabling him to spot clues he might have missed. It is a slow, contemplative suspension of the plot, and serves several useful functions. Importantly, Jack's introspection personalises an issue of potential political significance, but his reluctance to make eye contact with Tanner puts the other officer in a position of moral authority. Because Tanner ultimately reaffirms Frost's judgement of the situation, the event could be read as a strategic use of a black face to ideologically reinforce police handling of race relations more generally. However, the scene is juxtaposed with other, near-satirical sequences in which Superintendent Mullett fluffs, frets and overreacts, making preparations for 'race riots', and urging extreme caution if Jack needs to arrest anyone from the black community. Mullett thus embodies 'the police' as an institution (hamstrung by its own initiatives), leaving Jack and

Tanner free to reflect on the more complex judgements they need daily to make, and situating them both as outsiders, at one remove from the force.

Jack's first pairing with a female officer ('Widows and Orphans') enables him to negotiate a similarly careful line, this time between the reactionary and the merely residual. Just when he thinks he has the measure of DS Lawson, described as a 'looker' by another officer, and unable to shimmy up a drainpipe because she is wearing a tight skirt, she reveals to Jack that she is gay and lives with another woman. Although somewhat flustered by the revelation, Frost's moral and professional rapport with Lawson enables him to rise above his old-fashioned instincts, and when they work together again ('No Refuge') it is he who steps up to defend her from a charge of impropriety. He also has an occasional and semi-paternalistic relationship with WPC Hazel Wallace, who is later promoted to detective sergeant and seconded to work with him on 'Close Encounters'. Called in unexpectedly, she has to bring her baby daughter into the office, creating an opportunity for Frost to demonstrate the paradox whereby he is tolerant to her needs as a working mother, yet ill-equipped to deal with a crying infant when she leaves him to mind the baby. It is through such contradictions that Jack demonstrates himself to be old-fashioned rather than bigoted, warm if cantankerous, and with a sense of equality that easily counterbalances his more insensitive remarks.

Another interesting pairing is with DS Reid (Robert Glenister), who becomes something of a dangerous alter ego for Frost and enables him to demonstrate his own prowess as a judge of true character. In the two-episode story 'Benefit of the Doubt' (2001) Reid is introduced by Mullett as a temporary transfer with 'a shambolic career that has all the hallmarks of being a complete washout'. Jack is less dismissive, notices that Reid was awarded a medal for bravery during the Falklands War and later keeps quiet when he learns of the officer's (managed) drug and alcohol addiction. Shortly after sharing one of Jack's customary curries, Reid is seriously assaulted in a public toilet, an incident greeted with caricatured hysteria by the police hierarchy and press team, who assume that Reid was a 'bad apple' in the force and had been there to 'feed his habit'. Here, Jack is the expressly dissenting voice, as he speaks up in a crowded room to demand that a long-serving officer be given 'the benefit of the doubt', and stakes his own reputation on there having been no wrongdoing on Reid's part. Reid spends the remainder of the episode in hospital, soon to be absolved from all blame and warrant Jack's faith in him. The episode closes when Jack leaves his bedside, declaring his intention to 'slide off to the pub and have a liquid lunch': a benign phrase and a common one, but a means for Jack to align with Reid's weakness, and invite the viewer to do the same. Official doubt of Reid is thus something of a proxy for the mistrust that may have been extended to Jack, had his own procedural misdemeanours not always been compensated for by his superior prowess as a detective. The trust and recognition that is vested in him, he graciously extends to Reid: the line in the sand is drawn, not between ranks or official orders of merit, but between those who put their heart in the job, and those who merely follow the rules. In a later episode ('Hidden Truth'), Jack has to coax Reid out of the pub and persuade him back to work: it is precisely because they care, he reminds him, that they do the job in the first place.

Sometimes Jack's assistants are drawn from the regular jovial ensemble of Denton police station. Characters such as DS George Toolan and the archivist Ernie Trigg often make small contributions even if they are not active parties to the investigation, perhaps as a sounding board to enable him to express a particular moral view. In 'Held in Trust', Frost is framed in close-up, as he discusses with Toolan a missing child, concluding with restrained anger 'I think if the worst has happened to that little boy, we should cast aside any pretence of civilisation, and bring back the death penalty.' This cuts to a reaction shot of George, unsettled and in thought, as Frost walks slowly away, providing 12 seconds of screen silence in all. The remark is obviously provocative: an appeal to like-minded viewers or a display of bigotry? An indication that Jack has crossed the line, or simply a rather ponderous device to raise the emotional temperature? If the next few scenes are uncomfortable, the unsettled viewer is invited to realign when Toolan asks Jack if had really meant what he had said. Frost sighs: 'I tell you what I do believe ... that "life" should mean life. It's only fair.' Later still, Jack and DS Reid arrest Anton Caldwell (Nicholas Woodeson),

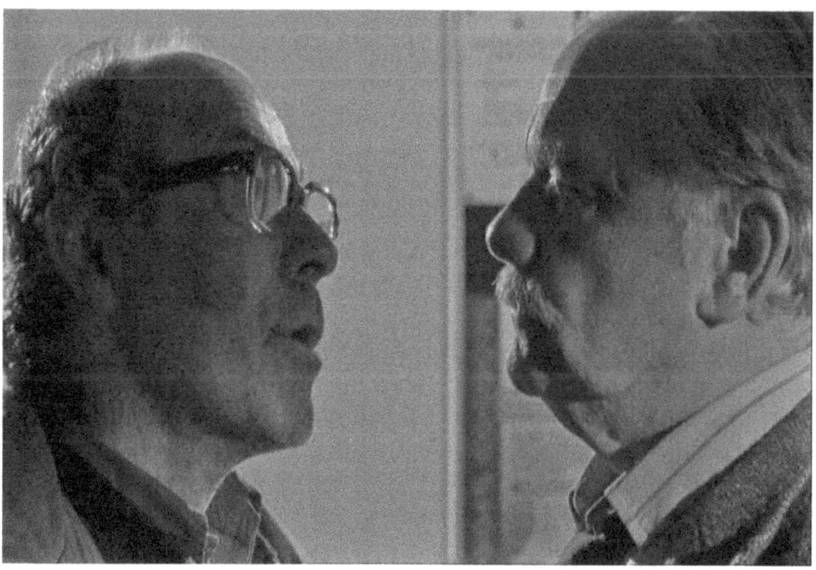

Figure 3.1 *A Touch of Frost* – 'Held In Trust' (2003)

who reminds Jack that 'you can't section someone for being a paedophile, just because my object of desire is different from yours'. Caldwell's dirty mackintosh and unshaven appearance are at odds with his eloquent summaries of his statutory rights, and Woodeson's performance exaggerates the man's oily affront to social and sexual norms. Perceiving that Reid has children, he leans over the desk, insinuating what he might have in mind; close-ups of Reid's narrowing eyes intercut with extreme close-ups of Caldwell's mouth, his tongue pushing suggestively at his stained teeth. Frost restrains Reid but later threatens the offender himself, framed at loggerheads to create an undeniably Manichean opposition. (See Figure 3.1.)

Notwithstanding this particular incident, the ongoing structure of moral allegiance in the series relies less on Jack's appeal to popular assumptions about criminality, and more on the visual and linguistic privilege extended to him, bolstered by the support of his diegetic colleagues. As Trigg declares when urging Jack to apply for promotion: 'this place would be a lot better with someone who knows what really matters, and I'm not the only one who thinks that you know'. As an instinctive judge of character Jack is rarely fallible, but in the more interesting and well-crafted episodes he is still allowed to make relatively serious mistakes. In the narrative absence of these, it is left to Jason's extraordinary character performance, range of facial gesture and compelling delivery to infer moral complexities above and beyond the bald truisms and unchallenging dilemmas.

The defining dichotomies of Jack's character (able yet unorthodox, instinctive yet flawed, gruff yet compassionate) are further delineated through his relationship with Superintendent Mullett (Bruce Alexander). Key differences in personality are suggested from the very beginning ('Care and Protection') when Mullett pulls into the police station car park in his immaculate red Jaguar (a clear allusion to Morse), carefully flicking an imaginary particle from above the rear window as he leaves. When Frost arrives (having missed the superintendent's briefing) he manages to reverse his old Sierra into Mullett's rear light, swears and kicks the debris out of sight under the vehicle. Thereafter the opposition is a constant (Alexander and Jason are the only two actors to appear in every single episode): Mullett is pernickety, clearly resents Frost's easy earthy popularity with his team, repeatedly berates him for failing to do his paperwork and once cautions a sergeant against showing him inappropriate loyalty. He is obliged nevertheless to tolerate Jack's organisational inadequacies, not least, as he reveals in this first episode, because the chief constable 'has a very high opinion of him ... he being our "local hero" so to speak'. Quite unlike Jack, Mullett sets great store by authority and reputation, is quick to invite the cameras for a press briefing and often seen at formal social functions, once telling Frost (quite without irony) that 'a superintendent has quite enough to do without worrying about crime' ('A Minority of One').

Mullett remains a thorn in Frost's side for 18 years, although he is also an occasional ally, stepping up to defend him when a bigoted HMI inspector calls him a 'dinosaur' ('Mistaken Identity', 2002), and recommending him for Chief Inspector ('Held in Trust'). Mostly, however, he is the management foil to Frost's superior hands-on policing, there to represent the police norms from which Jack must dissent. In 'Appropriate Adults' (1995), the two clash over the culpability of Billy (a youth with Down's syndrome circumstantially implicated in the disappearance of a young girl), but Mullet has the humility to regret his error once Billy's innocence is established, admitting to Jack 'I thought I'd been in this job too long to just snatch at a culprit'. In the ultimate episode, Jack is tricked into being the reluctant guest of honour at his own surprise party, also the occasion for overdue acknowledgement by Mullett:

> Of course, I would never have made a detective of his calibre myself, and over time he's taught me the value of instinct, gut feelings. I've even developed gut feelings of my own: so much so, that it is extremely rare that I don't know that Inspector Frost is up to something that I shouldn't know about. ('If Dogs Run Free')

For the most part he is a good-humoured adversary, disappointed that Jack should be so unwilling to follow the party line and quite horrified by his lack of protocol, yet a grudging admirer of his way with people and natural feel for the job.

Already representative of an older generation when the series began, and not afraid to declare himself frequently to be 'too old for this', Frost also taps into the anxieties of a 50-plus demographic around the day-to-day experience of what Charlotte Brunsdon calls the 'collapse of the postwar consensus'.[4] In 'Hidden Truth', he wrings his hands over an outbreak of gun-related violence, prompting George to remark: '*Dixon of Dock Green* days are long gone Jack', to which Jack retorts quickly: 'yes, I know. They shot him as well'. It is a neat allusion, revisited when Reid closes the scene by quipping 'Evenin' All' for the benefit of Frost's heartland of viewers who would be old enough to remember. Although the 18-year run of *A Touch of Frost* fell short of Dixon's record 21 years (and astonishing 432 episodes), it still boasted some 42 individual feature-length editions, attributed to 12 different writers and 16 directors. Even though these varied considerably in moral complexity, it would seem fair to note a distinct progression towards more predictably populist sentiments. The series was often championed by the *Daily Mail*, which ran an almost frame by frame picture account of the final episode, presumably in the expectation that Jack's long-running residual antipathy to the modern world would be especially missed by their readership.[5] Jack's legendary disrespect for procedure had by now settled into a more generalised expression of disenchanted middle

England: tired of management speak, political correctness and the technological wizardry of an internet age. A grudging accommodator of science and information technology when necessary, Jack was ever sceptical of it in the abstract and saw it as oppositional to a common-sense, human approach. Although the series kept pace with obvious developments in modern policing, such as the increasing importance of forensic evidence in securing convictions, Jack continued to dissent and rail against the new, dominant logic of technology-as-progress.

Press coverage of the debut of the series in 1992 had made much of Jason's departure from playing the comic characters for which he was best known,[6] and was described in the *Radio Times* as 'a leap that will leave public perceptions, temporarily at least, stranded'.[7] It is testament to Jason's skill as a character actor of some range that such reservations were quickly discarded, although the author of the original published Frost novels, R. D. Wingfield, remained famously unhappy with the way his character's dark humour had been toned down for television, and was often cited as saying: 'I have nothing against David Jason as Frost at all. He just isn't my Frost.'[8] Like Morse, whose translation from novel to screen required that his sexually predatory tendencies and taste for pornography be excised,[9] all traces of the lascivious admiration that Wingfield's Frost felt for young girls is removed. Instead, Jason's performance, more so even than Thaw's, suggests a general avuncularity. He is surprised, for example, when an 18-year-old girl turns up at his front door, believing him to be her father ('Benefit of the Doubt') and clearly disappointed when it transpires she is mistaken. In spite of a few intermittent relationships, the prospect of romantic satisfaction (another threat to his loneliness) is also continually postponed. In early series, Jack dates his wife's former nurse, Shirley, but the impossible demands of the job mean that he repeatedly leaves her sitting in pubs and restaurants or, on one never forgiven occasion, fails to accompany her to a funeral in Scotland. Later he has what seems to be a comfortably intermittent, casual relationship with a former prostitute, but true to character type, work is always in the way, and Frost remains haunted, not by the grief of widowerhood, but by the unhappiness of his marriage whilst it lasted. Although he continues to wear a wedding ring, it is as a reminder of his guilt not his happiness, for he insists he was about to leave his wife when she became terminally ill. True romance only becomes a serious prospect in the final episode when he wins over Christine, a local RSPCA officer, as well as her teenage children, only to be deliberately knocked down by her unhinged ex-husband immediately prior to their wedding.

This much publicised dramatic denouement brought *A Touch of Frost* to its end in 2010, when Jason was 70 years old, some 15 years past normal retirement age for a police officer, although still the junior of Ernie Trigg (Arthur White, Jason's brother in real life) who would have been 77 when he played the role of police archivist for the last time. Three endings were filmed, all possible consequences of the car crash, in which Toolan, Mullett and Frost himself were the respective victims. However, it was Toolan's funeral, and not Jack's that was used for the broadcast version. The closely guarded secret ensured high ratings and numerous tabloid and broadsheet articles lamenting Jack's departure, much as they had done for Morse ten years earlier. Although, as the acerbic Nancy Banks-Smith felt compelled to point out, '[g]ood detectives never die, of course, they just repeat',[10] Jack's retirement was also the winding-down of a residual, cantankerous voice which had kept a stumbling, exasperated pace with a changing social world, the few regrettable continuities of which had seemed to be poverty, injustice, violence and evil.

Lewis

Providing an exotic alternative to *A Touch of Frost* was *Lewis*, which resurrected from *Inspector Morse* the character of Robbie Lewis (Kevin Whately), then a sergeant but now a detective inspector. Production began with a feature-length pilot, broadcast in January 2006, and was followed by annual series of four feature-length episodes, plus a 'final' seventh series of three stories, broadcast in 2013 as one-hour instalments over a six-week period in a bid to boost ratings. The possibility of a spin-off series had been developed initially by Michelle Buck and Damien Timmer, two Carlton/ITV executive producers who had previously worked on *Morse* for Central Television, and Chris Burt, who has since produced all episodes of *Lewis* to date. The new series had the blessing of Colin Dexter, writer of the original *Inspector Morse* novels, and he was to continue to receive a credit for its creation.

Lewis was thus intended as it was critically received, as a very conscious replication of the middle-brow intellectual and aesthetic pleasures of its predecessor, marketed on the strength of its elegant cinematography and beautiful Oxford locations. These, alongside supporting casts of British quality actors (including such luminaries as Timothy West, Juliet Stevenson, Robert Hardy and Simon Callow), provide the most obvious on-screen spend, signifiers of its somewhat lavish production values. In spite of being 'hugely expensive,' as Kevin Whateley acknowledged,[11] the series nevertheless survived the swingeing ITV axe in 2009, eventually coming to an apparently natural end four years later.[12] As I shall demonstrate, where *Lewis* most distinguishes itself from its contemporaries is in its aspiration towards visual and narrative grandeur, and its reliance on heritage-inspired theatricality.

The pilot episode, written by Russell Lewis and Stephen Churchett, 'reeled in an almighty 11.3 million' viewers,[13] making it the most watched detective drama of the year, and raising the bar for future output. In a characteristic trope taken from *Inspector Morse*, the programme opens with 'a visual present of a fantasy past',[14] an aerial sequence panning Oxford's 'dreaming spires', but omitting the post-war buildings that interrupt certain high vistas of the city. The camera zooms down into a college quadrangle, and cuts to an interior shot of a student room in which a young man frantically scribbles mathematical formulae. It is an effective transition from tourist gaze to privileged insight, and indicative of the implicit invitation of the series to look beyond the much photographed architecture and access a rarefied world of genius and passion that – as the notices on many Oxford University buildings warn – is 'not open to the general public'. In some episodes almost every shot is location-specific, inferring that its events are exclusive to Oxford, unlike those that occur in generic 'everytown' Denton. Many extended sequences are shot such iconic buildings as the Ashmolean Museum and the Bodleian Library, and others incidentally confirm landmarks such as Hertford Bridge, and make use of college buildings to represent fictional equivalents such as 'Mayfield College' ('Life Born of Fire', 2008), or 'Gresham College' ('Dark Matter', 2010).

In *Lewis* genius is often associated with other forms of privilege, and the pilot narrative follows several murders that connect brilliant mathematicians with the wealthy Griffon family, producers of heritage racing cars. The young student glimpsed in the first sequence is later identified as Danny Griffon, and the first victim his fellow prodigy, Regan, whose murder is to be handled by Detective Inspector Knott, until he is suspended for drink-driving just as Lewis returns to the city from an overseas posting. Although Lewis is aware that his new senior officer, Chief Superintendent Innocent (Rebecca Front) would prefer to have him 'put out to grass', he is allowed to take over the case with Sergeant Hathaway (Laurence Fox) in support. Further murders pull Lewis and Hathaway deeper into a family saga with a typically classical flavour. Since his brother's death in a road accident, 'Rex' Griffon has been in charge of the family firm although his nephew Danny suspects him of having deliberately caused his father's death. Rex and his brother's widow, 'Trudie', are both living in the stately family residence, as is Tom Pollock, a financial adviser, whose own daughter Jessica is tortured by her unrequited love for Danny and later attempts to drown herself.

In case the similarities to *Hamlet* are missed by the viewer, some halfway through Hathaway jests to Lewis that 'something's rotten in the state of Denmark', and explains the resemblance. Again typically, the series thereby offers alternative points of alignment: the satisfaction of recognising a high-brow cultural reference and/or the opportunity, alongside Lewis, to make intelligent deductions once the allusion is explained. Lacking the passion of his predecessor for opera and choral music, Lewis is obliged to encounter and negotiate high culture obliquely, often mediated by his Cambridge-educated sergeant, who is usefully equipped with encyclopaedic recall of information about everything from Aristotle to Nietzsche, and neurology to Iraqi geography. Tempting as it may be to dismiss its name-dropping as mere quality-coding or middle-brow aspiration, such references are not entirely gratuitous in *Lewis*, for allusions to the arts are meticulously woven into its narrative and thematic concerns. Principal plots may be orchestrated around anything from Jacobean tragedy ('Wild Justice', 2011; 'Quality of Mercy', 2009), early Renaissance painting (Paolo Uccello in 'The Point of Vanishing', 2009), English romantic poetry (Shelley in 'And the Moonbeams Kiss the Sea', 2008), to nineteenth- and twentieth-century literature (C. S. Lewis in 'Allegory of Love', 2009; and Lewis Carroll in 'The Soul of Genius', 2012; two obvious puns on Robbie's surname). After all, as he often notes, 'this *is* Oxford' and their prime suspects are usually 'Oxford types'.

Admittedly there are also forays into culture of a different register, such as the ageing rock band held in awe by Robbie ('Counter Culture Blues', 2009) or the use of thinly veiled 'Cluedo' nomenclature in 'The Dead of Winter' (an episode from 2010 featuring a Colonel, Professor Black, Miss Scarlet and 'Father Jasper'), but these are less typical, and the suspects in both instances are still fabulously wealthy. In the pilot, the familial strife and revenge passions confirmed by analogy with *Hamlet* turn out to be part of the episode's strategy of smoke and mirrors: it is Pollock (the Polonius equivalent) and not Rex who is revealed to be having an affair with the widowed 'Queen' and indeed it is he who is also Danny's real father. The viewer with the cultural competence to decode the Shakespearian parallels is hoodwinked: the murderer is finally revealed as an outsider, a Professor Denniston, who killed to preserve his award-winning reputation as a mathematician.

The sense of grandeur conveyed by *Lewis*'s lofty references to great works reinforces its narrative diagnosis of the criminal act: murder is never the product of, say, banal loathing, petty covetousness or temporary intoxication, but a dramatic working through of excess passion. The revenge motive (and motif) developed as a red herring for the pilot, is worked through more fully in 'Wild Justice', also written by Stephen Churchett. Most of the action in this episode is situated in the fictional St Gerard's Hall, a university college populated by friars now facing the progressive challenge of two female candidates competing with the conservative Father Mancini for election as Vice Regent. A series of murders are committed, inspired by Jacobean revenge tragedies, both actual (*Titus Andronicus*, *The White Devil*) and imaginary ('*The Devil's Friar* by Fulworth'): an American female bishop dies after taking poisoned wine by a riverbank, a friar is found starved and half-buried in a kneeling position, the son of one female candidate is strangled by 'a true-love knot' and a former police officer is suffocated with a St Gerard's red and gold brocade cushion. In keeping with the inherent theatricality of the crimes, the *misé-en-scene* mixes the opulent (wood-panelled rooms, tapestries, velvet drapes, semi-fictional Renaissance art) with an aestheticised religious austerity in the form of black draping cassocks, candlelight, large wooden crosses and buildings to be entered by heavy archaic doors.

At one point, a ponderous meeting to confirm the candidates for the Vice Regency takes place around a table in a grand medieval crypt (Figure 3.2), although significantly, this scene is briefly interrupted by another in which Lewis and Hathaway discuss the case at Oxford police station (Figure 3.3).

From a seated discussion among the crypt shadows, rich wood and Gothic arched vaulting, to standing officers in a near monochrome space of glass walls and perpendicular lines: the juxtaposition creates a clear opposition between the modern upright force of law, and the archaic, dark, exotic other-world of the medieval college. When the scene in the crypt resumes, the meeting breaks into factions: the two female candidates (Caroline Hope and Professor Pinnock) parry over minor differences, whilst Brother Stephen questions Mancini about his strategies for succession. This time the opposition between modernisers and traditionalists is within the scene itself, the women in the full central light that is directed on the table, the Friars huddled in a shadowy corner, partially obscured by a coat rail. As ever, after a great many false clues as to the perpetrator (including one that points to Hope, a lecturer in Jacobean theatre, another to Brother Stephen) the denouement begins 30 minutes from the end. On this

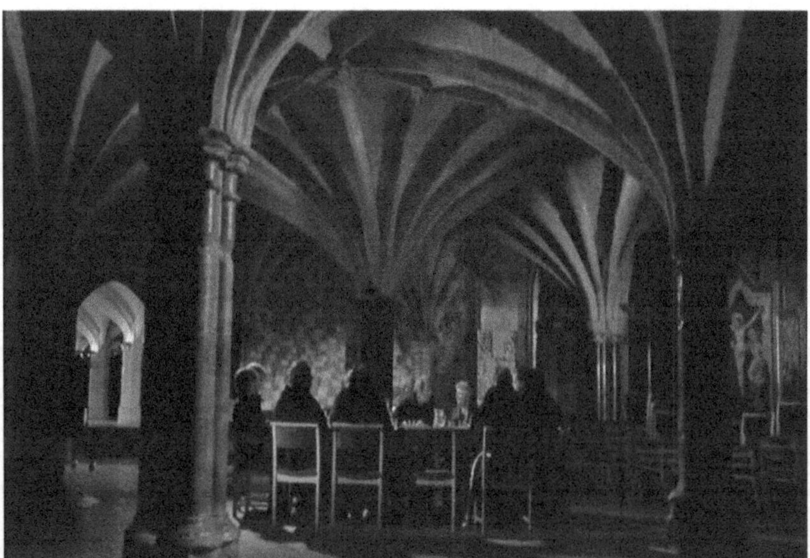

Figure 3.2 *Lewis* – 'Wild Justice' (2011)

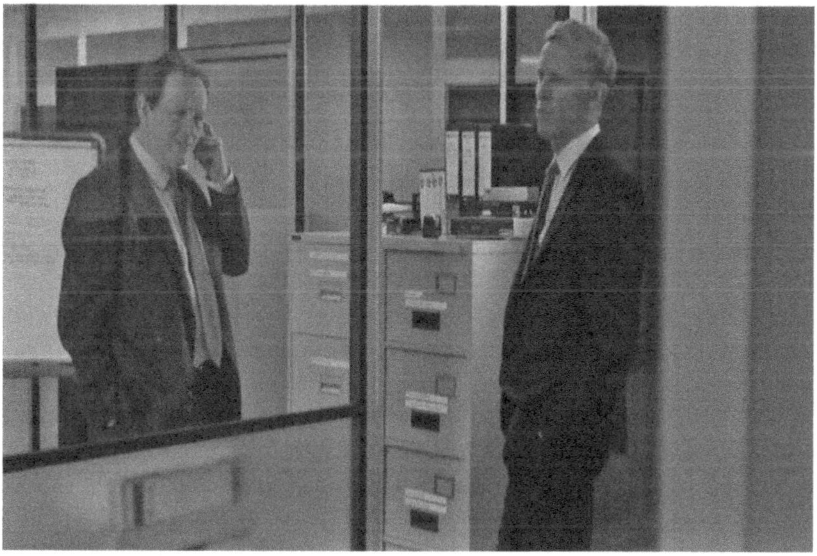

Figure 3.3 *Lewis* – 'Wild Justice' (2011)

occasion a chance misplaced apostrophe on a sign prompts Lewis to declare 'this is all about revenge!' and, in typically random logic, to connect the college servant, Felix, to the killing spree.

'Wild Justice' exemplifies the visual richness of the series and its tendency to position heritage and academia as exotic. The stage for murder is Oxford at its most vibrant, replete with displays of pageantry and hedonism, elaborate processions and ritual college dinners, as well as stage performances ('The Quality of Mercy') and fancy dress parties ('Falling Darkness', 2010; 'Old, Unhappy, Far Off Things', 2011). 'Wild Justice' was filmed in actual Oxford locations (including the medieval college St Edmund's Hall) but the diegetic Oxford is still a work of imagination, a richly romantic other-world in which human passions of jealousy, lust and desire lurk and are liable to spill over. In this Oxford, academics elide the personal with the professional and kill to protect threatened reputations, avenge old slights or rid themselves of errant lovers. Commonly they have radical pasts, sexual secrets (masked by protestations of celibacy or strident feminism) and generally suffer the sort of vaulting ambition that can only end in their downfall. Striding purposefully into this domain of dramatic hyperbole are Lewis and Hathaway, emotionally reticent, sober-suited emissaries of order and modernity. As Felix is arrested and taken away in 'Wild Justice', Caroline Hope recites the title's allusion to Francis Bacon in full: 'Revenge is a kind of wild justice which the more man's nature runs to, the more ought law to weed it out.' Hathaway pauses and remarks, somewhat lamely, 'maybe that's what we're for', before the close-up cuts to an aerial shot from which the two officers exit left frame, and the near victim exits right, leaving a momentary image of an empty grass lawn. Superficial as this mock gravitas might seem, it is also characteristic of the series's loose play with themes around divinity, life and passion that I shall return to presently.

Part of the broader extra-textual appeal of *Lewis* is that, however impossibly gorgeous its screen version of sun-dappled Oxford, a recognisably beautiful, ancient, heritage city of Oxford does indeed exist as an empirically verifiable space, and participating in one of its many 'Morse and Lewis walking tours' is a major attraction for fan-tourists. The singularity of *Lewis*'s Oxford mixes up actual buildings, pubs and traditions with fictional equivalents, much as the invented personae of the series operate within a logic of causality that references actual literary works, fictionalised authors, known astronomical configurations, made-up mathematical formulae and even fantastic medical conditions. The semi-fictive cultural geography of this diegetic Oxford may even be compared to the quasi-mythological space of the classic western, as its situational premise accommodates a range of character types and conflicts that may be implausible in a less imaginative rendition of contemporary space. In both instances, the quasi-mythologised order offers metaphorical possibilities by means of an analogous, rather than literal, correspondence to the concerns of the present day.[15] Unlikely as it might sound, the Oxford of *Lewis* may thus be closer to the Hadleyville of *High Noon*, than it is to the recognisably anxious territory of, say, London in *Prime Suspect* or post-industrial Manchester in *Cracker*. As Richard Dyer notes of the utopian impulse in myth, the very process of drawing attention 'to the gap between what is and what could be, is, ideologically speaking, playing with fire',[16] and it is perhaps because *Lewis* must continue to tread a careful line that excursions and even references to the world beyond the rarefied city centre are so very infrequent. When the beautiful student daughter of the American Secretary of State is recalled to the USA ('The Point of Vanishing') she sighs to Lewis 'I'm being airlifted back to reality', indicating a place or state of mind that, in *Lewis*, is always elsewhere. For the activity of humble, working-class 'ordinary' characters to matter to the narrative, they must either be victims ('Fearful Symmetry', 2012; 'The Indelible Stain', 2012), changelings ('Counter Culture Blues', 'Falling Darkness') or corrupted by the need to disguise their own class inferiority ('Whom the Gods Would Destroy', 2007; 'Dark Matter'). Unusually, as part of their investigation in 'Wild Justice', Lewis and Hathaway are obliged to visit a suburban house belonging to a retired police officer in Bristol. The difference is remarkable: a dreary bungalow on an indistinctive estate, shot in a palette of greys and blues that contrasts markedly with the warmth of the golden Oxford stone, and echoes instead the colours, if not quite the décor, of the police station.

It is, in fact, the bland generic space of Oxford police station – and not the internationally recognised city buildings – that anchors the narrative in the contemporary world, and grounds the heady heights of the fantastic storylines. The station helps to bridge the chasm that might yawn between diegetic Oxford and the physical spaces of everyday life elsewhere in the country, and makes coherent the dual fidelity of the series to both myth and reality. It is ever efficient and calm, a safe retreat, the monochrome furnishings relieved only by the cobalt blue glow of 'Oxfordshire Police' PC screen savers. Rarely seen outside of this comfortable zone is Chief Superintendent Innocent, who serves a similar narrative function to Superintendent Mullett in so far as she listens, chastises and insists on procedure. Like Mullett, she is the visible face of a police hierarchy and part of the wider establishment, complicit with University public relations ('The Indelible Stain'), and in danger of being compromised in her desire to shield local authority figures, once telling Lewis: 'I really can't have you harassing anyone of that standing' ('Whom the Gods Would Destroy'). After her initial hostility towards him, Innocent softens towards Lewis, freeing his opposition to the giddy excesses of the Academy.

Both police and police station exist in constant narrative and visual opposition to wildly extravagant crimes, such as that befalling the beautiful Czech barmaid who is discovered on the riverbank with her throat cut by a stolen Persian mirror ('Allegory of Love'). Indeed, crime in *Lewis* is of the same improbable and aestheticised order as it had often been in *Inspector Morse*, making Lyn Thomas's audience research into the earlier series also relevant here.[17] Amongst the focus groups Thomas documents, crime features so rarely as to warrant Joost De Bruin's surprise that the relationship between crime and fear was not even a discussion topic,[18] although the omission says more about *Inspector Morse*'s nebulous relationship to the contemporary social world than it does about Thomas or her interviewees. For viewers of both *Morse* and *Lewis*, the forms of crimes depicted in the series are as unlikely to touch their own lives as a Western shootout, suggesting that 'fear' of its occurrence will be negligible. In such a context of wildly unlikely criminality, Robbie Lewis is less an enforcer of social norms as the embodiment of them. Hathaway is equally restrained but takes up a more active mediation role in the space between his 'governor' and the academic world which his own genius and privileged past has enabled him to comprehend. Much like a Freemason's handshake, Hathaway is always 'recognised' by his own, and there are frequent exclamations of surprise that someone so well-read, devout and sharp should be a policeman at all ('Wild Justice', 'The Gift of Promise', 2011).

Partnership – God, Love and Discontent

As we shall see with other professional pairings, the two parts of a detective double act must be complementary. In *Lewis*, each is well aware of the qualities of the other, as Robbie once observes: 'Between us, we make a not bad detective. I'm the brains obviously', to which Hathaway responds drily, 'obviously' ('The Dead of Winter'). Although he often lacks the cultural competence to identify certain clues, Lewis is not the chippy working-class Northerner he is sometimes assumed to be by upper-class suspects, so foregrounding education rather than class as the fault-line between him and Hathaway. Spatial alignment is offered to both characters, enabling them to offer alternative, but rarely conflicting, moral viewpoints. If Lewis is 'everyman' he is also informed, intelligent and able to keep up, reminding his sergeant on one occasion 'I do know some big words you know'. Similarly, if Hathaway is 'gifted' and cultivated he nevertheless stands at some distance from those in the academy by dint of being competent, diligent, self-controlled and remarkably unambitious for worldly recognition.

Unlike Lewis, James Hathaway begins the series as an unknown quantity with an unrecorded past. We learn from the pilot that he abandoned seminary training for the police force but – cocking a snook at Morse's notorious atheism – retains a strong private faith. However, other traits, such as an unlikely passion for the guitar and world music are reserved and revealed (or rather invented) much later ('Your Sudden Death Question', 2010). Hathaway's private sexuality is at first left ambiguous, although brought to the fore in 'Life Born of Fire' after a former friend is driven to suicide by 'The Garden', a Christian movement that condemns homosexuality. The investigation prompts Lewis to enquire about Hathaway's preferences, but the younger man simply equivocates that heterosexuality is not necessarily indicated by a taste for 'Yorkie Bars' or the magazine *Loaded*. Nevertheless, he later he uses precisely these accessories, ironically of course, to signal that he is indeed heterosexual.

In 'The Dead of Winter' an investigation requires Hathaway to return to the country seat of Crevecoeur Hall close to where he had lived until the age of 12, when his father had been the Estate Manager for Lord Mortmaigne. This precipitates a sudden rush of narrative interest in him, showing him rattled when he learns that one of the estate girls is self-harming, and briefly reuniting him with a childhood sweetheart, Scarlet Mortmaigne. When Lewis learns of his romantic relationship with a suspect, he sends Hathaway 'on leave', but not before the younger man has snapped: 'I'm not sure I want to wake up in 20 years' time, old, and with nothing more to show than a life spent picking through other people's misery.' Although the revelation of private information prompted criticism from the actor Laurence Fox, who suggested 'the less you know the more you care',[19] the storyline concludes conventionally enough, with order and celibacy restored.

'The Dead of Winter' is also a significant episode for its careful delineation of the class differences between Hathaway and Lewis. Unusually there is a third party to the investigation, DC Hooper, who is abrasive and predictable in his class snobberies, makes numerous jibes about Hathaway's accelerated promotion as a graduate entrant and accuses him of 'cosying up' to the nobility of Crevecoeur Hall. Lewis himself has little contact with the aristocratic family who live there, other than being taunted by Lady Mortmaigne for his 'lower middle-class disapproval' of her adultery. Nevertheless, he is neither deferential nor tempted to demonstrate his contempt for the family's privilege, actually rebuking Hooper for having 'a small mind and a big mouth'. Hooper thus becomes a mechanism to strengthen the bond between the two men in spite of their differences, and their friendship grows in warmth (offset by witty repartee) thereafter. Ultimately, it transpires that the murderer at Crevecoeur Hall is another former childhood friend of Hathaway's, Paul Hopkiss (rather incredibly, the butler), brought up like him as a tenant child, but abused by Lord Mortmaigne. Clearly there is an enigmatic possibility that Hathaway may also have been abused by the aristocrat, but the question is left unanswered.

Whereas Hathaway's relative youth and proximity to the intelligentsia/aristocracy suggests that he may harbour latent passion, Lewis is distinguished only by loss: for his deceased wife, Christian faith, absent children. The Sergeant Lewis of *Inspector Morse* had been in tension with the bachelorhood of his boss, regularly seen to juggle his police duties with his domestic ones, concerned to get home and do his share of child care. In his bereaved and self-evidently older reincarnation in *Lewis*, Robbie's private life intrudes only when he is winded by the memory of Val and the injustice of her unavenged death, or unsettled by a telephone conversation with his distant daughter. Whately claims to have resisted an increased emphasis on middle-aged loneliness, and was relieved when his character's ongoing preoccupation with his late wife was allowed to dwindle.[20] However, the character has few interests outside work: considering then rejecting adult education ('Whom the Gods Would Destroy') or taking on an allotment he has neither the time nor inclination to maintain ('Life Born of Fire'), an experience that only marks a stage in his 'moving on' from bereavement.

For both characters, the possibility of progression is dangled and continually deferred, whether as career development (promotion for Hathaway, retirement for Lewis), or in ever unfulfilled romance. In spite of his happy marriage, there had never been any suggestion that Lewis might have much in the way of sexual imagination, but even when his grief for his wife Val abates, Lewis is denied the narrative opportunity to find a new partner. Whilst reinvestigating an old case, he meets up with a former colleague, Ali McLennan, who flirts and even, to his astonishment, kisses him, but by the next morning she too has been murdered ('Old, Unhappy, Far Off Things'). Gradually (and for the first six series, unproductively) the narrative hints at compatibility between Lewis and the forensic pathologist Dr Laura Hobson (Clare Holman). Hobson appears in every episode, white-suited and meticulous, a confidante as well as a colleague, often pointing out obvious details that Lewis lacks the necessary sensitivity to notice for himself, such as Hathaway's brewing affair with a fellow officer ('The Point of Vanishing'). By series 6, Lewis's inability to even contemplate romance has become a discussion topic, most emphatically in 'Generation of Vipers' (2012), which revolves around the death of a feminist academic, whose lonely hearts video appeal had been uploaded for public amusement on the satirical 'Barker site'. The investigation prompts many timely reflections on the single life, Lewis being unusually exercised by the humiliation she suffered after 'taking a risk', suggesting he is disinclined to take any himself. It is not until the penultimate episode of series 7 (for which Stephen Churchett again supplied the story)[21] that Robbie is allowed to recognise, let alone act upon his desires, and after an off-screen courtship, romance with Laura finally blossoms on-screen, much to the astonishment of their colleagues ('Intelligent Design', 2013).

Early commentators had been sceptical that such a character as Lewis could come close to the charisma of Morse, indeed by the second series Sam Wollaston was ready to dismiss him outright:

> He has sidekick written all over him, and always will. It's there, etched on his permanently bewildered expression, his unflinching loyalty to the force, his ploddy plodishness (surely Lewis is the origin of the word plod, for police). He may be a decent copper, but in every other way he's crap – crap at parties, crap with women, crap at picking a car, crap at every thing basically.[22]

It is an oddly bilious review that selects a set of heterosexual clichés of hard-boiled masculinity as an implied ideal, even though one would be hard-pressed to find a single television detective who meets more than one of these criteria. A counter view might be that Robbie Lewis is actually an example of brave characterisation, which opens up more subtle meaning possibilities for his particularly understated heroism. Lewis's is the voice of steady, decent people everywhere: his own lack of personal passion, including the progressive dissipation of his anger over Val's death, implies a retreat to quiet exasperation, passive resistance to the untethered volatility of brilliant, passionate people. Although Hathaway was regarded by Wollaston as the greater interest, for being simply 'more ... well, more Morse', it would be simplistic to see him as an inversion of Lewis's shortcomings when theirs is such an inspired transformation of the dynamic at work in the former Lewis/Morse partnership.

Without Morse's romantic yearnings, celibacy becomes increasingly important to the new partnership. Of course, emotional isolation is a generic convention, but given that in *Lewis* passion (its opposite) is the hallmark of the powerful, criminal 'Other', there is a heightened need for narrative delicacy around any demonstration of desire by the detectives. It is precisely their shared reserve and self-denial that positions them outside of the world they encounter and enables them to comment upon it philosophically. Lewis is hardened to the demands of the job (another generic trope of course), as is regularly emphasised, such as when he is asked how it feels to be 'surrounded by dead bodies all the time', and he simply quips, 'it's a living' ('Fearful Symmetry'). Hathaway, younger and less weary, is shown often to be troubled by the plight of victims, and so willing to take on the burden of guilt that he questions his aptitude for the job. Fittingly, when the series concludes, it is not just with Robbie reaffirming his intention to retire but with Hathaway declaring his to resign, in resentment at how the job 'makes you look at things differently'. Their parting exchange is in keeping with a quasi-philosophical tone throughout, usually underpinned by the mapping of interpersonal conflicts on to clashes of values (intellectual, cultural, class, religious), so allowing lofty questions of spirit to be appropriated as themes. Self-reflexive as to their duty as policemen, they assume a certain moral superiority to this world in which lust, power and murderous intent are often elided.

Of course, for a great many detective dramas, the resolution to a case is an occasion to reflect upon its moral example. In *Lewis*, such deliberation is existential rather than social in tone, and so plays quite differently to similar ruminations by other police officers such as Jack Frost, who tended to mourn the fragility of everyday life. Murders in *Lewis* bear an altogether different relationship to 'normality', they are the *haute-criminalité* of the outrages that litter the worlds of contemporary crime fiction, the outcome of intellectual glory, passion and delusion. Indulging in abstract moral and spiritual discussion is increasingly necessary for Lewis and Hathaway to counterbalance the grandiose representation of crime as a classically 'tragic' product of untrammelled passion. Like Hathaway's intention to resign ('I used to think that people were basically good. Now I don't and I don't know when that changed'), the near asceticism of the two detectives is a way of emphasising that the price of their essential opposition to criminality is the repression of their own humanity and/or desire. If murder is the terminus where the ambitious finally over-reach themselves, then 'dissent', in so far as it can be expressed at all, must be articulated in judgement of excess itself.

4

Ambivalent Voices: Moral Allegiance in *Prime Suspect* and *Cracker*

Emboldened by the economic and critical returns on its investment in quality drama, in the early 1990s the ITV Network Centre commissioned a raft of new peak-time crime series, including some which departed from the *Morse* model in their aesthetic recommitment to 'gritty' social realism and common willingness to address challenging subjects, such as racist or misogynist policing. The first five series of *A Touch of Frost* demonstrated some such inclinations, although as we have seen the show later underwent a significant, albeit gradual, softening of tone and visual style. Of the others, the two greeted with the most enthusiasm were *Prime Suspect* (1991–2006) and *Cracker* (1993–2006), each produced for ITV by Granada Television. Both of these series are determinedly (if unspectacularly) metropolitan in setting, and appeared to chime with the unease of a decade that had been ushered in by the poll tax riots of 1990, the resignation of Margaret Thatcher and the onset of a sharp economic recession to which unprecedentedly high crime rates were now being attributed. As liberal-left commentators warned of social breakdown and provided cautionary lists of the crime-ridden estates scattered across 'No-Go Britain'[1] it became clear that 'crime' had become the barometer of urban malaise.

Prime Suspect and *Cracker* are saturated with the social dissatisfaction of their era. Each is punctuated by references to homelessness, social exclusion, the welfare state and the broader disintegration of civic and community values. Willingness to tackle difficult topics was matched by a visual appetite for what Brunsdon calls the 'spectacularization of the body and site of crime',[2] a tendency shared with cinematic films of the time such as *The Silence of the Lambs* (Jonathan Demme, 1991) and an increasingly lurid cycle of literary crime fiction by authors such Patricia Cornwell, James Patterson and Minette Walters. As Mizejewski notes, 'the standard turf for 1990s crime stories' was: '[s]adistic violence, serial killers and dysfunctional bureaucracies', alongside a growing interest in forensics.[3] Where series such as *A Touch of Frost* and *Inspector Morse* remained mindful of their loyal cross-demographic audiences and continued to shy away from visceral images and bodily effluence, *Prime Suspect* and *Cracker* staked a claim to greater authenticity on their unflinching representation of rape, murder and, sometimes abuse *by* police, as well as the display of gruesome forensic evidence.

Particularly interesting with both series is how integral characterisation is to their mobilisation of socially reflexive critique, resulting in two of the most memorably complex performances of British television: Helen Mirren's celebrated portrayal of detective Jane Tennison in *Prime Suspect*, and Robbie Coltrane's troubled and charismatic psychologist, Dr Fitzgerald ('Fitz') in *Cracker*. As this chapter is intended to complement rather than rehearse the growing literature on either series, I shall focus on what I regard as a central, but neglected, critical concern: the articulation of expressive, contingent voices, made persuasive in each through a systematic structure of moral allegiance. In both, the acute moral superiority and professional judgement of the protagonist exists as a counterpoint to other, 'ordinary' police officers, thus carving out for the viewer a privileged, critical position at a time of equivocal feeling towards the police. Given their intense timeliness, it is also interesting to consider the way in which the revivals of each in 2006 – coming some time after their period of peak popularity and resonance – play in different ways to and with the accrued allegiances of earlier series. Ongoing, emotionally invested, relationships of trust underpin the *de facto* licence that permits these characters to express dissenting sentiments which transcend the personal, and raise complex ethical and political questions that the viewer is repeatedly invited to navigate.

Prime Suspect

Prime Suspect was created by the actor and writer Lynda La Plante with the assistance of DCI Jackie Malton, whose real-life experiences in the masculine stronghold of the Metropolitan Police Flying Squad have since been widely reported. A couple of years later La Plante parted company from Granada, having contributed three storylines and two full series scripts, but now citing differences over the direction wanted for the character of Jane Tennison.[4] Subsequent series employed male writers such as Paul Billing and Frank Deasy, and were produced by an almost all-male team. Up until 1996 it remained in regular production although, after a disappointed critical response to *Prime*

Suspect 5: Errors of Judgement there was a seven-year gap before *Prime Suspect 6: The Last Witness* in 2003, and another three before a further revival, firmly titled 'The Final Act' (2006). Most of the series were actually broadcast in an intensive mini-serial format over consecutive nights, but in series 4 changed briefly to a run of more conventional feature-length, self-contained episodes. Whether or not this was to suit the requirements of overseas buyers (see Chapter 1) or the result of Mirren's personal intervention[5] is not certain, but it later reverted back to its original formula.

The first few programmes are located in London, and make verbal references to police stations at West End Lane and Scotland Yard, as well as providing brief glimpses of city landmarks. Later, Tennison is relocated or 'loaned' elsewhere, for example to Hadley Green (*Prime Suspect 4*, 1995) and Manchester (*Prime Suspect 5*, 1996), and her return to the screen in 2003 saw her visiting Bosnia for an investigation that brought her into contact with recent war crimes. Consistently, however, the *misé-en-scene* is as dark as the crimes under investigation, transforming mundane spaces into sinister sites of mutilation: a lock-up garage bearing the evidence of sexual assault and torture, a charred council flat with an unidentified cadaver, a homeless boy dying of AIDS in an unofficial shanty town at 'the Bullring'. Moving from space to morbid space, Tennison seems to permanently dodge downpours, often shot in the murky evening light from behind a rain-splattered windscreen.

Unsurprisingly, given the relative rarity of female investigators in television crime fiction, *Prime Suspect* has been repeatedly examined in the context of questions of gender, although the 'radicalism' of a female character in a typically male role may have been exaggerated. In the first episode, senior officers articulate their reluctance to put a woman in charge of a murder investigation (asking one another 'are you prepared to take the risk?')[6] with a bluntness that seemed out of kilter with the political correctness of the early 1990s. It is debatable whether this was a shocking indictment of police patriarchy or simply a case in which 'drama is trailing reality'.[7] Arguably, the real blood had already been spilt in the professional gender battles of the 1970s and 1980s, although the equal opportunities case brought by Alison Halford in 1990 suggested that the macho culture of the police force may have provided the conditions for a continuing and entrenched form of institutional discrimination.[8] There had been female leads in British police series before – notably *Juliet Bravo* (BBC 1980–5) and *The Gentle Touch* (LWT 1980–4) – but the sophisticated private/professional conflicts that were later developed for DCI Jane Tennison made her character a cultural marker, a reference point for its time, part of a televisual working through of matters of public concern.

Picking up on the Equal Opportunities theme of the first series, *Prime Suspect 2* (1992) characteristically begins and ends with references to Freemasonry, and with scenes of senior officers (with links to Conservative politicians) sharing information about her, closing ranks to deny her promotion and conforming to an institutional logic of recognition that systematically undervalues a 'good detective' for what she is. In later series, Jane has herself become 'old guard' and no longer has to suffer openly sexist caricatures (at least she is not called a 'bird' or told the job is too dirty for her) but she is still alien to certain forms of male camaraderie, in spite of her ability to 'drink with the lads'. Mary Eaton describes this collegiality as 'canteen culture' and notes its continued importance in endorsing 'hegemonic masculinity' and perpetuating male authority some 20 years after the passing of equal opportunities legislation in 1974.[9] Indeed, as I shall later demonstrate, as late as 2006 the final episode contributed to a still-rumbling public debate as to whether professional women could really, ever, 'have it all'.

Crucially, for the viewer, Tennison's superiority of judgement and insight is consistently displayed in contrast to the officers around her, who make mistakes that undermine her or for which she, as their senior, must take responsibility. The structure of allegiance in *Prime Suspect 2* is also exemplary in this respect. At one point in the murder inquiry Jane interviews the chief suspect, David Harvey, on his death bed, coaxing from him an odious confession of rape and murder whilst she holds and strokes his hand. The sequence is cross-cut with another, this time conducted back at the station by DS Bob Oswalde, a black officer with whom Tennison previously had a sexual liaison and who has since been seconded to her team. Marginalised by Tennison and the menial tasks she asks of him, Oswalde has gone out on a limb, arresting Tony Allen, a young, terrified black man and subjecting him to prolonged, bullying interrogation whilst his parents sit in the reception area. Allen's mental state is a concern to both the custody sergeant and the demonstrably racist DI Frank Burkin, neither of whom think him fit to be detained, although neither is prepared to over-rule Oswalde and send the youth to hospital instead. Later, Allen commits suicide in his cell, and it is Jane who must deal with the fall-out, not least by informing the parents, to whom scant consideration has been paid by anyone else. As Jermyn has noted, the aggressive masculinity of Oswalde's approach is contrasted with the 'femininity' of Jane's, although hers is an uncomfortable act, and seems 'grossly misplaced'.[10] However, the *professional* difference between them is essentially a matter of judgement, not approach: Oswalde is not a routinely hot-headed officer but one whose perspective has become badly impaired. The moral implications of the incident are also more complicated than they appear at first sight: Tennison later holds Burkin responsible for failing to act upon his concerns; Oswalde is proved right in thinking that Allen had been involved in the murder of Joanne, albeit as a horrified observer; and the inquest returns an official verdict of suicide (although this does little to stop Oswalde torturing himself for his error of judgement). In any event, Tennison's feminine deceit is proven to be counter-productive once Harvey's confession, besides being legally inadmissible, is discovered to be a fabrication designed to cover up for his nephew. Amongst such ambivalence, all that carries any certainty is a generalised impression of police fallibility under the sort of pressures from which Jane too is not immune, although her relative superiority of judgement is never in question.

The ambivalence exaggerates another generic trope: typically, Jane's methods may be dubious but her 'voice' is usually affirmed as one of ethical principle. As direct speech this can sometimes jar, for example in series 5 (*Errors of Judgement*) when she chastises Ballinger for his morally compromised arrangements with a local gangster: 'you compromise and you deal and you bargain until there is no law, there is no order, there is no justice!' However, Jane's ethics are more complex than such bald utterances might suggest, and although she singularly refuses to ever take the line of least resistance against corruption, her moral perspective must still be retrieved by the viewer from the complications of dire mistakes, insensitivity and occasional willingness to condone breaches of procedure herself.

Within this logic, it is the strength of Jane's grasp of the moral endgame that is most telling, and in order to engage the viewer for the ends rather than the means, she is regularly made analogous to the victims of crime. In her analysis of *Prime Suspect 6: The Last Witness* (2003), Jermyn notes the expressive strategies of visual alignment used, citing the opening sequence which shows Tennison undergoing a medical examination via 'a series of dislocated close-ups of her hands, torso and feet, which foreshadow the post-mortem that awaits the victim's body'.[11] Similarly, Cavender and Jurik observe instances that infer 'connection and empathy' between Jane and both the dead and the living, such as when she mirrors the body language of Samira's sister during an interview, and they celebrate her clear sense of moral purpose in this episode even when she is suspended from duty.[12]

Nevertheless, it is important to recognise that Jane's moral courage is far from exceptional in the detective genre, and as I shall later elaborate, we must consider as problematic the claim that this particular series is a 'progressive moral fiction' or that Tennison is an unusual 'justice provocateur'.[13] Like all good TV detectives, Jane relies upon instinct, enabling her to distinguish the truth from the obvious, the guilty from the usual suspect. Although often marginalised amongst men within the frame, she is also privileged, as Jermyn has noted elsewhere, by the visual tradition of a lingering close-up on her face for an 'extra beat' at the resolution of a scene.[14] As we have already seen with *A Touch of Frost*, this 'beat' is a conventional opportunity for the viewer to contemplate facial performance and infer an accord between themselves and the protagonist. More distinctive to *Prime Suspect* is the expressive coding of Jane's 'instinct' through various visual and performative motifs such as seeing and touching, the empathetic nature of which provides means of alignment to Jane herself in a way that is quite different from conventional visual strategies of optical and spatial alignment. It is 'the insistence on looking, or refusal to look, at women ... [that] ... is marked as a central motif in *Prime Suspect*'s gendered aesthetics and its investigation of male structures of power'.[15] As Jermyn further elaborates in her monograph, Tennison's 'willingness to touch' is similarly indicative of how she can also be 'movingly empathetic and human'[16] and can demonstrate types of behaviour that might be difficult to imagine of her male colleagues.

In *Prime Suspect* 6, 'seeing' also takes on thematic significance, not least in a scene where Jane attends an optical examination with 'Lukic', a man she suspects to be both a Bosnian war criminal and a recent murderer, now practising as an optician. When she is shown news footage of the atrocity for which she believes him responsible, and learns that it had been considered 'too harrowing to be shown in British homes after dinner' (the same time, of course, when *Prime Suspect* would have been transmitted), the viewer is actively denied the chance to look, being shown only Jane's reactions as she watches the video. As in previous episodes, Jane's subsequent refusal to settle for an easy solution to the case is a direct result of her ability to 'see', but it means that she becomes isolated from her colleagues and compelled to desist by senior officers.

It is nevertheless worth remembering that, if a willingness to look and touch is coded as feminine in the series, it is through the narrative and visual oppositions of the text rather than through correspondence with a conventional set of feminine attributes. The sequence of Jane watching the video is immediately juxtaposed with the response of Detective Chief Superintendent Larry Hall (Mark Strong) to whom she has shown it, but who denies her permission to visit Bosnia to further the investigation. As Creeber observes, in the very first episode Jane had made a 'slow arrival' into a 'typically masculine environment' as a direct counterpoint to DCI Shefford's bullying, tough persona, which is in many respects 'an Identikit picture of previous fictional male detectives'.[17] By contrast, Hall is one of a new breed of politically astute male senior police management, but a continuation with the earlier, macho/masonic closed-ranks is implied. In a direct allusion to *Prime Suspect 3* (1993), when he was just an inspector, Hall tells a more junior officer: 'I used to work for Jane Tennison. Now she works for me.' By inferring that Tennison does not and has not played the orthodox (male) game and has therefore been overtaken by other (male) officers, her lone stance (a generic trope) becomes associated with an implied femininity. Whereas *The Gentle Touch* had arguably left male territory to the men – by reinforcing DI Maggie Forbes's rather different, softer, approach in parallel rather than in conflict with theirs – Tennison's character is altogether more contradictory, and the challenges the series makes are often to extra-textual or generic viewer expectations. In the first series, her insistence on looking closely at Della Mornay's decomposing corpse is meaningful only because DCI Shefford had earlier shaken his head and refused, presumably out of squeamishness (a 'feminine' trait?) to look at Karen's body. In *Prime Suspect* 6, Jane's willingness to look (at the footage) is underlined by her willingness to act and defy what she regards as politically compromised authority. This is conventionally heroic behaviour, gendered here as feminine only through opposition with men who cannot or will not do the same.

There is a similar reversal of gender expectations in the reworked series, of the conventional conflict between work and private life. Typically, it is the male officers whose personal lives are shown to impinge on their work[18] whilst Jane, conversely and repeatedly, allows her job 'to screw up another relationship' ('The Scent of Darkness', 1995). The increasing narrative interest in Tennison's romantic life (allegedly at Mirren's instigation and a bone of contention with La Plante) is in itself revealing. It is perhaps as if having introduced an ambivalently feminine voice into a male genre, the series is required to pick over its ramifications. As Jermyn observes:

> While the romantic ineptitude of the lone detective may be a familiar scenario from Sam Spade to Inspector Morse, its implications shift when the cop in question is female, since it means that her very being and legitimacy as a woman becomes the subject of enquiry.[19]

The cultural example that Tennison provided for the renegotiation of this conventional trope both coincided with and gave rise to extra-textual public discussion around working women. Unlikely as the comparison might sound, this brings her closest in social function to Gene Hunt in *Life on Mars* (see Chapter 5): not so much a provocateur of justice but a provocateur of discourse; a catalyst and working through of social changes that have already occurred. The ability to assume a certain discursive centrality is facilitated not by subjective identification in the psychoanalytic sense proposed by film theory, but by the characteristic offer of an ongoing position of shared allegiance that encourages contemplation rather than immersion.

Jane's life is repetitive but it does also convey a sense of development: lovers come and go, but some relationships extend beyond the narrative arc of the episodic crime investigation, implying a private life lived off-screen while Jane gets on with each job in hand. However, the repetition of relationships becomes cumulative as well as cyclical, each time their prospects of success seem less and less likely, and Jane is allowed to age in a manner that, say, Frost is not. When she discovers herself pregnant in *Prime Suspect 3* and subsequently goes for an abortion in *Prime Suspect 4: The Lost Child* (broadcast 16 months later in 1995), it is clear that this may well have been her last opportunity to become a mother, even though the only question she asks of the doctor is 'when can I get back to work?'. On her return, she has to take over an investigation into what is revealed, ironically, as the murder of a toddler. Although her emotions over her own 'lost child' do not cloud her judgement, the viewer's privileged view of her being visibly affected (for example, whilst looking at a baby photo in the case file) is made public when she becomes uncharacteristically tearful in the incident room.

In common with similar storylines in both *A Touch of Frost* and *Cracker* (see below) the case of a missing child inspires scenes of mob outcry over child protection, a known sex offender wrongly accused, mock news footage and the formulation of hasty police judgements. However, with a not-long-since-potential mother in charge, all of this is rather differently inflected. Moreover, however compromised Tennison may have been by personal circumstances, it is DI Tony Muddyman who loses control and assaults the prime suspect, and Tennison who is sensitive enough to appreciate that he must himself have been abused. It is also Tennison who coaxes the child's *mother*, Susan, to admit that, for her, motherhood had been a constant endurance (the baby 'would *not* be satisfied, would *not* let me sleep'). When Susan finally breaks down and confesses to murder ('I'm the victim! Suffocated since the beginning'), it morally complicates the parallel story of Tennison's 'lost' chance at motherhood, much as Jane's own silent, lonely expressions of loss (clutching a teddy bear) work against the possibility of reading her character as cold and detached. The emotional ramifications of being 'wedded to the job' are revisited in other episodes, such as when Jane is suspended temporarily from duty in 'The Scent of Darkness' and begins to drink heavily. In this case it is only the willingness of her colleague, Richard, to support her unofficial investigation that allows her to regain self-control. Thereafter the devil is always at the door, and the incident foreshadows murmurings of a drink problem that becomes fully realised in 'The Final Act'.

Prime Suspect: The Final Act

Although the first *Prime Suspect* had introduced Tennison as an emergent figure, a newly promoted DCI hungry to prove herself, in 'The Final Act' some fifteen years later she is being described in essentially residual terms, for example by DCS Mitchell as: 'Old School, that's Tennison. On the force what 30, 35 years? Battered, burnt-out. Dinosaurs. What did they do when they leave? They drank themselves to death that's what'. From a figure yet to be reckoned with to one whose promise was now spent, Jane's career trajectory seemed to have played out on screen (albeit with ellipses). If it had been a life intensively lived, the inference was that it had hitherto been under-examined, and its injuries were soon to overwhelm her. In keeping with this, the narrative style of this final episode moved away from an emphasis on revelation (the horrors of crime, the police behind closed doors) to a greater emphasis on reflection. It was to prove controversial that this ultimate and most self-reflexive of editions should be so haunted by past episodes, as it meditated in turn on a career spent in a particularly brutalising sort of public service.

A sense of passing was always part of the promise of the revival, and the opening shots of Mirren in 'The Final Act' inevitably provoke comparison with previous appearances: certainly this is not the character described as 'every man's fantasy powerful woman'.[20] Instead, her pallor is as harsh and grey as the lighting, as she wakes on a sofa dressed in pyjamas at the beginning of a scene which progresses at a markedly slow, gloomy pace in contrast to the inter-cut shots of a frantic discovery of a missing girl. Jane investigates her own night before, piecing it together from clues: a bruise on her forehead, an empty bottle of spirits on the coffee table, the telephone left off the hook, the toilet seat left up. Dressed and ready to leave, she opens an empty fridge and a spent carton of orange juice, obliging her to down a tall glass of vodka undiluted. The entire *misé-en-scène* (her work suit, the kitchen) is cast in monochrome shades and lit by a steely grey light: this may recognisably be the Tennison of former editions but older and worse for wear than ever before. A history of allegiance with this character would in itself generate an expectation of sympathy, and the full impact of the sequence could be realised only with prior knowledge. Moreover, Jane's evident uncertainty about herself in this sequence is contagious, further inviting the viewer to judge, albeit with compassion, rather than to align (perceptually or emotionally). It immediately reinforces the theatrical resonance of the title ('Final Act') for it is now possible to infer the intended parallel between Jane and a classical tragic hero approaching that critical moment of recognition (of the flawed self) that Aristotle called 'agnorisis'.

It is evident from the first few minutes of screen time that this final drama is to be more than usually about Jane herself, elevating the generic trope of a detective's dysfunctional private life to centre-plot. This, her last case before retirement, concerns a missing teenage girl, Sally Sturdy, and a range of potential suspects including the girl's father Tony Sturdy, two teenage boys/friends called Curtis and Lester, and her head teacher, Sean Phillips. Familiar to fans of *Prime Suspect* would be the manner in which certainties about a given subject at any time are confounded by new forensic discoveries. Also well-precedented – but rarely to this extent – is the intermarriage of personal and public storylines, although in this instance Jane's private tragedy is not so much juxtaposed with as played out *through* the murder investigation. She becomes unusually attached to 14-year-old Penny, Sally's best friend and the daughter of Sean Phillips, with whom her badly managed relationship becomes a figurative squaring up to her younger, lost self. Equally significant is Jane's relationship with her father (Frank Finlay), for whom she was once the little girl he didn't ever want to see 'what people were capable of', last seen in *Prime Suspect* 6 encouraging her lonely crusade: 'you know what's right, and you'll do it'. In 'The Final Act', it is his death that precipitates one of the crisis points in the narrative when, on leaving him in hospital, Jane is confronted by the gun-wielding Curtis in a sequence that ends with the shooting of her old adversary, now friend and fellow alcoholic, Bill Otley.

Throughout the first of the two parts, Jane's performance at work is consistently undermined by small but telling narrative incidents and her growing awareness of her own fallibility. On one occasion, there is a shot of her sitting behind the steering wheel of her car as she unwraps and eats a supermarket sandwich. At this point the camera is positioned apparently inside the car, towards the dashboard facing the passenger seat, but we then cut to a shot of the same action, this time with the camera positioned head on, observing Jane through the familiar barrier of the rain-splattered windscreen, at the very moment that she pulls out a quarter bottle of wine. It is an apparently small incident that disrupts the spatial alignment and well demonstrates an aesthetic project which continually complicates (and sometimes confounds) the structure of allegiance. Shortly afterwards, an interrogation of Sally's father (at this point under suspicion) dissolves in disarray after he points out that it is Tennison, and not he, who is smelling of alcohol. Sturdy's continued and well-founded antipathy towards her contrasts self-consciously with the moral certainties of her previous relationships with prime suspects. Later, he shows her a home videotape of Sally kissing her head teacher after a basketball win. It is a moment that seems to promise itself as a narrative turning point, a new investigative lead and an opportunity for Tennison to salvage his respect, yet it is foreclosed when she rejects the evidence instantly, urging Sturdy to take it no further. Challengingly, Jane is now refusing to 'see' what others can.

Throughout this first part, spatial alignment is used not to support allegiance but to offer privileged insight into the distress Jane feels at her *own separation from* the woman she once was. This private duality and self-disgust invites contemplation and retrospection, and generates qualified pity. In the second part the narrative and moral orientation shifts markedly, this time supported by less ambiguous methods of optical alignment. Broadcast a week later, it plays with a differently configured recognition of Tennison than anticipated by the first episode, given that she has since been re-established as an increasingly fallible and unreliable party. Nevertheless, new expectations are again confounded, this time by a frantic chase sequence that suggests less time for the maudlin introspections of the previous week. When Curtis is tracked down at his sister's apartment, he has just been shot on the toilet by his young niece who is still wielding the weapon, thus allowing the old Jane to show that, in spite of being 'the cop supposedly without maternal instinct, [she] knows how to talk her down'.[21] Although the storyline of Jane's private anguish continues to unfold slowly, in the second episode there are more reminders of Jane's professional competence, and some exquisitely understated moments that complicate easy judgements: a purchased bottle of whisky left (as yet unopened) on the table;

the ring of her mobile phone as her father's coffin is ceremonially brought into the crematorium; the sincerity of her promise to Sturdy ('I give you my word'); and the simple gesture of faith in her from a colleague who refuses to believe that she would offer alcohol to Penny.

Jane's fallibility gradually becomes less about her alcoholism and more about her affection for Penny, a girl who repeatedly reminds her of her younger self and against whom the evidence is mounting. 'She stole my heart', muses Jane, 'who'd have thought' – from which an audience might well infer that it is precisely being in possession of a heart that drove her to drink in the first place. Penny's intense affection for her father, apparently irrational rejection of her mother and strong moral instincts (even though she is later revealed as the murderer) chime with more than Jane's professional sentiments. Indeed, her career achievements begin to pale, her evident personal scars emphasising the price that she has paid *for* others: for victims avenged and crimes averted.

Viewed positively, one could read this closing edition of the show as a tribute, an elegy to a generation that made it unnecessary for Penny's generation to fight the same professional battles. The converse is equally possible, of course, typified by Libby Brooks's response in the *Guardian* which regarded it as 'a depressing ending for a character who was emblematic of women's struggle to succeed in the workplace'.[22] This tendency to distinguish a character's allegorical trajectory from their nuances of characterisation is significant, for as Annette Kuhn notes of the American police characters Cagney and Lacey, these 'cannot be conceptualized as realistic images of women, but as textual constructions of possible modes of femininity... they do not function as role models but are symbolic realizations of feminine subject positions with which viewers can identify in fantasy'.[23]

The complex system of allegiance developed in the ultimate *Prime Suspect* offers shifting positions of relative sympathy with Jane, whilst eliciting distress at the price she has paid. It fits, in this respect, with what Murray Smith calls a 'graduated' moral structure – as opposed to a Manichean one – for it 'situates characters within a more finely calibrated spectrum of moral gradations, and thus tends to elicit mixed and qualified emotions' that marry up somewhat with psychological states of approval and disapproval.[24] Remarkably, Jane's present condition (loneliness, alcoholism) thus becomes contingent rather than defining: this is not, in other words, a study of an alcoholic, as her alcoholism is but the dramatic manifestation of the emotional price she is paying. As Brooks also noted: '[t]he early Tennison knew what she wanted, and went for it gladly. Her final incarnation was a woman of regret'.[25] Rather than the demise suggested by Mirren's infamous 'slip' – that this would be the character's last ever outing unless she came 'back from the dead'[26] – the viewer is left with a closing sequence in which Tennison leaves the station early to avoid her own retirement party. She departs both as a woman who has foregone too much and as an officer who has given too much, although she is at least spared the ritual humiliation of the male stripper in police uniform, whose arrival she notices, half-smiling, as she simply walks away.

Cracker

Cracker was *Prime Suspect*'s most commonly cited contemporary, having arrived on domestic screens a couple of months prior to its third series and concluding within a fortnight of 'The Final Act'. Initially there were three series, all broadcast in a different format to *Prime Suspect* as each comprised three separate stories, broadcast across two or three weekly one hour instalments. This amounted to a total of 21, high-ratings episodes going out over a period of just over three years (September 1993–November 1995), helping it to achieve quite an intense cultural impact. After a one-off special in 1996 ('White Ghost'), British production of the series ceased for an entire decade until Fitz was brought back from his narrative exile in Australia for a final, two-part edition, 'Nine-Eleven', broadcast in November 2006.

As with *Prime Suspect*, the series is embedded in a city location, in this instance Manchester, but although Fitz has been described by Steve Blandford as a character 'haunting a post-industrial landscape',[27] the actual spaces encountered during investigations are more varied than this might suggest. Murders do occur in grim, graffiti-strewn estates and back alleyways ('To Say I Love You', 1993) or a corner shop in an old working-class neighbourhood ('To Be a Somebody', 1994), but they also take place in comfortable, quiet, suburban settings ('The Big Crunch', 1994), similar to Fitz's own domestic situation. A rare reflexive incident occurs in 'Brotherly Love' (1995) when Fitz and DS Beck visit a derelict industrial site, now home to a number of men living rough, including Barney, a charismatic singing Scottish tramp who reminds them of what the place once stood for: 'My father used to work here – him and thousands of others!' It is one of only occasional nods to the once industrial prowess of the North, to all those who flocked to Manchester for the sort of work made virtually obsolete by 1980s monetarism and the near collapse of industrial manufacturing. In 2006, Fitz's return to Manchester sees him astonished by the regeneration of the city in his absence, spatially encoding the character as out of sorts, and self-consciously out of his time, and it is interesting that this of all the episodes should be the most reflexive in its routine deployment of space.

Cracker was originally developed in response to an ITV call for replacements for *Inspector Morse*, although Gub Neal, its original producer, has since spoken of an appetite amongst the development team to do something 'much more original than yet another Morse'.[28] The most apparent innovation of the new series lay in the choice of a forensic psychologist rather than a regular policeman to play the central role, a decision that coincided with a growing cultural interest in forensics, and that had been taken to ensure a grittier take on contemporary crime: the inclusion of all that was 'grubby, dirty, dangerous and didn't sit very comfortably on the palate'.[29] Neal had previously worked on *Prime Suspect 2* where he had begun to form the possibility of a series around a psychological profiler, an idea he took to the writer Jimmy McGovern who created the series assemblage and central character, Fitz, and wrote six of the original screenplays as well as 'Nine Eleven'.

McGovern made no attempt to emulate the procedural authenticity of *Prime Suspect*, and Fitz was allowed to access police files and interview suspects with a freedom that would not in reality have been acceptable under the Police and Criminal Evidence Act. Defending the improbability of the first series, McGovern insisted:

> There are a number of incidents in all three stories that are somewhat far-fetched, but then you could say the same about Greek tragedy or a Stephen Spielberg film. Good fiction must be believable, but with a suspension of disbelief. The desire for procedural correctness mustn't deny the poetic interpretation of characters as people.[30]

The poetic licence granted to Fitz is to be profoundly, engagingly flawed, and allowed to express a highly persuasive take on life that solicits viewer trust in his intellectual and ethical position, and may excuse his maverick behaviour.

Memorably, Fitz's screen debut in 'The Mad Woman in the Attic' (1993) shows him breaking off a telephone call to his bookmakers to give a (late, improvised) university lecture in which he advises students to discard their Spinoza, Freud and Descartes until they have confronted the darkness of their own souls. Further into the episode he is seen berating a friend over dinner for lecturing on female oppression whilst employing a woman to clean her house on a minimal wage, and the scene ends – not for the last time – with Fitz drenched by a woman's drink. From the first, Fitz displays an 'essentially predatory' intellect,[31] that articulates a complex social conscience but dispenses with the political dogma of an earlier decade, emerging as very much in tune with a particular, challenging, cultural moment. As McGovern has noted: 'He was the kind of man it was so easy to attack in the late Seventies. You could use all kinds of misogynist, sexist, racist labels against him then but it was not so easy to attack him in the Nineties.'[32] If the political identities and certainties of the past had lately become more complex, then Fitz was an eloquent witness for his time, and it is the character's sharp wit, verbal dexterity and penetrating insight that mark him as distinctive. When DCI Wise asks, rhetorically: 'Are you infallible?' Fitz simply quips, 'Yes, the other guy is an imposter' ('The Big Crunch'). He is always a step ahead of received wisdom, fuelled by fascination for destruction, Catholic self-loathing and an innately superior psychological understanding of what might drive a disturbed culprit to kill, and kill again.

Serial killers are plentiful in *Cracker*, not least because the format of the show relies upon cliff-hangers (Who will they kill next? Will they be caught in time?) to sustain suspense from week to week, but the essential and constant enigma that preoccupies the central character and propels the narrative is neither 'who-dunnit?' nor even – as with *Prime Suspect* – '*Did* they do it?', but a simpler, psycho-social interrogative: 'Why?' In pursuit of this question a structure of allegiance is constructed, according to which Fitz's private life unravels in parallel to successive police investigations, and which depends upon the viewer having access to both Fitz's private dysfunction *and* the mind of the murderer. 'To Say I Love You' provides an excellent demonstration of this with a plot involving Sean and Tina, two alienated youths, whose sexual relationship spills over into a killing spree of retribution against loan sharks, family members and the police themselves. The early exhilaration of their coupling is contrasted with stages in the breakdown of Fitz's marriage to Judith, as when the sequence in which Sean steals a bus (on which Tina, breathless at back, exclaims: 'It's like Bonnie and Clyde!') is inter-cut by shots of Fitz banging angrily at the door of Judith's parents' house, where she is seeking refuge. Serendipitously, Fitz is arrested for harassment and incarcerated, although his release is quickly engineered by DS Beck who wants him to interrogate Sean, conveniently in the very next cell. Fitz quickly recognises the extent of Sean's stuttering, angry, psychological disturbance and asks for him to be remanded, pending further reports, arguing 'I'm talking prevention here'. Yet Beck refuses, and Sean is released with disastrous consequences.

Although Fitz's superior insight is endorsed officially by his professional and academic qualifications, it is rarely expressed as scientific, and seems rather to arise out of the *emotional* disposition he shares with the culprit, in this case Sean. Two consecutive sequences affirm this. In the first, there is a barking dog in the stairwell of the graffiti-strewn stairwell of the high-rise where Tina and Sean live; Sean barks back at the dog, chasing the animal away. In the second, Fitz arrives to visit his daughter Katie at his in-laws house, where he too is seen to growl aggressively at their barking dog. Sean is a loose cannon, restless and retaliatory, who enjoys fury because only then can he speak without a stutter. Fitz too is wearied by the drive to make sanitised middling versions of us all, and likes to bite back: for him, dysfunctional personal relationships, anger and addiction are natural responses to modernity, injustice and the moral bankruptcy of capitalist institutions, and this rationalisation he shares with many murderers represented in the series.

Crucially, at the same time as Fitz's personal life places him in sympathetic parallel with the experiences of the perpetrator, his judgement puts him in tense counterpoint to other police officers. The team with which Fitz works is headed by DI Bilborough (Christopher Eccleston), a well-liked but weak and hot-headed officer who is killed at the end of series one ('To Be a Somebody'), after which DCI Wise (Ricky Tomlinson) takes over. The only female in the squad is DS Jane Penhaligon, affectionately dubbed 'Panhandle' by Fitz, and who frequently supports him when his would otherwise be the lone voice, cautioning against errors of judgement made by other officers. Their ongoing flirtation eventually develops into a sexual relationship in 'The Big Crunch'. However, Fitz's most morally revealing relationship is with DS Beck (Lorcan Cranitch) from whom he experiences growing antagonism, and whose own oppositional voice serves to distance Fitz from the prejudiced and retributive distortions of official justice. The full import of Beck's character becomes apparent in series two ('Men Should Weep', 1994): the team debate a rape case during which Beck insists that women 'allow themselves' to be raped, and he goads Penhaligon into admitting that even she has fantasised about being raped. Such troubling equivocation of what is, and is not rape, is further complicated when Fitz later makes a radio appearance during which he declares:

> Show me a man and I will show you a potential killer, a potential rapist. I am one for goodness sake. I don't do anything about it myself, of course, because I'm frightened of other men, frightened of being caught. ... But I think he's still inside me – the killer, the rapist. Buried deep, growling occasionally.

It is characteristic, rhetorical Fitz and typical of how he can take a proposition with a small element of truth, and work it up into a provocative polemic: the devil, he likes to argue, is in us all. However, the speech follows a scene in which, unbeknown to Fitz, Penhaligon herself is raped by a masked attacker (later revealed to be Beck)[33] which destablises the sophistry with which all the men have been qualifying 'rape'. It also opens up an uncomfortable tension between Fitz's knowledge and his rhetoric, emphasised when he persistently telephones Penhaligon, champagne at the ready, unaware she has been taken to the station rape suite, and by the way in which Floyd, the original serial rapist, takes one of Fitz's on-air remarks as a suggestion that he should henceforth kill his victims after raping them. The inference here is that Fitz is unable to communicate the particularities of his worldview without disastrous consequences.

Nevertheless, it is Fitz's deductive insight that leads to Floyd's arrest (just before he attacks Judith), putting him again in opposition to Beck, who not only commits rape (rather than citing the possibility as rhetoric), but whose reasoning is morally and unsettlingly unsound. For Beck, the problem is that policing has become caught up in a wash of feminisation and 'compassion' for villains: 'Forget the bloody compassion! Let's get back to the way things were'. For him the presence of a psychologist has always been emblematic of the engulfing tide, for as he put it to Bilborough, 'it's getting like we can't shit without Fitz' ('One Day a Lemming Will Fly', 1993). On his return to work in 'Brotherly Love' Beck's latent anger and guilt become retributive, and infuriated that a suspect may go free, he becomes a 'rogue cop', marching him to the top of the Ramada Hotel and dragging him over the edge with him to oblivion. Fitz's particular ethical trajectory is thus defined by Beck's opposition, as well as by the parallels between him and the perpetrators he helps to catch. These counterpoints are essential: Fitz is flawed and the line that divides him from deviance is a fine one, so his morality must be reaffirmed in contrast to those who are patently wrong.

Tellingly, the only occasion when moral allegiance with Fitz is systematically destabilised comes in 'One Day a Lemming Will Fly' when, like the rest of the police team, he succumbs to operational pressure to secure 'a result'. An incident is again precipitated by Beck, who arrives at the police station gate angry not to have been the one to bring in the suspect, Nigel Cassidy, for questioning over the death of an 13-year-old boy. Besieged at the car park gates by an angry mob, and knowing Penhaligon and Fitz will soon arrive with Cassidy, Beck incites the crowd by telling them 'we've pulled in a shirt-lifter'. When the car finally approaches the gate, the mob descend in a sequence that cross-cuts between shots of vengeful faces (optically aligned with Penhaligon and Fitz in the front) and reaction shots of Cassidy in the back seat, panicked and terrified, as he attempts to dodge breaking glass and grabbing arms. It is an ugly disturbance that could have been prevented rather than stoked by Beck.

Later, Cassidy has to be taken to a hotel room for his own safety, a narrative premise that enables another extraordinary, intense scene, this time featuring only Fitz, Beck and the accused. The sequence lasts over 13 minutes, and is intercut only by two very brief scenes (each around 30 seconds) in which Bilborough is called to the hospital to attend his wife in labour. Beck is odious from the outset, checking the hotel cable channels for pornography to watch, subjecting the other two to his best bigoted *bon mots*: 'Two queers doing it, that's two women going spare. But two lesbians doing it, that's two men going short'. At this stage Fitz is casual, passive even, but later, when Beck begins to bark accusations at Cassidy, Fitz turns the tables, suggesting Beck's homophobia stems from teenage doubts about his own sexuality. Beck gestures at Cassidy ('*this* is the suspect") and continues, but Fitz persists in his harassment. After the next cut, the two men cease to occupy the same shot: Beck is standing, eyes addressing Fitz down and to the left of the frame in a shot that is almost, but not quite, optically aligned with Fitz's viewpoint. The angle contrasts with the head and shoulders shot of Fitz, who sits calmly, looking way above and to the right of his frame, a reverse exchange that offers the viewer allegiance with Fitz in opposition to Beck's aggressive posture and flustered demeanour. After this, the dynamic between the men shifts and turns. Beck defends himself, claiming Fitz is 'twisted'; Fitz rehearses Cassidy's emotional motive for murder; and at one point, Cassidy and Beck are framed together accusingly, in mutual contemplation of Fitz's marriage and sexuality.

Aside from its intense theatricality, the scene constitutes an elaborate game of alignment, brought to fruition when Fitz finally coaxes a confession from Cassidy. Fleetingly, Fitz's face betrays him: he swallows, his nostrils flare and his mouth gives the merest flicker of a satisfied smile. Troublingly, it is not until the case is wrapped up back at the station with the usual drinks and farewells that Fitz speaks to Cassidy again, this time in a cell, only to realise that the confession was false, a gesture by Cassidy to share his guilt. However, Bilborough refuses to accept the retraction, rushing to announce to the press that Cassidy has been charged. Although moral allegiance is reinvited with Fitz, who attempts to rectify the situation ('I don't give a shit about the result. He didn't do it. It's the truth that counts!'), it is clear that it was vanity about his own interrogative powers that led him to make a mistake that he now cannot undo. Although the scene has profoundly troubling implications,[34] the series returns and survives it, perhaps because, as we have already seen, fictional crime detection is primarily concerned with moral trust, fantasies of protection and the articulation of dissent. It is not, for the most part, willing to engage in the spectacle or aftermath of formal justice and punishment. Crucially, Fitz's retraction reaffirms his distance, and thus enables him to continue at one remove from the operational logic of policing that was a matter of public unease at the time.

More commonly, Fitz's moral ambivalence is designed to challenge the *a priori* assumptions of the viewer rather than undermine their allegiance with him. In 'The Big Crunch', Judith has again left him, taking their daughter Katy, whom he then resorts to seeing as she comes out of school. As he queues to buy Katy an ice cream, Fitz finds himself wrongfully arrested following a tip-off to police by a school bus driver that he may be a predatory paedophile. It is an amusing incident, particularly when Judith is required to identify him at the police station ('severe yellowing to the fingers of the right hand, exhibits tremulousness when deprived of alcohol, permanently wrinkled suit, old appendix scar'), yet it serves more serious purposes. First, it satirises the hysteria of the time in response to the prospect of paedophiles in the community when, in this case, the predatory seducer and murderer of young girls is revealed to be an apparently upstanding head teacher and Christian preacher. Secondly, as the recipient of a false accusation, Fitz is a proxy for the assumptions Beck later makes about Dean, a suspect with learning difficulties who is also pushed into 'confessing'. This time there is no uncertainty about Fitz's judgement, and it is he who immediately recognises that Dean does not fit the killer's profile. In a direct allusion to a real-life case, he chastises DCI Wise for accepting the confession:

> Stefan Kiszko spent sixteen years of his life banged up for a crime he couldn't possibly have committed. Looks odd, sounds odd, he must be

> the killer. And do you know what finally sent him down, hmm? A hastily sought and eagerly accepted confession, that he only signed because he was confused, frightened and just wanted to go home to his Mammy.[35]

Through reference to topical cases and his personal demonstration of how easily mistakes can occur, Fitz claims the ability to 'see' just such a miscarriage of justice before it occurs. Whilst it also retreads the enduring conceit of his superior (prescient) insight, such speeches also make explicit the function of the detective as 'provocateur' and, as with Tennison, expectations that they may demonstrate this moral possibility also inform viewer re-recognition of the character in later episodes.

A good example of how re-recognition may become invested with moral expectation is suggested by 'Nine-Eleven', broadcast in 2006 and almost certainly the last ever edition of the series.[36] The opening credits certainly promise a return to topical form, juxtaposing shots of Fitz with news footage reporting the death of British soldiers during the war with Iraq, ongoing since 2003. Scenes of a murder are quickly juxtaposed with a sequence in which Fitz observes from his taxi the radical regeneration of Manchester during his on- and off-screen absence (reportedly in Australia), so building an unambiguous moral framework of 'returning hero' versus 'murderer at large'. Typically, for *Cracker*, the viewer not only witnesses the crime, but is granted clear spatial access to (and sometimes optical alignment with) the murderer himself, soon to be revealed as Kenny Archer (Anthony Flanagan), a uniformed constable who is later assigned to protect the wife of the victim. Interspersed with plot developments are scenes that establish that Archer is a former soldier, a victim himself of an earlier 'war' trauma in Northern Ireland, to which attention then shifts.

The identity of the murderer becomes known some time prior to the structural climax of the investigation/chase, although there is very little tension or anticipation around this revelation. Halfway into a scene in which the senior police team declare themselves unable to offer any leads, Fitz steps forward and with typical accuracy, surmises the man for whom they are looking. His speech is watched through glass office walls by Archer, whose fixed stare is matched in a sequence of looks with Fitz's eye-line – in a sequence inter-cut with shots of residential Manchester, and more flashbacks of Archer's war service. Whether or not Fitz's look is directed at Archer is ambiguous, but given that he has so far attracted no official suspicion and given away few clues, it is highly implausible that even Fitz should identify him from looks alone. Until this point, the most obvious function of the sequence has been to contrast Fitz's competence with the smug inadequacy of DI Walters (Richard Coyle) but then Fitz requests a word and the narrative jumps to a scene in which he is interviewing Archer, whom he has clearly deduced to be the perpetrator. It is an implausible leap that relies entirely on how Fitz's judgement appears to match the privileged foreknowledge of the viewer (through spatial alignment with the 'villain') but has little to do with optical or spatial alignment with Fitz. Indeed, the viewer has effectively been excluded from the process of deduction, making moral allegiance possible only by an appeal to trust *already vested* in Fitz, even though it is precisely such a returning viewer who is likely to have anticipated a demonstration (and not simply an assumption) of Fitz's ability.

Some months later, Jimmy McGovern was to publicly regret the revival, admitting to a journalist:

> He was of a certain time and place and we shouldn't have brought him back. I'm a granddad now, and he was a granddad too. Despite the fact that Antonia Bird did a wonderful job, as did Robbie, and John Chapman was a great producer, the fault lies with me.[37]

McGovern's elision of his own age and sentiments with those of his character creation is revealing. For some time before transmission, the prospect of a revival had been excitedly anticipated by the press and in on-line chat rooms, indicating more than a craving to relive pleasures past but an active expectation that Fitz would apply his customary insight to recent news events. Presumably it was such commentary and diagnosis that McGovern found so difficult to write, with the result that, like his author, Fitz's certainty of his own judgement and the passion with which he had been wont to rage against injustice were here fatally undermined.

McGovern's regret also alludes to the production alchemy that is always easier to identify in retrospect than it is ever to engineer or predict, but appears to have been remarkable effective for the initial three runs of series. Gub Neal has suggested that a critical decision was made counter to McGovern's original vision of the character (as 'thin and wiry') with the casting of Robbie Coltrane, a comedy performer perhaps best known as an actor for his role in *Tutti Frutti* (BBC 1987). It was Coltrane, Neal argues, who brought crucial 'vulnerability and sensitivity' to the 'level of fury' evident in McGovern's script: 'He could do all that bile, he could do all that anger, he could do all those things and you were still with him.'[38] If it is Fitz's vulnerability that allows him to speak 'the unspeakable' and still generate affection then it is indeed Coltrane's multi-layered performance that brings wit to the darkness. Moreover, it is Coltrane's performance that makes both attractive and plausible Fitz's dexterous and persuasive exposés of the criminal mind, and carries the political anger which suggests that social injustice may be similarly predictable. By eliding Fitz's psychological understanding with his diagnosis of social problems, the series aspires to national reflexivity, feeding into debates about benefits, unemployment, homophobia. Being timely and edgy sometimes brought with it controversy, an example being 'Men Should Weep', criticised for its representation of

Floyd, a predatory rapist and unfortunately the only fully developed black character in the series to date.[39] However, the narrative logic is at least consistent with the diagnosis of criminality in the series, for it is Floyd's experience of racial discrimination and the scars he bears (from the attempt to bleach himself white to be like his mother) that feed and warp the reasoning that he later uses as self-justification for an odyssey of rape and murder.

A similar causal logic underpins 'To Be a Somebody', which traces a direct connection between deviance and social injustice in the figure of Albie (Robert Carlyle), who is grieving for his recently deceased father and broken marriage. As Fitz later clarifies, Albie attempts to justify his initial shocking murder of a Pakistani shopkeeper and turn it into a crusade, by casting his murders as revenge for the injustices of the Hillsborough stadium disaster of 1989.[40] It is still, of course, a brutal, racist crime, but a remarkably complex moral structure to this episode nevertheless allows Albie to act as 'an articulate spokesman for working-class anger and alienation',[41] assuming the manners and appearance of a skinhead to demonstrate a point: 'Treat people like scum, they start acting like scum.' Fitz demonstrates his usual powers of perception, piecing together an accurate interpretation from the crime scene, and engaging in eye-to-eye, verbal combat with Albie in the interview suite, enabling him to prevent the explosion of a letter bomb sent to DS Beck. Yet the episode ends with the explosion of a similar bomb sent to a former *Sun* journalist, providing a degree of ambivalent, moral retribution outside of the formal closure to the investigative narrative. Typically, it also accommodates lighter scenes, such as a rare trip to the supermarket by Fitz, compelled to justify his place in the 'eight items' queue by arguing that three bottles of whisky and six frozen lasagnes each 'constitute one item'. This incident allows Fitz to express his own constantly simmering frustration with the everyday world, his resistance to norms, railing against irksome pettiness, and in such eloquent confrontations there is clearly a vicarious satisfaction to be had. However, the interlude further contrasts with the event that sparked Albie's first murder, committed after the shopkeeper would not trust him to owe four pence on credit. Whereas Fitz articulates his dissent as barbed sarcasm, Albie's anger becomes warped, mapped onto a larger sense of injustice, and reaches a giddy, murderous extreme.

In so far as they work through the relatively commonplace experience of injustice (albeit to murderous excess), it could be argued that perpetrators in *Cracker* are like Nuttall's 'expendable army', sent ahead as hypotheses for a 'game in which the muscles of psychic response, fear and pity, are exercised and made ready, through a facing of the worst, which is not yet the real worst'.[42] Fitz's insight and witty expressions of dissent are both part of a fantasy response to this hypothetical demonstration of the worst, and one is always aware that he too is there but for the grace of his redeeming intellect and personal charm. Certainly, some of his more wildly provocative rhetoric does not bear a great deal of scrutiny, beyond the seductions of a willingness to say the unsayable, and according to Duguid's interpretation, the conversations he has with Penhaligon and Judith put him 'frequently and plainly in the wrong'.[43] However, in his delineation of the boundary between dissent and deviance, he is exemplary, and to engage with the character of Fitz is to mobilise some of his emotions and guess at the pleasures of behaving badly. Most remarkable is how such anger and excess actually serves a role designed to anticipate and identify excess itself. Fitz's moral voice in *Cracker* is ambivalent yet indisputably heroic, although this is not so much in spite of but *because* the criminal 'Other' so, he likes to argue, is very much within.

By way of final observation on both *Cracker* and *Prime Suspect*, it is perhaps worth revisiting the paradox that they should each have been so rooted in the morally ambivalent structure of feeling particular to the early 1990s, yet also have endured so remarkably as 'classic' texts, and providers of mighty, memorable protagonists. If Tennison's 'Final Act' was the more satisfying of the two revival narratives it may have been because the formerly fascinating pleasures of watching her in combat had here been substituted by the equally absorbing spectacle of her decline. Such a spectacle also sought to mobilise contemplation and invite the viewer to reflect on the woman she had been and the battles she had fought. Fitz was denied this final unravelling, which for Jane was also in some respects an obituary. His impotence was not a stage in a tragic resolution but simply a discharge of viewer expectations, leaving him perpetually stranded in the Fourth Act: past that brink of angry middle age, mourning as much as re-enacting his compulsions and destined to remain forever on the brink of self-destruction.

5

The Reactionary Voice: *Life on Mars* and 'The Gene Genie'

In the new century, the steady shift away from 'gritty realism' paved the way for more innovative and playful interventions to the detective genre, the most notable of which was *Life on Mars* (BBC 2006–7). Created for the independent production company Kudos by the writers Matthew Graham and Ashley Pharaoh, the series idea was first offered to and rejected by Channel 4 before eventually being commissioned for BBC1, and it was to distance itself from other police series by an imaginative premise that was quickly, if imprecisely, described as 'time travel'. The temporal logic was established neatly in the first few screen minutes when Sam Tyler (John Simm), a newly promoted and thoroughly modern DCI, well versed in current policing methods, is knocked down by an oncoming vehicle, coming to on a building site in a year that later reveals itself to be 1973. Finding himself in possession of an authentic warrant card and an Allegro, Sam makes his way to the Manchester police station where he is accepted grudgingly as a transfer from 'Hyde'. The narrative drive of both series is Sam's ensuing desire to return 'home' to the present day, although each episode also has its own self-contained storyline of crime detection and the usual apprehension of perpetrators. Typically, and in spite of the enormous culture shock to finding himself a working member of a 1970s police squad, by the end of the first episode Sam is already apprehending local villains alongside his senior officer, DCI Gene Hunt (Philip Glenister).

Aside from its fantasy premise, *Life on Mars* is also a hybrid of crime fiction forms, fusing the ensemble, police squad episodic action story with the tradition of an autonomous, virtuoso detective or duo. The period setting of the 1970s frees the series from some contemporary conventions, such as the often tiresome details of technology and forensic science. Instead, it revels in the 'daft but wonderful'[1] wheeze of sending a twenty-first-century detective back to a period associated in the popular imagination with raffish bank heists and organised vice, paying homage to 1970s crime classics such as *The Sweeney* (Thames Television 1975–8) and *Get Carter* (Mike Hodges, 1971). Such reflexivity enables *Life on Mars* to elbow past 1990s gritty crime drama without reneging on its objectives. Despite its two white male central characters, the narrative challenges the selfsame 'overtly white, masculine era and style of policing' that, as *Prime Suspect* had implied, needed 'be tempered with greater accountability and diversity'.[2] The hybridity and imagination, representational politics, nostalgia and fan activity around *Life on Mars* have all since brought it growing academic attention.[3]

Formally, *Life on Mars* interweaves episodic investigative storylines with ongoing, progressive narrative enigmas that ensure committed viewing and led to heated speculation in response to Sam's explicit question: 'Am I mad, in a coma, or back in time?' Although press and viewer attention was certainly influential,[4] a second series of eight episodes was commissioned while the first was still in post-production. After first transmission, newspaper reviews were positive but cautious, although the consensus was that the show might, after all, manage to negotiate the risk of its own conceit. Thus, it was 'more than just a jolly tongue in cheek romp into the past', and 'could have slid into a boring session of sniggering at the '70s. But something much cleverer was going on'.[5] Thomas Sutcliffe of the *Independent* conceded that '[e]verything suggested it would be an embarrassment, but it works',[6] as did *New Statesman* critic Andrew Billen, who acknowledged that the premise may be 'silly' but 'so are those that kick-start *Hamlet* and *Macbeth*. It is what you do with a premise that counts, and *Life on Mars* looks as if it's about to do rather a lot'.[7]

And so it did, in so far as such things can be measured by practitioner and viewer approval: *Life on Mars* was nominated for a BAFTA in the Best Drama Series category in 2007 and won numerous other accolades, including the nation's most creative television show in *Broadcast*'s Creative Report 2007, being voted 'Most Popular Drama' at the National Television Awards in 2007 and winning an International Emmy for Best Drama Series in both 2006 and 2008. Importantly for my purposes, *Life on Mars* also provided for general cultural circulation the most iconic and unlikely small-screen detective hero of the decade in the form of Hunt, fond of referring to himself as the 'Gene Genie'. It is partly because of Hunt that I have singled the series out for extended analysis in this chapter, as he is the detective who most obviously seems to buck the legacy of Morse and whose personality exceeded the series, prompting a spin-off sequel (*Ashes to Ashes*) and feeding into British public, interpersonal, even party-political discourses. However, more than any other detective of the period, Gene's 'voice' has to be heard through the place and time of his environment and its manifest contrast to the present day, suggesting that the spatial *construction* of both past and present in the series needs to be examined in some detail.

Space, Place and 1973

The conceit of time travel requires more than viewer immersion in a historic diegesis, it also invites reflection on the *passage* of time from past to present. In *Life on Mars* the differences that time has wrought since the 1970s are mediated by Sam Tyler's reactions, taking on a growing and complex thematic significance. Of course, 'time' itself – being both invisible and abstract – poses obvious challenges to audio-visual representation which must somehow mark it materially and sensuously. The most evident time-signifying strategies in *Life on Mars* would include its evocative soundtrack, a carefully selective *mise-en-scène* and the use of colour-coding. The 1973 sequences are all saturated in earthy, lived-in hues of browns, beige, green and orange, suggesting a vivid era, albeit one drenched in the fug of a nicotine wash. This is in sharp contrast to the few sequences set in the present, all of which are relayed through a clinical spectrum of steely grey to glassy blue. The enactment and detritus of everyday life in either period is mapped onto this dichotomy, in which all that was grubbily warm and hearty is opposed to that which has been bleached-out and constrained.

Sam's realisation that he has gone back in time is the pretext for a lingering observant cinematography that invites a similar attention to detail from the viewer. Indeed, the camera prowls the everyday artefacts of Sam's new world with almost predatory fascination, noting everything from the peeling ceiling and oversized floral wallpaper of his bedsit, to the 'Pye' radio speaker in Hunt's brown Ford Cortina GXL. Tim Edensor's work on the everyday has stressed the significance of such mundane artefacts to national identity, and he situates them alongside the common and institutional temporal routines of daily life, its cultural practices, representations and spaces: 'familiar objects endure in everyday lifeworlds, are part of *the way things are*, discreetly contributing to forms of shared solidarity. Situated in familiar spaces, they provide orientations for movement and action'.[8] These objects can indicate shared ways of being that inform a sense of belonging, and whereas this might be specific in its class or ethnic connotations, it is often national in character. Consumer goods from the postwar hiatus between rationing and rampant global branding (roughly from the late 1950s to the mid-1980s) may hold a privileged status for audience members of a certain age, and such forgotten items are given a carefully calculated emphasis in *Life on Mars* that transcends background naturalism. The series works to consciously evoke the everyday national past with an emphasis on routine and shared recollection that is quite different to, say, the discreet authenticity assumed by commodities in the 1940s *mise-en-scène* of *Foyle's War*.

A lingering camera further enables the spaces around these objects to assume a similarly 'other-worldly' quality that extends even to places that Sam encounters repeatedly, such as the CID offices or his bedsit home. In comparison to his formerly smart office with high-tech urban vista, he is now based in a dark, smoky, low-ceilinged bunker, cluttered with brown paper files, shabby office furniture, manual typewriters and shirt-sleeved workers all in a thick fug of cigarette smoke. Scenes in this cloistered, almost daylight-free space are regularly followed by scenes shot in the corridor just beyond, which is an equally dingy space into which muted sunshine often spills from one side, lending it a near-mystical quality by reducing the depth of field and shrouding character entrances and exits in something resembling a fantasy waft of smoke.

In the first episode, Hunt directs Sam to the cluttered lost property room to interrogate suspects because it has 'thick walls', providing a marked contrast to the contemporary purpose-built interview suites that have become a staple of police series iconography with their two-way mirrors, tape recorders and webcams for third-party moderation. Indeed, although the 1973 station has holding cells, suspects are occasionally detained in the CID offices themselves, as the gangster Steve Warren discovers when he finds himself handcuffed to a filing cabinet in the centre of activity (series 1, episode 4). It is a busy, ramshackle, gutsy use of space in which snap decisions are made, revelations are arrived at spontaneously, and 'procedure' is largely disregarded. A similarly cavalier treatment of forensic evidence is often played for comic effect, whether that involves cigarette ash in the mortuary, or a drip from Gene's fried egg butty on a body at the crime scene (series 2, episode 5).

Continuing post-war austerity limps shabbily through all these 1970s spaces. Most of the action and apprehension of criminals takes place in exteriors or in public spaces that architecturally belong to an earlier Victorian/Edwardian epoch and recall Manchester's once affluent industrial past, long prior to its recent regeneration, and often dilapidated in appearance. In so far as they feature, domestic interiors are made up of muddled colours, doilies and unfashionable ornaments, and almost every episode entails a visit to a villain or a victim that requires an establishing shot of a red-brick terraced house in a late Victorian street. Although there are still many such terraces in Manchester (an association culturally reinforced by the long-running soap opera *Coronation Street*) they are also a common sight in other British cities, as the homes of a now disappearing urban industrial working class.

Typically, Gene and Sam visit one of these terraces in search of Patrick O'Brien, an Irish labourer they believe to be lodging there (series 2, episode 3). This street has one dead end and there are very few cars parked; washing is hung on lines across the road and kitchen chairs are parked outside, next to the front door; a rag and bone man with a barrow flits briefly to the left of the frame; children play in the road; a couple of women wearing button-up smock aprons chat to the right. A similar, but empty street could have served as authentic background, but it is these incidental details that recall the lost everyday, evoking commonplace activities and routine practices that disappeared without anyone seeming to notice that they were going. Examples of Victorian industrial architecture still survive today of course, but they are shown to have been inhabited quite differently then, meaning that both space and artefact work together to appeal to collective memories and evoke a former, *shared*, working-class culture. The evocation underwrites the narrative in interesting ways as well, for as Gene and Sam turn to leave after O'Brien's closing speech (on the industrial exploitation of the Irish), an Indian couple arrive to move into their new home, foretelling how one migrant community came to be replaced by another.

On a couple of occasions, Sam visits his own childhood home, located in another very similar red-brick terrace (series 1, episodes 4 and 8). The location is important, he is a Manchester lad too, like Gene, and although this may seem like another country, it is still recognisably his past and his country. Although, as John Curzon observes, the adult Sam is very clearly aligned with the 'New North' through the continuous interplay of surprise and recognition at his material surroundings,[9] his narrative journey obliges him to rediscover his regional past and feel at ease within it. The insistence that both men belong to Manchester emphasises the new/old dichotomy rather than an easy insider/outsider spatial opposition. Nevertheless, as a creature of his time Hunt is at home in the 1973 spaces in a way that Sam cannot be, showing a profound attachment to his patch, his city, in a way that modern professionalised policing would actively discourage, even in the name of 'community support'. By contrast, in spite of encountering his own mother, Sam's essential detachment is sustained by continual visual reminders of how much the period setting differs from the present. Indeed there is something rather incongruous about a visit to the perennially archaic setting of Manchester Crown Court (series 2, episode 7), peopled then as now by lawyers in wigs, and resembling rather closely the conventional settings familiar to contemporary drama series. Period order to this episode is only restored by a visit to The Railway Arms, a spartan smoke-filled pub run by the genial Nelson, a visible world away from many contemporary pubs and bars.

Particularly important to the iconographic and thematic strategies of the series is Manchester's industrial heritage, and as Curzon notes, the exact year 1973 is significant as it 'marks a decisive turning point in the emergence of the "post-industrial society", and the decline of a factory based working class in the Western world'.[10] At one point, Gene and Sam go to a murder scene in Cresters Textile factory,[11] where they must directly confront the breakdown of industrial relations in the wake of successive trade crises (series 1, episode 3). Taking its prompt from increasing mechanisation, the plot dramatises a set of conflicts between local and immigrant labour, unions and management, calling attention to the historic significance of these now regenerated spaces. Indeed, Sam 'recognises' the factory as the location of his twenty-first-century apartment, telling Gene, 'this is all going to be flats in thirty years'. Later he contemplates the large brick tower outside, of which one of the workers, Ted Bannister, comments 'the heat just bleeds through the bricks, makes it a living thing'. Sam is sympathetic but Gene latches instead on to Bannister as a key suspect, having already decided the murder must have been committed by 'a Union man with an axe to grind' and noting that Bannister is a 'commie bastard'. To the contrary, it transpires that Bannister's loyalties are so considerable that he later confesses to something he has not done in order to keep the factory open and his family in work. It is all a stark generational contrast to the attitude of his son Derek, the real culprit, who had resorted to armed robbery of the factory wage packets that rightfully belonged to his own friends and family.

The suggestion of a decline in moral values from one generation to another intersects here with the emerging conflict between Gene and Sam regarding the place of emotion in crime detection, and the dichotomous relation that Gene's gut instinct bears to Sam's more scientific propositions. It is telling that exchanges between the two should resonate within a historical context of national change, thus aligning Bannister's emotional principle with Hunt's reckless instinct, and opposing both to the rise of individualism and self-interest, emergent qualities that presumably had to be countered by growing professionalism of the type that Sam demonstrates. After Derek is shot Gene offers Sam a deal: 'I'll listen to your little tape machine now and again, OK, so long as you, just sometimes, listen to this!' (at which point he clicks his fingers to his temple), and later they celebrate by symbolically opening a tin of 'Party Seven' together. Typically, a narrative resolution to an episodic interpersonal conflict is thus achieved, but without failing to remind us that there actually was no such historical compromise to prevent the irreversible loss of urban industrial communities and their values.

In spite of what appears to be a thematic concern with the industrial North and an emphatic spatial fidelity to Manchester (in so far as it is possible to recreate the city as it would have been), Susan Sydney-Smith has argued that *Life on Mars* is a revealing example of the *failure* of British crime drama to 'negotiate with "the real"', providing instead 'a nowhere place in a nowhere space, where time seems to stand still'.[12] The argument is not demonstrated, the series briefly cited simply in unfavourable comparison to the particularity of place in an earlier canon of celebrated films, but it clearly ignores the signifying possibilities of *generic* space in television crime fiction. Such a view also underestimates how, as Charlotte Brunsdon shows, it has always been possible to 'discern a fluctuating, but persistent, articulation of two kinds of space in the British crime film' that repeatedly slips from the geographically specific into a generic (Hollywood influenced) or abstract/expressionistic space.[13] Certainly, Sydney-Smith's verdict seems overhasty, for although *Life on Mars* does not fetishise its setting as if it were the Oxford of *Lewis*, the location is neither arbitrary nor incidental.

Indeed, the city of Manchester, by turns grand and dirty, affluent and poor, is an apt metaphor for the equivocal national relationship with commerce, as demonstrated by its trajectory from Victorian expansion to post-industrial decay and deliberate, late, regeneration. Far from being set in a 'nowhere' space, the lived realities of this particular urban environment are inferred to be of both local and generically national importance, as emphasised by the themes of home-coming and cultural change.

The Ensemble

Although, as I shall show, the characters of Sam and Gene are best understood in opposition to one another, their individual significance is relative also to the broader ensemble of the police squad, which offers a remarkably fluid field for allegiances and generates the sense of jostling camaraderie that may be part of the pleasure of the series for a social audience. Indeed, in this sense *Life on Mars* inverts the allegiances of the 1970s caper film, in which social pleasure is usually vested in a rogue ensemble of robbers, for here it is the police squad that is endowed with outlaw charisma. Of the regular characters, Ray (Dean Andrew), Chris (Marshall Lancaster) and Annie (Liz White) are the most crucial for delineating and complicating the opposition between Gene and Sam. With Phyllis, the station officer, as her only female colleague, it is Annie who must stand in as the token 'plonk' and provide a prospective love interest for Sam (a storyline further developed in the second series). She is manifestly of her time, not least in how she good-naturedly tolerates sexist banter, arbitrary allocation to child road safety duties, and Gene's demands to 'fetch the Garibaldis'. Liz White's softly spoken and placid performance provides an interesting throwback to *The Gentle Touch* In marked contrast to later, post-Tennison, female detective characterisations (a category to which one suspects Sam's 2006 girlfriend Maya would belong), Annie is neither sharp nor sassy, but all calmness, smiles and neatly blow-dried hair. She quickly becomes a friend to Sam and indulges, if not quite believes, his wild time-travelling tales.

Unlike Chris, who is quickly recruited as a potential disciple for Sam, Ray is a key opponent. Intensely and unequivocally loyal to Gene, he also usefully mitigates Gene's bigotry by acting as its logical extreme. When DC Glen Fletcher arrives, as an 'extra pair of hands' who happens to be black (series 2, episode 2), it is Ray not Gene who makes the racist jibes. In fact, Ray's moral standing had already been seriously compromised in the previous series, after Gene had left him interrogating a suspect, Billy Kemble (series 1, episode 7). In this earlier narrative, Gene and Sam later return to the station to find Kemble dead, and Sam is asked to conduct an internal inquiry to find out the causes – a responsibility which brings him into direct conflict with the other members of the team, and occasions many dialectical exchanges with Gene. As Sam asks: 'if we can't police ourselves, how are the public supposed to trust us?', to which Gene responds, 'the public don't give a damn what we do, as long as we get results'. The internal investigation becomes all-consuming, and Sam soon believes he must destroy Gene's corrupt world in order to return to his own, thus neatly eliding the enigma of the series with its recurring concern with police ethics. Eventually Sam discovers that Kemble had died after ingesting too much cocaine, forced upon him by Ray to make him talk. As Ray was emulating Gene's methods, culpability for this catastrophic misjudgement appears to lie with him: 'I'm to blame for this. I left a weak man in charge. You see, these lads, they think they're made in my image, but they've never learnt where to draw the line, and it scares the shit out of me'. As Gene concedes, Ray's excess is the logical conclusion of his own brand of policing when it is practised by those unable to 'draw the line'. Characteristically, Gene resolves Ray's transgression by dealing with it himself, and he unilaterally demotes him, fines him half his wages and bans him from The Railway Arms. 'This has been shaming,' he announces, 'we are never to talk of this again'. Sam's attempt to take it further is unsuccessful when Superintendent Rathbone destroys the tape-recorded evidence he gives him, a symbolic failure of Sam's attempt to change history by prematurely destroying this world of institutionalised corruption, perhaps proving Gene's point that they cannot 'change this world ... only learn how to survive in it'.

It is in this fashion that the supporting cast help to delineate and enrich the conflict *between* Hunt and Tyler. Theirs is a productive and dialectical partnership, not least because it always takes both of them to apprehend the villain and they are always both present at 'the kill', suggesting that this otherwise unlikely confrontational coupling is, in fact, mutually complementary. The first episode introduces Sam as an officer who has lost his 'feel' for the job, to the frustration of Maya who rebukes him: 'Screw his psych evaluation! You used to believe in gut feeling – what happened?' Sam therefore arrives in 1973 with much to learn, not least because he is failing to conform to the generic model of the television detective as *essentially* intuitive. Reading the series through the prism of the detective genre would suggest that Sam's journey is an extended lesson obliging him, amongst other things, to identify why he has ceased to trust his intuition. He must learn to rediscover his humanity, his instinct and his passion: all defining qualities of the television detective, and ones that Gene is able to provide in abundance. Gene thus takes on the function of providing a fantasy solution to a national predicament, allowing Sam's loss of 'gut feeling' to suggest such changes have also occurred on a broader social scale, as 'feeling' has been obviated by procedure, regulation and surveillance.

The balance of sympathy between the two men is endorsed stylistically. Optical alignment is reserved for Sam and only in those sequences when he is distressed and 'between worlds', such as when he believes himself personally addressed by presenters via (diegetic) television or radio sets. Conventional shot-reverse-shot dialogue sequences between Sam and Gene are usually reserved for any arguments that take place between them, and the two men are often framed together in a two shot, or the team arranged in a mid-shot. Close-ups are rare and usually reserved for objects rather than faces. Although in narrative terms Sam is clearly the protagonist, the camera is always neutral, thus whatever viewers might make of any dialogue between the two men, Sam is neither privileged nor Gene objectified, even at the moment of his most bigoted diatribes.

Gene continually justifies his excesses and contempt for Sam's methods by reference to the changing face of crime. When a murder weapon is found by some derelict arches (series 2, episode 1) Sam wants to leave it for 'forensics' to dust, but Gene suggests they frame someone from the 'we don't like you list', responding to Sam's insistence that they follow procedure with: 'Cobblers! The world's getting tougher, the police have to match it!' Indeed, Gene's position exemplifies what Lez Cooke notes as the 'self-righteous belief' of 1970s police detectives 'in the validity of their own methods, even if those methods involved a degree of violence and a bending of the rules'.[14] In this context, the retroactive character of Sam is used to actively challenge the relationship between police drama and the broader social anxieties to which it, as a genre, had then responded. As Sam constantly observes, the 'solution' to increasing lawlessness that was demonstrated by 1970s policing caused a new set of problems, and the genre that imitated them is also shown here to be misguided, however affectionately recalled. In fact, it is the affection of the series for popular culture and everyday life that enables it to re-view the crime of the period in a rather different light to the original films and television series from which it borrows stylistically. As Leon Hunt notes, 'the fear that Britain was becoming 'ungovernable' and 'a scarier place to live'[15] is evident in many discourses of the decade, not least the two *Sweeney!* feature films themselves, for as he concludes, 'these were not happy times and these are not happy films'.[16] Although a naïve reading of *Life on Mars*, such as that offered by Garland and Bilby, might dismiss its reliance 'on our nostalgia with a collectively (mis)remembered history of British society',[17] the evident warmth of the series is neither facile nor rose-tinted. *Life on Mars* is not a simple parody of, or homage to, a 1970s cop show, or even the 1970s themselves, but a complex reflexive *re-exploration* of the time and its artefacts.

The interweaving of cultural, generic and social critique around the theme of policing epitomises the complex sleight of hand with which *Life on Mars* manages to be critical yet not cynical, simultaneously celebrating the popular culture of a decade whilst remaining dubious as to its quality and presuppositions. Thus, although it is laden with affectionate allusions to everyday television of the 1970s – *The Galloping Gourmet*, *The Morecambe and Wise Show*, a lengthy animated parody of *Camberwick Green* (series 2, episode 5) – such 'nostalgia' coexists in constant tension with the evident problems of the past. Moreover, as Matt Hills argues, its positioning of media technology is complex, television itself becoming 'uncanny', presented in the form of 'potentially interstitial, monstrous disruptions of Sam's world'[18] and throwing us back to a time when the technology itself was considered 'spooky and fantastical'.[19] To return to Richard Sparks's argument that crime drama tends to address the tension *between* anxiety and resolution,[20] one could suggest that it is precisely in the tension between anxieties of (cultural, social) loss, and the impossible, fantasy solution to it (a return to the past?) that *Life on Mars* is expertly located. At the same time as it is trading in shared cultural trivia, it reminds that cultural attitudes were responsible for many atrocities, and whilst offering Gene as a historical reminder of all that Sam's world has lost it is always simultaneously rendering his character problematic. The world may have been getting tougher, but responding to criminality on its own terms was to render the police unable to resolve anxiety because it led, as Sam continually points out, to a collapse in public trust. In an IRA-themed episode (series 2, episode 3), Sam has to restrain Gene from kicking and beating the Irish suspect that Gene 'knows' is guilty:

> SAM: And what if he's innocent! What if he gets sent down and the conviction's overturned? Because then you may as well become a recruitment office for the bloody terrorists. And as for the public's faith in the police, no-one will trust us, no-one.
> GENE: We're the police, everybody trusts us.
> SAM: Not where I come from they don't.

Typically, this exchange dramatises competing ideals of resolution rather than simplistically contrasting right with wrong. In a later, if less morally fine-tuned storyline (series 2, episode 6), Sam begs Gene not to hand over a suspect to the murderous intentions of a peculiarly overblown character, Toolbox, warning him: 'When you look in the mirror, there'll be a different man looking out at you'. To this Gene responds 'I've become that man already, I've had to be'. Later Sam softens, touching his colleague's arm in a gesture that invites the contemporary viewer, potentially shocked at what Gene had been about to do, to engage in a similar process of forgiveness.

The surface polarities occupied by Gene and Sam thus mask a more complex relationship between them that negotiates some of the key thematic oppositions in contemporary detective drama: corruption versus accountability, instinct versus procedure, emotion versus control. Its unpacking of the dilemmas around modern policing is intricately and reflexively bound up with an equally complex and often humorous exploration of masculinity. Gene often equates Sam's methods with femininity, notoriously calling him a 'Nancy boy'. When Sam suggests that Ray may need counselling following his close encounter with a car bomb, Gene retorts: 'He's a police officer, not a fairy' (series 2, episode 3) and in the following episode, when Sam recommends surveillance, Hunt demurs that it 'doesn't sound very manly'. However, for all his macho posturing, Gene is never a ridiculous figure: he is brave as well as rash, protective as well as sexist, and as he points out to Sam, even in the 1970s they did not give away DCI badges 'in them lucky bags'. He is seen to deserve his team's trust, attracting the grudging admiration of those who come across him or fall foul of him. When, in episode 5, a pub customer comments to Sam, 'your mate's got some balls', Sam can only agree, 'if they were any bigger, he'd need a wheelbarrow'. Importantly, Hunt's masculinity has to be placed within a broader context in which men are everywhere resorting to crime to support their families, thus emphasising the hostility of the terrain in which they all must survive. He treads a fine line, nevertheless, and in one memorable rant, refers to the gangster Steve Warren as 'a bum bandit. Do you understand? A poof, a fairy, a queer, a queen, a fudge-packer, uphill gardener, fruit picking sodomite' (series 1, episode 4). It is a tirade that shocks with its expletives but is contained, if not cauterised, by the comedy inherent in its own taboo-breaking excess and Sam's measured faux-naïve response ('he's gay?') which diffuses the power of the obscenity.

Revealingly, Hunt's homophobic rant was omitted from the American version of the series (ABC 2008) which managed the same storyline entirely with coy references, raised eyebrows and whisperings behind hands. One may assume that caution was exercised because of the target 'middle American' Fox Channel audience, but it would in any event be difficult to imagine Harvey Keitel pulling off something so ugly, given the lack of humour in his performance, and his creation of an altogether colder, more disturbing Hunt, whose shortcomings are harder to overlook. Unlike Keitel's 'bad cop' interpretation, nothing about Glenister's Hunt is apathetic: when he declares it time to postpone a murder hunt till the following day it is neither laziness nor tiredness, but a rather energetic commitment to 'beer o'clock, Gentlemen'. His exuberance is even attractive to Sam, inspiring him to try it on for size in episode 3, chirping 'morning, love' to a passer-by, and chastising a teenage boy for riding his bicycle on the pavement.

The attractions of Gene's vernacular are reinforced rather than undermined by the witty subversion of his unreconstructed sense of masculinity, not least his self-image as maverick western law enforcer. For example, the second episode closes with a scene in Hunt's office where he is framed repeatedly alongside or below a poster showing the gun-toting sheriff and outlaws of *The Good, the Bad and the Ugly*, yet it began most memorably with a comedy sequence of a canal-side chase in which – his pasty pale middle-aged paunch displayed in all its glory above his retro swimming trunks – he quickly begins to flag and has to be elbowed aside by Tyler, easily the fitter man. Hunt is self-deluded and flawed, but sufficiently competent (and dangerous) to prevent him becoming a simple figure of fun, and Glenister's delivery of the more offensive quips relies on a similar, ebullient mix of brazen energy and cynical sarcasm. He pushes the joke far enough to make the transgression clear, but with sufficient innocence to infer the progressive superiority of a knowing viewer, who may well think he knows not what he says. In April 2007 a BBC spokesman responded to complaints by school teachers of homophobia by insisting: 'DCI Hunt is an extreme, tongue-in-cheek take on a stereotypical 1970s bloke and the audience understand and revel in his direct approach to his job and life in general'.[21] 'Life in general' is the revealing term here, for Glenister's instinctive realisation of the character pulls off the paradox of a constant (and constantly endearing) gusto for life, as well as (or in spite of) a generalised discontent with modernity-at-large that tends to brim over when he rails against drug-dealers and rapists, or patronises petty thugs.

Hunt's discontent is always there, encouraging him to articulate populist antipathy to everything from unionised labour ('Bolsheviks') to the 'lucky' residents of newly built estates: 'Bloody council spends my taxes housing the scum of the city in penthouses. All mod cons, city views, jammy bastards' (series 1, episode 7). As I shall discuss further in Chapter 8, estates such as the one to which he refers here – with their outside walkways, impoverished and/or anti-social tenants and resident gangs – have become the very stuff of contemporary crime shows, a synecdoche for the problematic underclass of society. For the viewer privileged with hindsight and an intertextual familiarity with televisual spatial coding for the representation of crime, Gene's outburst is evidently far off the mark. Gene is safely of his time, unaware that the clock is ticking against him and his kind. When Sam describes him as an 'overweight, over the hill, nicotine-stained, borderline alcoholic homophobe with a superiority complex and an unhealthy obsession with male bonding', Hunt responds with an exquisite mix of innocence and sarcasm, 'you make that sound like a bad thing' (series 1, episode 8). He is not, then, an offensive bigot, but a humorous, affectionate, caricature of a near-bigot, a differentiation achieved partly through Sam's sighing sarcastic rejoinders. When Hunt wants to round up half the Irish population of the city Sam retorts, 'why don't we interview that well known terrorist suspect, Dana', and at the close of one of his rants against everything and everyone, he simply prompts 'I think you left out the Jews' (series 2, episode 3).

All these strategies of containment ensure that Gene is both licensed and contextualised, enabling the series to engage reflexively with bigotry rather than simply reproduce it. The 'metalanguage' of *Life on Mars* is equivalent to neither the 'voice' of Gene nor Sam, as neither is so privileged within the narrative structure; instead it is produced dialectically for the viewer through the conflict and conciliations between them, and is further circumscribed by their space, time and ensemble. The hazardous moral line that Hunt treads is repeatedly tested, but each episode concludes with the reassurance that it *is* still there, just as doubt may be cast on Sam's mental and physical health, but his judgement of a crime situation is usually sound. In order to collaborate, the pair must arrive at compromises that allegorise a rapprochement between past and present.

In its diagnosis of history, the series returns the viewer to pivotal moments in the national past, not to re-observe particular emblematic events (such as Bloody Sunday), but to more regular occurrences (a small explosion from an IRA car bomb), in order mark the mistakes that were made in response, the moments when British society shifted, when the rot began to set in. In episode 5, Sam signposts a turning point in British football culture, one that fed the sort of public and police assumptions about fans that resulted, indirectly, in the tragically mismanaged Hillsborough stadium disaster of 1989. As he tells a fan who is clearly spoiling for a fight: 'United and City fans used to walk to the game together… [then] … people like you came along… How long before something terrible happens and we are dragging blokes out …' Sam's fantasy function captures a broader social desire to go back and correct history, to reverse the procedures and pressures that resulted in catastrophic miscarriages of justice.

Nostalgia, Pleasures, Meanings

It is in such ways that the series manages to be analytical as well as evocative, and so transcend the fuzzy nostalgia that often accompanies period drama, most obviously the police drama *Heartbeat* (ITV 1992–2009) in which the 1960s seemed to roll on indefinitely, the stage for comforting storylines and a hit parade soundtrack. Of course the period detail is all here in *Life on Mars* to be fetishised and remarked upon, music in particular being crucial to the series's emotional, and to some extent commercial, appeal. However, its selection did rather more than retread predictable 1970s pop singles, and included a number of album tracks such as Uriah Heep's 'Traveller in Time' (from *Demons and Wizards* 1972), alongside less obvious hits, ranging from John Kongos's 'Tokoloshe Man' (1971) to the sitarist Ananda Shankar's 'Snow Flower' (1974).

Like the everyday objects discussed at the beginning of this chapter, these semi-forgotten tracks are emotional cues that provoke surprise as well as nostalgia, bring to mind a past that is at once banal *and* exotic, imagined *and* yet somehow unexpected.

Amy Holdsworth has argued that the series defamiliarises the past at the very same time as it recreates authentic period detail, and presents a 'shock of the old' mediated through John Simm's performance as Sam: 'the intensity of the experience captured by Simm is expressed through the character's interiority, his vulnerability and his swagger – he closes his eyes as if he can't believe it, he gulps, he squeezes the bridge of his nose, he sneers'.[22] Acknowledging that the series was designed to *challenge* nostalgic representations of the 1970s, Holdsworth nevertheless insists that 'it is Sam's central ambition to "get home" that makes the series, first and foremost a nostalgic narrative', and she charts the shifting idea of 'home' through the two series as pivotal to this imperative.[23] Whereas Sam began *Life on Mars* wanting to get back to the present, throughout the six minutes or so of screen time that follow his awakening from a coma in his contemporary hospital bed (series 2, episode 8), the emphasis is firmly on the shortcomings of the present: he surveys the colourless skyline, sits on a bench surrounded by random individuals communing with their phones, sits in dreary meetings about the ethics of policy custody. He also visits his mother, to whom he relates that, in the place he went to, he had been 'alive', 'in some ways more than I've ever been', and from whose window he looks out in a now classic motif of social entrapment (Figure 5.1).[24] Haunting the whole sequence is the

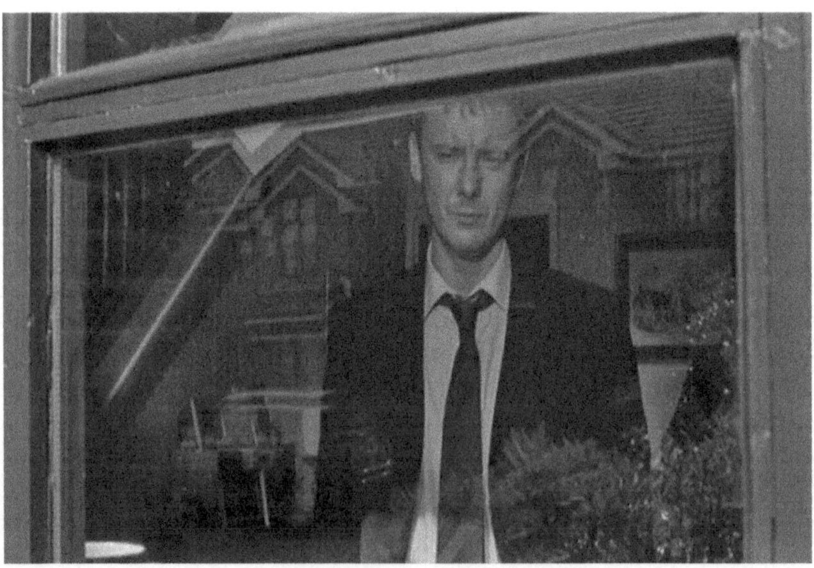

Figure 5.1 *Life on Mars* – series 2, episode 8 (2007)

achingly wistful rendition of 'Somewhere over the Rainbow' by Hawaiian ukulele musician, Israel Kamakawiwo'ole.

Thus it is not relief but regret that engulfs Sam and, after some time in which he is demonstrably unable to settle or 'feel', he leaps from a roof top. In the next sequence he is returned to the scene he had left: a railway tunnel in which Gene, Annie and the squad are still under fire from an armed gang of robbers, the bright natural greens of the setting acting as a reminder of the vibrancy of the period. Whatever Sam's leap meant in narrative terms (and it was subject to much on-line debate), the affection of the series for the oddities of the early 1970s is ultimately reinforced by Sam's profound disappointment with the present. Since rejecting the present is to critique the present and to imagine instead a better world, nostalgia can also take on qualities that Svetlana Boym regards as essentially utopian, save that 'it is no longer directed toward the future. Sometimes nostalgia is not directed toward the past either, but rather sideways'.[25] The key here is that nostalgia may express an aspiration for a better world through the expression of lost possibility; it does not necessarily entail a literal desire to return to the way things were. Indeed, as Pickering and Keightley point out, to conversely valorise the present over the past is to endorse an ideology of progress, and the reversal of this is a rejection of that somewhat discredited premise. Nostalgia is thus not a simple longing for the unattainable, a hopeless 'sigh and lament', but may instead 'recognize aspects of the past as the basis for renewal and satisfaction in the future', and thus become 'a means of taking one's bearings for the road ahead in the uncertainties of the present'.[26] This would seem to be the very resolution that is negotiated by *Life on Mars*, not simply because of its elegant and open conclusion, but through the constant dialectic of Gene and Sam's relationship, which suggests repeatedly that the past is something that should neither be romanticised nor forgotten, but worked through.

Gene's 'voice' is only reactionary in the context of the present, for it is not anachronistically enlightened, unlike the 1960s protagonist of *Inspector George Gently* (BBC 2007–), who must constantly shake his head in disapproval of the racist or sexist attitudes prevalent in his own time in order to mediate these for contemporary audiences. As the mediation function in *Life on Mars* is taken care of by Sam Tyler, Gene is free to simply 'be', and so remind us that the spirit of correctness can be lost in the detail and that the vibrancy of social life may be lost through excessive regulation. In this sense he is perhaps closest to *Cracker*'s Fitz, whose energy needs to burst through systems of control and who, like Gene, presents the viewer with an opportunity to indulge in acts of vicarious rebellion: to break rules, behave badly, be politically incorrect and yet still remain essentially decent and ethically sound. However if, as the previous chapter argues, *Cracker* through Fitz was able to pose the question 'why' in respect of the social and psychological problems of its time, the questions posed by *Life on Mars* are framed through the collision of Sam's predicament with

Gene's historic generic model, demanding of the *present*: 'How did we get to where *we* are?' and even 'Do we want things to be as they have become?'

The frenzied cultural currency the series enjoyed, and which I shall now discuss briefly, suggests that these are questions of some timeliness in the wake of the past twenty years and what Andreas Huyssen describes as its 'slow but palpable transformation of temporality in our lives, brought on by the complex intersections of technological change, mass media, and new patterns of consumption, work and global mobility'.[27] However, that *Life on Mars* should have generated intense day-to-day discussions amongst viewers as well as by self-identifying fans is also to some extent the consequence of its own construction, to the producers' 'astute assessment of the tastes of television audiences'.[28] Indeed, as one *Guardian* reviewer declared: 'If some crazed scientist were to genetically engineer a drama to have an obsessive cult fanbase it would come out looking like *Life on Mars*', adding, 'it practically demands you engage with it in a way you don't with other shows'.[29] Such demands were met via The Railway Arms website, on which fans offered theories of the hidden meanings of the series and the ultimate 'truth' of Sam's circumstances (dead, in a coma, hallucinating, time-travelling), but also reminisced about white dog poo, Wagon Wheels, Raleigh Choppers and of course, Gene's favourite tea, 'oops (tinned spaghetti hoops). Although reminiscence might seem to require first-hand knowledge of 1973 and be therefore confined to a demographic born prior to, say, 1967, there was no shortage of those born later who also confessed to nostalgia for the period, including a considerable number, evidently in full-time study, who were eagerly anticipating the release of Lacey and McElroy's edited study of the series. In fact, a common concern was that others, particularly those with some public influence, should also value *Life on Mars*, and links to newspaper reviews and other sources were widely exchanged and commented upon.

Other 'hot topics' and recurrent threads on the site related to filming locations in Manchester, anachronism spotting, Ford Cortinas and Sam Tyler's jacket.[30] As Brett Mills has noted, one of the website's four main categories of debate is dedicated to the American remake of the series, including a sizeable strand called 'American remake – shudder' that was used to air fans' concerns about the series's core Britishness being threatened by a US version, long before production even began.[31] If, as Chapman argues, the many ambiguities of the series were part of a deliberate opening up of a debate over its meaning, then this suggests a conscious relinquishment of authorial control. This was certainly apparent in some of the direct exchanges between creator and fan, such as one on the BBC's official *Life on Mars* site, which typically ended with Matthew Graham regretting that he had failed to live up to the complex musical allusion that had been read into the series's premise: 'Paul, I love where your head is at and wish I could do your theory justice but I'm afraid that I'd never heard of "Denis Law and Ali McGraw" until I read your question. Sorry'.[32] Nevertheless, in a sea of conflicting interpretations and debate, statements of authorial intent can become disproportionately privileged, and any comments made by the writers were also eagerly exchanged amongst fans as 'clues' as to the 'real' meaning of the series. Less easily contained is the broader resonance of a work, its open-ended capacity to chime perhaps with viewers' personal experiences of 1973, or their dissatisfaction with the present, to which the iconic figure of Gene Hunt was to represent a fantasy response.

The exchange of fan discourses on sites such as The Railway Arms reveal a considerable female fan base for Gene's anachronistic machismo, echoed by the still sizeable presence of a Gene Hunt Appreciation Society on the social media site, Facebook. Self-appointed to speak on behalf of 'millions of British women', for one print journalist:

> the only riddle was why the hell did anyone think this was Tyler's show when a brief psychological profile, cursory examination of the evidence and old-fashioned gut instinct showed that there was only one man in the frame and that was DCI Gene Hunt.[33]

Anticipated or not, when *Life on Mars* was first in production, Hunt's sex appeal was quickly recognised and developed more concertedly in his next televisual incarnation. The two series of *Life on Mars* were followed by three series of its sequel, *Ashes to Ashes* (BBC 2008–10), described by its executive producer Jane Featherstone, as 'the next chapter in the life of Gene Hunt, as seen through the eyes of a modern, no-nonsense woman'.[34] Adopting a similar temporal strategy to *Life on Mars*, the new series narrative begins in the present and revolves around DCI Alex Drake, a police psychologist familiar with Sam Tyler's case, officially recorded as suicide. Drake is shot during a hostage situation before waking up in 1981 clad in an excessively short red mini-dress and faux fur, to the sounds of Ultravox's massively successful single of that year, 'Vienna'. The series is thus structured around a similar enigma to *Life on Mars*, relying upon the same narrative pretext (is she dead/in a coma/back in time?) as well as on the continuing psychological imperative to resolve the trauma of her parents' unexplained deaths, which also occurred in 1981, just as Sam had to resolve the mystery of his father's disappearance after 1973.

Although *Ashes to Ashes* will not here be subject to the same level of analysis as *Life on Mars*, I would like to reference its opening episode in acknowledgement of how Hunt was developed as a cultural icon in a manner that exploited the paradoxical combination of sex appeal and a 'Neanderthal' machismo that had been more of a by-product than a premise of *Life on Mars*. Within minutes of waking, Drake is involved in an aggressive encounter with Edward Markham, a city trader and key player in the drug trade, a situation from which she is rescued by Hunt, who arrives in a red Audi Quattro to the hook ('Look out, Look out') of Duran Duran's hit, 'Careless Memories'. When the Quattro screeches to a halt the near frame is dominated by Drake's provocatively angled legs, a shot followed by an anticipatory close-up of a snakeskin cowboy-booted foot as it steps from the driver's seat and establishes itself outside of the car (see Figure 5.2). This unmistakably libidinous invitation is then reinforced when the camera pulls back to show Hunt's recognisable physique within the diegetic frame of Drake's legs (Figure 5.3).

Viewer recognition here is clearly being mobilised through a humorous intertextual play on Hunt's pre-existing cultural status and the character's love of the Western. It is interesting that he is so obviously objectified, his body revealed in parts, the equivalent of the male gaze once argued by Laura Mulvey to dissect the female subject, integrating

> into the narrative a different mode of eroticism. One part of a fragmented body destroys the Renaissance space, the illusion of depth demanded by the narrative, it gives flatness, the quality of a cut-out or icon rather than verisimilitude to the screen.[35]

Drake of course is framed in a similar fashion, so the entire sequence assumes a cartoon-like quality, in which viewer pleasure is inextricable from its reflexive

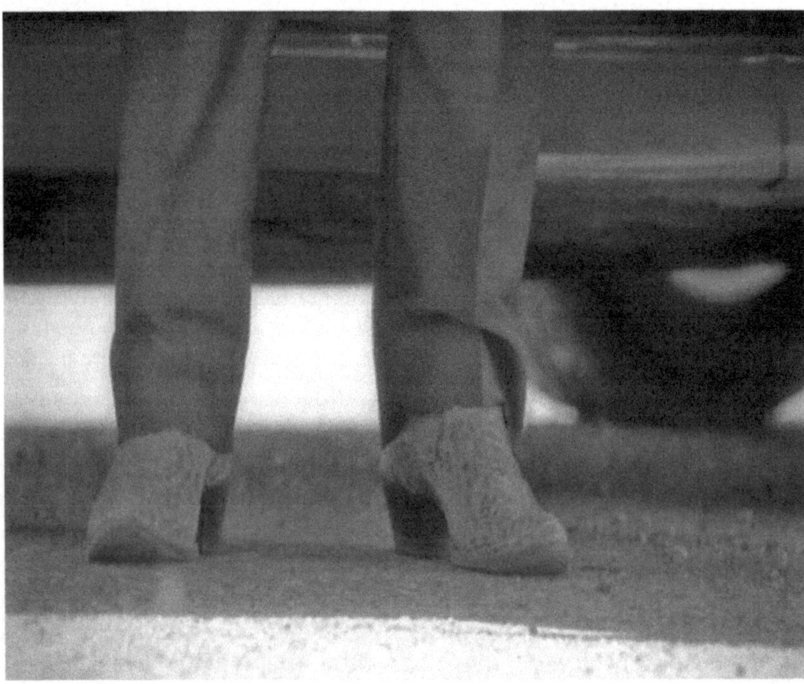

Figure 5.2 *Ashes to Ashes* – series 1, episode 1 (2008)

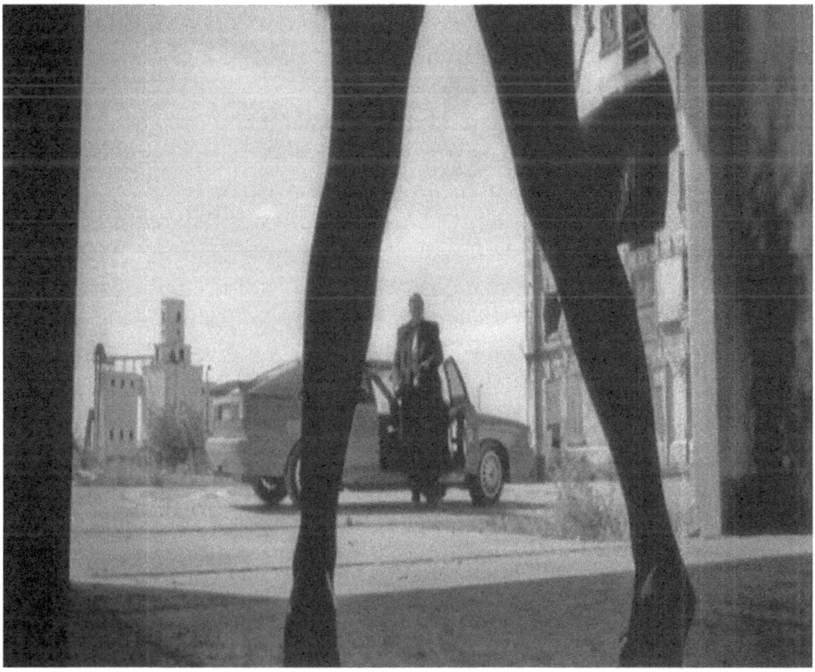

Figure 5.3 *Ashes to Ashes* – series 1, episode 1 (2008)

play on action-romance movie conventions, and from re-recognition of Hunt as returning hero (see also Chapter 2).

Whereas *Life on Mars* had balanced the relative prominence of Tyler and Hunt within their dialectical friendship, patriarchal order is restored here. Drake is positioned as a potential love interest, destined to find that Hunt has more to teach her than she can have imagined, and this gives a rather different inflection to the thematic conflict over policing methods. Although the opposition between Hunt and Drake is analogous to that between Hunt and Tyler – for example substituting her expertise 'on the criminal mind' for Sam's insistence on 'procedure' – Alex's drift into 'psychobabble' thus inevitably becomes gendered as female gibberish in relation to Gene's no-nonsense vernacular. On-line discussion about the new series by *Life on Mars* fans was mixed, if approving, mentioned here only for the number of complaints about Hunt having 'gone soft' and the new format having been feminised or made 'girly': 'Imagine a new *Fawlty Towers* where Sybil has left Basil and Manuel has been replaced by a Swedish sexpot. This is how I feel about *Ashes* to *Ashes*'.[36] As the three series of *Ashes to Ashes* progressed, the 'will they/won't they?' possibility of an actual sexual encounter between Drake and Hunt was exploited by extra-textual speculation in the press and on the message boards. This was stoked by the narrative, which often resolved episodic plots with drunken nights at Luigi's, an Italian restaurant that became the squad's after hours social venue of choice, analogous to the diegetic Railway Arms in *Life on Mars*.

Although the sexual promise of Hunt's character is clearly being played for full effect in *Ashes to Ashes*, his status as an emissary from a world we have lost continued to resonate in his encounters with various 1980s villains. Hunt is explained as having left Greater Manchester Police for the London Metropolitan force the year before, following Sam's death in 1980 'during a jewellery blag'. No longer married, Hunt has adjusted to various other changes since the 1970s, although his customary abrasiveness is still there, not least because 'scum is scum, wherever you go'. Yet self-awareness had crept in, and as he acknowledges to Drake: 'You know, they're sharpening the axe for coppers like me. But ... up until the last second, I will be out there, making a difference.' Of course he does, week on week, but since *Life on Mars* there has been a shift: Hunt is less a creature of his time and his city, although again, such anachronism was not without its attractions for female fans.[37]

I will conclude by briefly mentioning a notorious instance of Gene Hunt's sexualised and ideologically ambivalent charisma, offered by the General Election campaign of 2010, when the character's image was used for a Labour Party poster. The poster was designed to discredit David Cameron by association with Thatcherite policies and bore the legend: 'Don't let him take Britain back to the 1980s' beneath an image in which his face had been grafted onto Hunt's body, sat on the bonnet of the familiar Quattro. The joke showed a poor grasp of Hunt as object of desire, met with immediate cries of 'own goal', and within a few hours the Conservative Party had reappropriated the image to make a virtue of the association. Cameron professed himself 'flattered' by the comparison and the rival poster repeated the image but changed the border to blue and bore the legend: 'Fire up the Quattro, it's time for a change', thus glossing over Hunt's reactionary qualities, and exaggerating instead the dynamism of his masculinity. Most obviously the example demonstrates the cultural resonance and iconicity of Gene Hunt, but may also be seen as indicative of the wider aspirations that can become invested in the role of detective. If the quasi-heroic police-detective continues to suggest a fantasy solution, then the imaginary sphere for its application is clearly not restricted to 'crime', but extends its emotional promise to broader socio-political aspirations.

6

Emergent Voices I: *Wallander* and *Vera*

Given the unabated appetite of British television commissioners for new crime drama over the past twenty years, there will of course be a great many detective shows which have as yet gone unmentioned. Rather than attempting to 'sweep up' all those omitted, the following two chapters will review a number of recent series, selected as indicative of the directions in which the TV detective may now travel. Although it would be foolhardy as to predict influence (still less longevity), the output of the past few years suggests the emergence of a generic cycle at least as heterogeneous as any previous, no matter how much some critics like (as they have so often liked) to generalise about 'typical detective drama'. If this invocation of 'typicality' implies an evasion of aesthetic experiment, and if the series discussed here seem visually 'stylish' in comparison to their predecessors, then on both counts it is worth remembering that the strengths of television were once perceived to lie elsewhere: notably in its intimacy, temporal rhythms, immediacy and resonance with the everyday. It was in playing to these strengths that British TV drama production cultivated a 'style that effaces itself in order to witness character and environment rather than to draw attention to the mediation of the narrative by specific audio-visual forms'.[1] I would argue that such a style needs to be remembered in turn as a different mode of quality to that vaunted as 'cinematic', one that facilitated intense character performances and a narrative address to matters of public concern, and I would hope that some trace of these attributes remains in evidence in the texts considered here.

The British series *Wallander* (BBC 2008–) is based on Henning Mankell's Swedish novels featuring the police detective character Kurt Wallander, and stars Kenneth Branagh, a (since) knighted actor and director with an established and somewhat high-brow cultural reputation, in his first role as a returning character in a television series. Although a potential such project was already under discussion, a chance meeting allowed Branagh to recommend himself for the part, and collaborate with Mankell on the adaptations. To date there have been three runs, each of three self-contained feature-length editions, all produced for BBC Scotland by Yellow Bird and Left Bank Pictures.[2] I shall later compare *Wallander* with another eponymous drama, *Vera* (ITV 2011–) of which there had been two series broadcast at the time of writing, but a third and fourth subsequently scheduled for 2013 and 2014, all comprising four feature-length episodes. Starring Brenda Blethyn in the title role, *Vera* adapts the Vera Stanhope crime novels written by Ann Cleeves, the first of which was published in 1997, although a number of episodes were specially written for television.[3] In common with several others originating over the past five years, such as *DCI Banks* (ITV 2010–) and *Case Sensitive* (ITV 2011–), these two series evidence the continuing reliance of contemporary broadcasters on literary crime fiction as a source of critically tested material.

Mankell's Wallander novels and short stories had previously been adapted in their original Swedish language as nine feature-length films for Sveriges Television (STV) starring Rolf Lassgård between 1994 and 2007. A second Swedish version, also produced by Yellow Bird, starring Krister Henriksson as Kurt Wallander, was specially devised for the screen by Mankell and places greater emphasis on the routine work of the police ensemble around the protagonist.[4] Interesting as it would be to compare the three performances of the character by Henriksson, Lassgård and Branagh, this chapter will be less concerned with questions of adaptation or interpretation than with the particular contribution the BBC series makes to an emergent cycle of British detective drama.

Wallander both epitomises and develops the early twenty-first-century foregrounding of a widescreen high-definition aestheticised landscape, and cements its visual rupture from television crime drama of the 1990s. The British cinematographer Anthony Dod Mantle, renowned for his association with Lars von Trier and the Scandinavian Dogme film movement, was hired to establish a visual style for the series, and acted as Director of Photography on two early (2008) episodes ('Sidetracked' and 'One Step Behind'). The relatively new technology of the Red One camera was used for shooting, as it achieved a high-resolution 35mm look when pressed for money, time and natural light.[5] Careful composition and framing, often of spectacular sequences, quickly became a hallmark of the series, as was its vivid and expert colour grading. These stylistic features are typified by the opening pre-credit sequence of 'Sidetracked' in which shots of a girl wading through a field of vivid yellow shoulder-height rape are cross-cut with images of Kurt Wallander, racing to the scene, the darkness of his dress and car interior a marked contrast to the rape field beyond. Images of a chained, tethered black dog and concerned farmer build on the suspense, alleviated fleetingly by the farmer's disappointment that Kurt has not arrived in a marked police car. Wallander wades through the crop towards the girl, begging her to talk, but he is quite unable to do anything to stop her when, in extreme anguish, she drenches herself in petrol and sets herself on fire.

The lurid and horrifying brilliance of a self-immolation in a yellow rape field exemplifies a strategy in which close-framing and a muted, dark colour palette (most notable in the greys and murky browns of the interiors and sombre dress of most characters) is punctuated periodically by spectacular set pieces. These often include a natural landscape: perhaps a windswept dune beach silhouetted against a fading northern Scandinavian light, a green-grey cliff-top that throws into relief a tatty bunch of vividly coloured flowers left at a makeshift shrine ('Faceless Killers', 2010) or a scattering of red poppies in a bleached-out wheat field ('Dogs of Riga', 2012). The same wild and desolate environments produce odd natural mutations, or suffer the scars of humanity's self-torture. An odd character trait of Kurt's father, Povel, is to compulsively paint the same scene over and over again, and this lends the Swedish landscape further thematic and narrative significance. Ironically, after Povel's death in 'The Fifth Woman' (2010), Kurt sees one of these near-identical pictures hanging on Vanja's wall, occasioning him to repeat his father's insistence that 'we each had our own landscape – that's what we had to endure'.

Languorous slow pans of sky and countryside invite awe of a fragile beauty that may be violated at any time by an act of savagery. A predatory, mobile camera is often used to observe such activity, its view impeded by an obstacle or window frame, providing optical alignment with neither perpetrator nor police, but with a hypothetical, unseen witness. Moments of violence stand out in contrast to the excessively careful composition of almost every other frame, including those in which Kurt himself is the primary interest. In *Wallander*, long takes of human subjects frame them with such calculation that sequences begin to approximate a form of meticulous filmed portraiture. A welcome variation to the static pace is occasionally signalled by the ringing of Kurt's phone, perhaps prompting a frantic car journey to another location, and there are also a number of action sequences involving the stalking of an armed suspect or a face-to-face combat. However, for the most part the camera work is heavily stylised, inviting scrutiny, and appearing to contain the action rather than follow it. The series also demonstrates many of the general realist features that Paul Cobley notes as having become newly associated with Scandinavian crime, such as 'bleakness, slow pace, low-key attention to detail', that may appear to circumvent 'the relentless formulaic sameness and melodrama of popular narrative' yet are really as 'entrenched' as the conventionalised realism against which they profess to rebel.[6] There is potentially something of an aesthetic tension here, pitting the fine colour grading and self-conscious static portraiture against the renewed commitment to realism, one implication being that 'the real' becomes strange and fascinating, newly positioned as an object of contemplation.

The most obvious way in which *Wallander* differentiates itself from the conventions of the British detective series is through a narrative logic prompted by the casting of familiarly British (and British-accented) actors but in an unusually non-British setting. As with all screen genres, innovations that attempt to negotiate a new representative relationship with the world beyond may entail the breaking of 'rules' which in themselves seem unimportant, but may have consequences for other functional and emotional expectations of the genre. We have already seen how the relative simplicity of casting a female DCI in *Prime Suspect* – a decision that, in principle, should hardly have been radical in late twentieth-century Britain – meant that other conventional traits of the detective, such as a typically dysfunctional private life, carried a slightly different significance, and this presented new narrative opportunities. The geographical logic of *Wallander* is analogous to this, as its Swedish setting effectively opens up a different set of meaning possibilities that break some of the TV detective's ties to an essentially national set of socially specific preoccupations.

Mankell's books are steeped in Swedish culture and developed out of a long literary crime tradition that contrasted 'the seemingly idyllic Sweden with the horrible murders, vice and crime that resided beneath the surface', sometimes charting the descent of the country's bourgeois welfare state traditions into a totalitarian dystopia.[7] Remaining faithful to the feel of Nordic crime, the UK series was shot primarily in the Skåne province of Sweden, using real-life locations such as the actual port of Ystad (also used for previous screen incarnations of the novels). In keeping with its topographical logic, its use of generic places so common as to be interchangeable amongst almost all other British crime series (office, police station, household, crime scenes) are emphatically 'othered' in *Wallander*. The exactitude of the imagery makes space for carefully selected everyday Swedish artefacts (signs, documents, cars emblazoned with 'Polis') and traditionally rustic and/or open plan suburban architecture that is quite distinct from the densely populated conurbations or estates upon which British crime drama has been conventionally dependent.

For British audiences, although such details do mark the diegesis as 'foreign', the use of the English language and casting of British actors means it is not recognisably a *Swedish text* (with all the extra-textual significance that this would involve), and thus makes it difficult to sustain the diegetic conceit that this is all somehow about Sweden. The logic of using British performers with 'no funny accents'[8] for storylines that frequently critique Scandinavian xenophobia, also posed practical difficulties. Kurt leaves the country on only one occasion, to pursue a case with connections to Latvia ('Dogs of Riga') for which authentic Latvian locations were used and a generically Eastern European supporting cast, although the Latvian police officer Liepa is actually himself

Scandinavian (Søren Malling), possibly known to British viewers from his role in *The Killing*. For the most part, however, *Wallander* provides a mix of performers drawn from the more familiar repertory of British TV drama that in itself has connotations. Whatever the logic behind the casting of, say, Saskia Reeves as Kurt's girlfriend, Vanja ('An Event in Autumn', 2012), she brings an added semiotic significance for genre fans, having also played a former sergeant and romantic interest in *Lewis* as well as John Luther's senior officer in *Luther*. Similarly and somewhat ironically, Kurt's ex-wife – who appears in 'The Fifth Woman' (broadcast 17 January 2010) – is played by Phyllis Logan, shortly to become engaged to Jack Frost and walk with him into retirement (*A Touch of Frost*, 'If Dogs Run Free', broadcast 4 and 5 April 2010). I mention these not just as amusing coincidences; it is familiar faces such as these that help to brand British dramas as British, and thus to assuage the proprietary concerns of national audiences keen to see 'UK content' maintained in the new digital political economy of broadcasting.[9]

Positioning British actors within diegetic Sweden may also exacerbate the topographical limbo that prompted a certain amount of consternation amongst fans and reviewers, a number of whom preferred their intelligence to be 'flattered', as Rachel Cooke put it, by watching the subtitled Swedish version rather than 'listen to Branagh and his colleagues talking in flat voices, as if they were reading a poor translation'.[10] For others, even the ringtone to Kurt's phone (an object regularly privileged by lingering close-ups) seemed so tantalisingly exotic as to merit a furious collective on-line investigation to discover the national provenance of both it and the phone itself.[11] Confounding viewer expectations in this way may also challenge the customary association between 'homegrown' crime fiction and the everyday social experience of crime. This is not to say that *Wallander* does not still offer opportunities for British audiences to reflect on British crime, to 'compare and contrast' as Branagh himself suggests,[12] but it is to argue that the referential relationship between on-screen and everyday space that so privileges the nationally inflected anxieties addressed by detective series has, in this instance, been severed.

In other respects, letting go of the familiar topography of British television crime licensed a whole new level of signification and rich visual symbolism, freed from the strictures of reference and the anxieties around national everyday spaces. In addition to the aching wildness of the remote Scandinavian landscape, other natural motifs are deployed, perhaps as reflections of Kurt's state of mind, or to mirror the narrative in some way. One memorable metaphor is presented by a white horse in 'Faceless Killers', in an episode that weaves together the murder of an elderly couple with an acute stage of deterioration in his father's dementia. Kurt is clearly haunted by the plight of the horse, an elderly creature which had bolted from the couple's farmhouse when they were assaulted, and which he encounters at significant moments. Once, shortly after a confused, pyjama-clad Povel is rescued from a countryside wander, Kurt spots the beast in an open field, leaving his car so as to contemplate it in its liberty (Figure 6.1). Later, after his father has accepted defeat and admitted himself to a care home, Kurt comes across the horse again, this time lying still in the road following a collision with a vehicle. Enjoining both sequences are instrumental riffs that flow into one another before blending into the closing title music and vocals (by Emily Barker), adding to the sense of seamless inevitability. For Povel, like the horse, the journey into the open was very much a last gasp, but it is Wallander who is defined by the encounter, enabling him to respond emotionally in a way he cannot seem to express to, or about, his father.

Mankell's books are not serial in form, and the sequence of stories in the BBC version is not the same as the order in which they were originally written (or, indeed, first filmed with Lassgård), but a number of continuing serialised storylines were added to the episodic narratives in order to develop a personal trajectory for Kurt across the run. In some cases the investigations detailed in the novels have been altered to make them contemporary, for example 'Dogs of Riga', written in 1990 and inspired by real events in Latvia at the time,[13] required significant changes to decouple the plot from the immediate aftermath of the Cold War. Other storylines have been updated to reflect the new technology used in both crime (global terrorism and electronic banking in 'Firewall', 2008) and its detection.

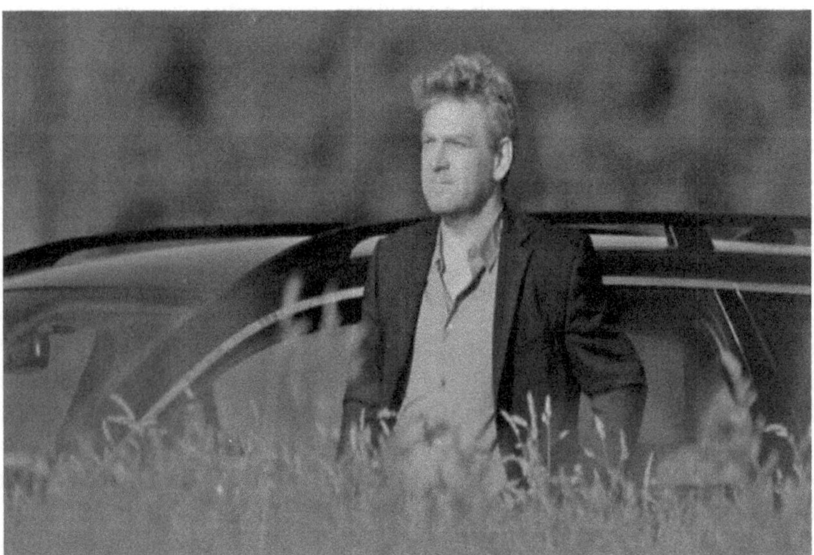

Figure 6.1 *Wallander* – 'Faceless Killers' (2010)

The need to detach the stories from their original topical context also disengages the series from the routine social problems that preoccupied an earlier cycle of British TV crime drama, and allows it to reach towards a more generalised, transcultural, set of meaning possibilities. Perhaps by way of substitution, the series encodes a rather old-school liberal-humanist fascination with the existential crisis in which Kurt is almost permanently embroiled. Branagh's performance expressly connects this crisis to Wallander's internalisation of the events he witnesses, about which he is prone to express despair in humanity or civilisation in their broadest forms. Thus, it is not so much the personal circumstances of the girl in the rape field that intrigues him in 'Sidetracked' as the hand-wringing question: 'what kind of world are we leaving a 15 year old girl that she would burn herself to death?' Whereas in *Prime Suspect* such an incident may have been symptomatic of historically particular failures of social care, or attributed in *A Touch of Frost* to a Britain 'going to the dogs', it is here a sign of worldly malaise, humanity itself in crisis. The particularly horrific crimes with which Kurt must deal (bodies impaled by makeshift spikes, scalpings, stabbings, immolation) infer a generalised depravity and bleakness that is given lyrical equivalents in the music, landscape and its disturbed inhabitants. All around Kurt Wallander are odd people, battered and worn down by old grievances and tortured relationships, removed from their local associations and aggregated into what his daughter Linda refers to as 'this stuff'.

Certainly, there is no utopian or heroic dimension to Kurt, who far from offering a fantasy solution to socio-historical problems, becomes instead an Ibsenite figure burdened by the weight of humanity's despair, condemned to shuffle helplessly around this northern land that is, by turns, gloomy, exotic and achingly beautiful. The Wallander of Mankell's novels is an essentially practical man, caught off guard by occasional existential reflections, but in this adaptation even storylines derived from a novel concerned with topical phenomena, such as immigration and racism in 'Faceless Killers', become overshadowed by Kurt's personal struggle, which in this episode involves facing his own latently racist instincts and feelings towards Linda's Syrian boyfriend, Jamal. Branagh's Wallander is not recognisably a small-town police officer caught up in 'a time characterised by a sort of criminality that nobody had experienced before',[14] so for him the political must be either acutely personal or universal (the xenophobia in us all) rather than historically and geographically specific.

Typically, Kurt's private life (or the lack of it) shows something of the same familial dysfunction that led to the crimes he investigates in his professional capacity. His demeanour is world-weary rather than angry but he is prone also to outbursts of despair that meet a match in his father's dementia. Kurt begins the first series reluctantly separated from his wife yet pleased to host a visit from his daughter, but their relationship quickly becomes difficult and unsatisfactory. In 'Sidetracked' his predicament is summed up by a police profiler with whom he has been working, who tells him 'you seem to be in crisis at the moment', and smiles wryly at Kurt's fantasies of 'getting out' and breaking the hold the job has over him. His private tragedy is slow-moving and inches forward over time as a psychological journey marked by occasional events, but remaining characteristically cyclical.

In 'Firewall' Linda berates him for suffering alone at the end of each day, urging him 'you've got to move on Dad!' and signing him up to an internet dating site, where he falls prey to Ella (Orla Brady), a beautiful terrorist who targets him to get access to police intelligence. Kurt seems relieved at the opportunity to share with Ella his terminally weary reflections on human life: 'I don't really think that there is a bigger picture. This is where we live – here, now. These are our lives, and they're fragile and precarious, and miraculous and all we have.' Ella is evidently curious and framed in a shot which accommodates her whole face and neck, but Kurt is in close-up, and for most of the speech his craggy unshaven face exceeds the frame, inviting a direct glimpse at his thoughts through his eyes, whilst still aligning the viewer with Ella's reactions, inviting that he be seen as if by others.

With some good reason, Kurt's immersion in the horror with which he must deal necessarily takes his character to the point of being self-absorbed, self-pitying and rather bad at self-care. In 'One Step Behind' he is diagnosed with diabetes, which has presumably developed as a result of his poor diet and taste for red wine. In a separate, emblematic gesture, Linda fills his fridge with sprouting beans and exotic vegetables, which makes Kurt smile fondly, although he does not seem to know what to do with such healthy bounty. Later, in 'The Man Who Smiled' (2010), he returns from a stay in a guest house where he had been trying to come to terms with having previously (in 'Faceless Killers') killed a man carrying an unloaded gun. On his return to his home, he again opens the fridge, but the contents are putrid and the smell is foul.

Even by the standards of the lonely maverick detective, Wallander's private ever-unravelling existential crisis is pronounced, and the theme of neglect is crucial to the suggestion that his identity conceals a vacuum, one hardly offset by the fullness of his days and demands of work as it is these that impede his character progression. Although a clear and careful personal trajectory has unfolded across the nine episodes to date, this gives but an illusion of movement as the 'developments' in Kurt's private life are actually repetitive in nature. He makes periodic attempts to make peace with his father (before he dies), with his wife (who intends to remarry) and with Linda (with whom he has circular arguments about loneliness, work, family; and from whom he becomes estranged then, later, awkwardly reconciled). The ending to 'The Fifth Woman' offers one of the most peaceful and positive images of the series, following an encounter at his father's funeral with his ex-wife (who berates him for still wearing his wedding ring) and a flicker of possible new relationship with Vanja, a florist. In the concluding brief sequence, she waits whilst Kurt leaves flowers and the ring on his father's gravestone before they walk off together, dwarfed by an overcast sky. The next episode ('An Event in Autumn') sees Kurt moving in with Vanja and her son, optimistically announcing it as 'a new start' after an interim lapse (both on- and off-screen) of over two years. However, within screen minutes the dog has discovered a body in the garden and the phone begins to ring, announcing further intrusions. As the reviewer Tom Sutcliffe noted, 'even dedicated viewers may have been surprised at the audacity with which the drama wiped the smile off Kurt's face again'.[15] After this, Kurt's domestic comfort begins to crumble, a process typified by his once again falling asleep in his chair after a bottle of red wine. To disintegrate with such circularity brings to mind Jane Feuer's observation that 'a static conception of character is a more damning description of bourgeois social relations' than one which is able to 'progress'.[16] Kurt insists he does not enjoy this return to form and rejects Vanja's accusation that he is 'putting on old clothes', yet his work defines his identity and he cannot move beyond it.

Kurt's personal reiteration preserves the imperative of stasis inherent to series form, although in another sense *Wallander* moves beyond convention, by reinforcing the detective as an object of such considerable interest for its own sake. In 'Before the Frost' (2012), the final episode of series 3, there are two sequences that exemplify the systematic prioritisation of Kurt's subjectivity above other meaning possibilities. Near the beginning, Kurt visits his colleague Ann-Britt (Sarah Smart) who is still in hospital rehabilitation after an incident (in 'An Event in Autumn') for which he feels responsible. Ann-Britt is first heard but not seen, her sighs of effort audible when he arrives at the treatment room, whilst the camera remains trained exclusively on him. When she does come into frame, it is only by means of shots in which she is obscured, or visible only from her reflection. The pair converse, but always in the reflective shadows of the glass, and only briefly together in the same shot when divided by the cross-frame of a window when she tells Kurt quietly that he does not need to keep visiting, 'it's time for everybody to get on with life'. For much of this exchange, the camera lingers on Kurt, his choking back of emotion, his need to agree with her, his hands nervously rubbing together in his lap. He pauses as he takes his leave, shot again from the rear, looking off to the left. In the entire two-minute sequence, Ann-Britt is alone in the frame for a total of only 14 seconds, in all of which the view of her is impeded by reflections cast beyond the window glass. Ever having been – even as Kurt's most prominent colleague – a mere sympathetic foil to his anguish and worries, Ann-Britt is reduced finally to a ghostly figure of his consciousness, an ethereal reminder of the dangers he risks daily and the responsibility he must bear.

Later in the episode, there is a brief sequence in which Kurt sits, without speaking, with a woman whose mother had earlier disappeared and who, it must be assumed, has now learnt that a body has been discovered. We do not see her face at all, she is identifiable only by the domestic setting in which he met her previously as, again, it is Kurt who is centre frame, shot from behind her bowed head, looking down at her with concern. Cut then to a shot of the two of them either side of the kitchen table on which the woman's head is still down, now covered by her arms, then again to a brief shot of her hands, crumpling a paper tissue. Her sobs begin shortly before the sequence and carry across all the cuts, and they are still audible when Kurt has left the house, the camera steady on his back as he walks away. Like Ann-Britt, the grieving woman is an object of Kurt's concern but one so scarcely identified and differentiated beyond her grief that she becomes a mere piece of diegetic furniture, there solely to demonstrate 'this stuff' and the effect it has upon him.

As the director Esther May Campbell admits, Branagh is necessarily 'visually indulged' in all episodes, as 'producers panic when you're not looking at Ken's face'.[17] Indeed, Branagh's Wallander is so privileged by style, script and structure as to suggest a reversal in function to that of an earlier generation of detectives, designed as 'palpable devices to explore something that is more interesting than themselves'.[18] In *Wallander*, Kurt is the primary, sometimes the only, object of interest, embedded in a more complex and comprehensive structure of subjective alignment than is usually necessary to promote moral allegiance. The suffering of the world is not merely knowable through his eyes, it is appreciable only through its consequences for him. Social malaise, crime and dysfunction may visibly exist beyond the character, but their broader social, cultural and political significance is never so important or interesting as the protagonist himself, represented by a devotedly attentive 'house style' of cinematography which fetishises his absorption in the suffering of others.

Indeed, in its representation of Kurt as constantly both *falling* and in other ways, *fallen*, *Wallander* might even be interpreted as a generic allegory, taking the detective over and over again to the brink of oblivion, pushing him beyond hope in his private relationships. Certainly, it is in this series that the character type – ever trapped partway down a tragic spiral – comes closest to the modernist bourgeois hero torn apart by the contradictions of 'self' first noted by Lukács (see Chapter 2). Although reviewers of *Wallander* were quick to dub it the 'Norse Morse',[19] Kurt's lack of resilience clearly exceeds Morse's (albeit profound) dissatisfaction. Unlike Morse, Kurt is also beyond passion: he drinks but less for pleasure than out of stress or habit and, unlike the Wallander of Mankell's novels, he neither socialises nor listens to opera. He is as passionless as Lewis, but more manifestly centre stage, and his relationships are marked by an emotional neediness that is quite chaste in its performance. Although in his coupling with Vanja, Kurt is briefly on the verge of achieving the romantic solace he appears (at that point) to crave, their on-screen presence is at best cosy: Branagh's face registering relief and affection in his moments with her, but never for one moment a flicker of sexual desire. Similarly, Kurt's seduction of Baipa Liepa ('Dogs of Riga'), conveyed in a brief morning sequence in a hotel room, is limited to an affectionate glance at her still sleeping form. Coming as they do in the third (intended as the penultimate) series, such instances begin to bring closure to Kurt's reluctant post-divorce trajectory, but they do little to develop his characterisation outside of his defining sadness.

The ITV series *Vera* shares with *Wallander* certain aesthetic qualities that make it an interesting point of reference, and was similarly presented as a series of feature-length films. Production was part funded by Northern Film and Media, a creative industry development agency for the North East, and it is the remote Northumbrian landscape that is one of the distinguishing features of the series. Much use is made of local landmark attractions, including Chipchase Castle ('Sandancers', 2012) and Holy Island, Lindisfarne ('Hidden Depths', 2011). By turns bleak and magnificent, northern English skies fill the frame, thundering above cottages and farmhouses and rendering tiny and insignificant the odd, lonely characters with which Vera must deal. After the death of her father immediately prior to episode 1, Vera takes up residence in his lonely farmhouse, full of foul-smelling and half-complete attempts at taxidermy but few modern conveniences. It is the same house in which her mother died when she was just ten years old, and her occasional discovery of items (and secrets) hidden amongst her father's personal effects reminds us that the space for her is redolent with memories of her sad childhood.

Vera repeatedly constructs visual oppositions between the natural and the manmade, for as with *Wallander*, the murders under investigation are often shocking and made all the more brutal by the achingly beautiful setting in which bodies are found. Nevertheless, the opposition is evocative rather than thematic, used to underline the horror of the crime but inferring no particular thesis as to its causes. An impressive cinematographic strategy used in the series is to jointly frame the prosaic and the wondrous, as typified by a sequence in *Hidden Depths* in which a slowly back-tracking camera reveals the Angel of the North appearing to rise majestically above a modest group of houses, and again, in a scene where Vera sits on a bench to share a packet of (out of date) cakes, dwarfed in scale by an enormous freight ship (Figure 6.2).

Contrasting landscapes are also used to create interesting narrative parallels. Typically, *Silent Voices* (2012) begins with a pre-credit montage in which, first, a woman is shown diving into a deep natural pool from a grassy ledge next to a spectacular waterfall. A succeeding and contrasting crane shot looks down above the lanes of an indoor swimming pool, one woman swimming breast-stroke from right to left of frame, another kicking her way ineffectually into the frame from left to right, balancing with a blue float. As the camera swoops down to eye level, we see that the struggling swimmer is actually Vera herself. The parallel is sustained through fast intercutting of the first swimmer (as she is

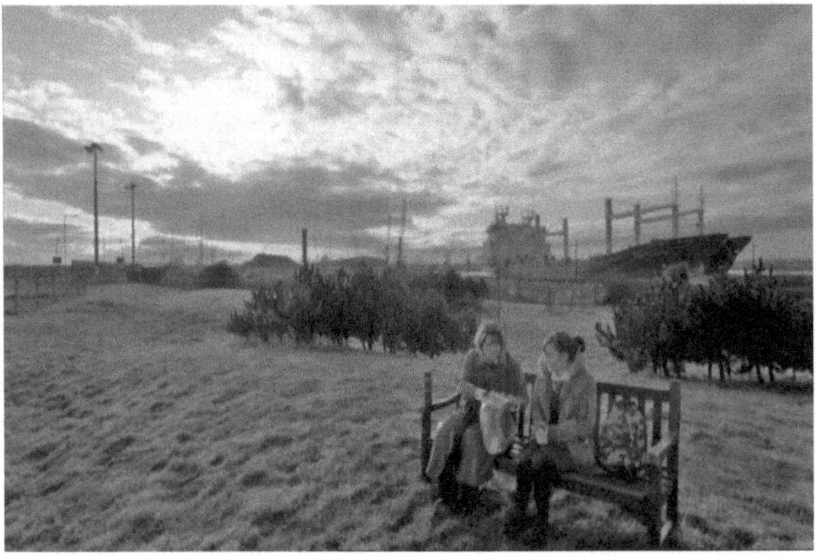

Figure 6.2 *Vera* – 'Hidden Depths' (2011)

pushed under and drowned by an unseen assassin) with an equally flurried sequence in which Vera, red-faced and anguished, struggles to dodge an aqua-aerobics class to complete a length. Typically, the juxtaposition thus creates a sympathetic alignment with and between the two women, at the same time as contrasting their differences of competence. The contrast does not carry through thematically: Vera may puff when she runs and is as unhealthy in her diet and drinking habits as the rest of her detective peers, but she is not at odds with the natural world. Quite to the contrary, she is seen to be rather at one with the wilderness of this, the least densely populated county in England.

In its expressive deployment of place, *Vera* is a relatively faithful visualisation of Cleeves's vivid narrative topographies, and perhaps the evident similarities to *Wallander* should not be surprising, as the author admits to having been inspired by Nordic literary crime fiction, particularly its bleakness, sense of loss, and the relationship between characters and an often hostile landscape.[20] Revealingly, *Vera* also uses a number of the same motifs as *Wallander*, flying birds, carrion crows and stuffed raptors being among the most obvious, as are quietly swishing wind turbines, lapping shores and the horns of passing freight liners.

As a central character Vera bears little similarity to any of her female antecedents, although she does have a more than passing resemblance to the grumpy, middle-aged, lonely Morse prototype. Looking every inch the eccentric in her shabby mac and crumpled batty hat, she is also gruff, tactless and frequently involved in minor conflicts with her colleagues, including DS Joe Ashworth (David Leon), DC Kenny Lockhart (Jon Morrison) and DC Holly Lawson (Wunmi Mosaku) who, to Vera's great regret, requests a transfer to Manchester in the fifth episode. Such confrontations are usually forgiven, Stanhope is also a fierce critic of herself, and often regrets her insensitivity to those around her. As with *Wallander*, a slow-moving personal storyline is stretched across the run of the series run to sustain serial interest and, like Kurt, Vera is prone to self-neglect. In 'Little Lazarus' (2011) she develops chest pains and Joe takes her to the hospital, although the outcome of her consultation is unclear. In the next series – ironically, during a 'celebration' supper that Joe's wife Celine has prepared for her ('The Ghost Position', 2012) – she blurts out that she has been diagnosed with angina, and then leaves abruptly for her dark and lonely house, an emphatic visual contrast to the warm glow of Joe and Celine's family home.

The opposition between Vera and Joe echoes *Wallander*, although we know only from report that Ann-Britt has to juggle domestic demands with work. Joe is a more developed character, whose life with Celine and their young daughters is lived out in front of Vera, a periodic reminder of what she never had. On duty, Vera is clearly privileged in terms of spatial access, although the structure of moral allegiance is quite open and narrative interest extends to others in the team. By way of further contrast to *Wallander*, there is a scene in 'Silent Voices' when Vera tells a daughter that her mother's body has been discovered. Vera and Joe hover at the edge of the frame, quietly sympathetic and in professional charge, but the camera remains with the girl's reactions (disbelief, nausea, anguish), intercut with images of her relationship with her mother, such as a set of holiday snaps, the pair of them all smiles, loosely fixed to the door of the refrigerator. In this as in other examples, Vera is aligned with the victim in order to illuminate their distress, not to appropriate it as her own. Her loneliness is significant, but established with some narrative economy, and rarely distracts from the criminal investigation.

I suggested previously that viewer engagement with detective characters may be in part libidinous, and that there can be a romantic aspect to viewer investment in these series, particularly if the central performer is charismatic. Certainly this much is suggested by the testimonies of female respondents in Lyn Thomas's 'In love with Inspector Morse',[21] or by the press and fan commentary circulating around Gene Hunt. However, I would also introduce the possibility that romantic viewer inclinations for the detective may be the emotional manifestation of a more general dissatisfaction with the contemporary world. As established previously, the police detective may be seen as an expression or fantasy response to the injustices that underpin discontent, and although this idealistic function is not necessarily romantic in origin it may often become so. However, for all the personal attributes that Vera and Kurt have in common with irritable, middle-aged Morse, it is difficult to imagine a significant proportion of the audience professing itself 'in love with Wallander' or 'in love with Vera'; which is actually to say less about the physique of either actor (both of whom had to be dressed down for their parts) than about the way in which their sexuality has been obviated and made redundant by the narratives. When Kurt removes his sweaty shirt and wipes his armpits with the office curtains ('The Man Who Smiled') and when Vera approaches a long-estranged police colleague only for him to exclaim: 'Christ!' at her presumably altered appearance ('The Ghost Position'), there is in both cases an active and express closing off of romantic possibilities.

Furthermore, where *A Touch of Frost* developed Jack's avuncularity as well as his late middle-aged romantic dalliances, *Wallander* denies its protagonist the possibility of any satisfactory relationships at all. Kurt is an unsuccessful lover and often a disinterested one, but he is also a disappointing son and a dysfunctional father, as played out repeatedly in arguments with Linda. Stanhope's childlessness is equally significant: where the viewer of *Prime Suspect* had been privy to Tennison's painful choice of career over motherhood, the viewer of *Vera* is presented with the accomplished fact of the post-menopausal single woman, awkward amongst family and social groups alike. Although Vera does show herself to be capable of sensitive relationships with minors (as witnesses and victims), she is not altogether comfortable in the role. Like Kurt, she is a highly sympathetic figure who has paid a hefty personal price for the job she does, although her personal tragedy is still secondary to the role she plays in mediating the troubled world beyond. Vera's private demons are put back in their narrative place, often offset by a sharp Tyneside turn of phrase, a bit of office banter, a witty exchange with the forensic surgeon Billy Cartwright (Paul Ritter), himself a master of morbid and sexual innuendo who is usually paying the price (in venereal disease and paternity claims) of passing sexual encounters.

Engaging as the team around Vera might be, the investigative resolutions brought about can also seem tardy and tinged with sadness, a suggestion cued partly by composed music almost as tense and mournful as that which underscores *Wallander*. Vera's own lack of satisfaction at each episodic closure is to some extent mitigated by Joe, who like DS Hathaway in *Lewis*, is granted sufficient youth and virility for occasional acts of daring, not least a spectacular dive into the reservoir to rescue a woman from inside a plunging car ('Silent Voices'). Through Joe, the utopian impulse is preserved in *Vera* even if the character of Stanhope, like Wallander, would otherwise seem only to realise the logic set in motion by the Morse detective cycle: a logic in which the detective's potential for heroic agency is overshadowed by the metaphoric and narrative reiteration of his or her empty, savaged private life.

Of course vulnerability is attractive and unhappiness has its fascinations, as one critic of *Wallander* noted: 'in the furrows and stubble of Branagh's pudgily perplexed face, all of this misery was an absolute delight'.[22] However, considered in relation to the other more resilient, combative, witty or reassuring figures encountered in this study, the relentless emphasis in both *Vera* and *Wallander* on the price exacted by the police profession is still curious, and could be read perhaps even as symptomatic of social apathy towards injustice: where Fitz and Tennison were once angry, Vera and Kurt are tired, defeated. Such characterisation may also crystallise a timely and (re)emergent expression of how the division between life and labour brought by modernity continues to exaggerate the experience of interpersonal bonds as 'bondages'.[23] That these professionals should reach middle age so compromised by their public service may thus be read as a critique of society and workplaces more generally, albeit of an altogether different order to the politicised dissent articulated by the 'voices' of the early 1990s.

7

Emergent Voices II: *Luther, Scott & Bailey* and *Line of Duty*

Following directly on from Chapter 6, I shall here examine in detail two further contemporary series that each suggest quite different directions for the genre than those considered previously. First I will analyse *Luther* (BBC 2010–), a programme noted for its debt to cinematic as well as television crime genres; and secondly, *Scott & Bailey* (ITV 2011–), a series self-consciously oppositional to *Luther* in style and narrative emphasis. The chapter will conclude with brief reference to a third text, *Line of Duty* (BBC 2012), broadcast initially as a five-part mini-serial at the end of the 20 year period under consideration, which may be read as a reflexive meta-commentary on the cultural functions and significance of the detective character.

Luther

The BBC's express desire to restrict its output of crime drama resulted in a select roster of detective shows, in which *Luther*, like *Wallander*, enjoys a privileged place. *Luther* was created and written for television by Neil Cross[1] and produced in-house for the BBC by Katie Swinden.[2] At the time of writing there had been two series, comprising ten one-hour episodes in total, with a third, four-part run confirmed for 2013. The series is set in London and revolves, typically enough, around a maverick eponymous hero, in this case DCI John Luther, a brilliant, volatile, philosophically incisive, loose cannon, described by one senior officer as 'nitro-glycerine'. Although there is little or no explicit narrative reference to his racial identity, it is not incidental that the role is played by London-born

British-African actor Idris Elba, known internationally for his role as gangland leader 'Stringer' in the much lauded American series *The Wire*.

Elba may not be the first actor of colour to play a detective lead in a British drama, but the field has certainly been dominated by more than its quota of middle-aged white men. Earlier series featuring non-white police protagonists included *Gangsters* (BBC 1976–8) set in a Birmingham Asian community, *The Chinese Detective* (BBC 1981–2) and *Wolcott* (ITV 1981) which revolved around the activities of a black CID officer in opposition to the drugs trade of a largely black criminal community. More recently, the equally short-lived mini-serial *Moses Jones* (BBC 2009) cast Shaun Parkes as the titular character, embedded as an undercover detective infiltrating a criminal African community within the London underworld. However, for most of the period, British television remained 'hideously white',[3] and with the possible exception of *Moses Jones*, these earlier series indicate the very limited possibilities available for ethnic minority characterisation in crime drama. Jim Pines observes as typical how the introduction of a black female officer to *The Bill* in 1994 became a means of simply managing other stereotypes, of reinforcing the police force as competent, fair and able to manage community race relations.[4] Unlike white police–gangster settings, the construction of both black villains and black heroes had continued to draw heavily and unimaginatively on a set of pre-existing stereotypes, and Pines concludes that, in most cases, producers and writers 'simply graft black-related situations on to storylines, rather than engaging "experimentally" with the possibilities that generic conventions offer'.[5] Pines's argument suggests an ideal against which some aspects of *Luther* may be briefly considered, namely the challenge to get beyond 'race relations' narratives and tackle a 'wider diversity of black and white experiences, expectations, desires and fantasies',[6] perhaps by experimenting with the very tensions that have come to surround racial representation in television crime.

Luther certainly suggests an early promise to grapple with some of these same tensions, not least with an opening chase sequence which makes deliberate self-reflexive play on the generic representation of heroes and villains. A suited white man races through a derelict industrial building, struggling to escape his pursuer, a black man who is introduced by the camera in pieces: the back of his head and torso as he strides along, then a shoulder, an obscured aerial view, a side shot and finally a close-up of a fragment of his face, just eyes and nose as he frowns intently at the man he has chased into a corner. It is revealed, again through fragments (of dialogue and cut-aways to police at a crime scene), that the white man is Henry Madsen, a serial child-killer, and his pursuer is John Luther, the detective who dug up Henry's last victim with his 'own hands'. Once he has all the information he needs, Luther stamps on Henry's hand, causing him to fall to likely death: a demonstration of justice, arguably, but not in a form that the law would uphold. As with a previous generation of crime drama, notably *The Sweeney*, Luther's methods are demonstrably and procedurally unacceptable but potentially justifiable – by a more abstract moral reasoning – as fitting to the crime in hand. When John is allowed to return from suspension he is reminded of the rules by 'DSU' Rose Teller (Saskia Reeves), who goes through the motions of warning him to 'observe case management protocol', and reminding him: 'any pro-active strategies to be signed off by me'.

In spite of its early play with genre conventions and implicit challenge to viewer assumptions, the carefully calculated assemblage of the first series of *Luther* nevertheless sidesteps rather than contests the problematic race relations conventions of an earlier decade. Luther has an upper middle-class Asian wife (but no sign of Afro-Caribbean friends or relations), never has to apprehend a black villain or visit a black community and for the most part he works with an exclusively white murder squad, only occasionally encountering (or being framed near to) another black officer, usually in a minimal speaking role. By virtually isolating the central character from any significant others who are black, the first series evacuates all the narrative opportunities that might conceivably present themselves to a black London police detective of such interesting and enigmatic design. Unlike *Line of Duty* (see below), there is no reference at all to the London Metropolitan police force as an ('institutionally racist')[7] organisation, the ranks of which such a maverick character would have had to claw his way up. It is worth remembering that in *Prime Suspect*, notwithstanding its 'systematic roll-call of categories of persons – other than white men – who might be considered capable and trustworthy' of policing,[8] Tennison had never simply happened to be a female in a male genre. In *Prime Suspect*, murder investigations had intersected with narratives of institutional corruption, Freemasonry and machismo, conventions of 'seeing' had been gendered in interesting ways, and the occupational hazard of romantic dysfunction had played out rather differently and often in contrast to male colleagues.

There is little such tertiary social significance in *Luther*, perhaps due to anxiety regarding the stereotypical black cops of an earlier generation: 'noble figures whose mission is to clean up the criminalised black neighbourhoods'.[9] In this and other respects, the second series is more mature and confident, as typified by the introduction of DS Grey (Nikki Amuka-Bird), a female black officer. Grey's most visible function is to mitigate the representation of Luther as the lone maverick in a white world, but there are complications to her character which open up more complex possibilities of racial identification. Grey is keen to impress DCI Luther, but being efficient, well-trained and a stickler for procedure she has the integrity to protest when he trusts instinct over the available evidence. When Luther sets off the station fire alarm as a diversion, it is significant that it should be Grey – symbolically clad in regulation high-visibility jacket – who is the only one to suspect him, and it is she who later reports his suspicious behaviour. Although her motive is clearly professional rather than malicious, Grey's 'disloyalty' contrasts with the unquestioning faith in Luther shown by DS Ripley (Warren Brown), and for her lack of trust she receives allegorical punishment, finding herself reprimanded by a superior officer when no evidence can be found.

About John Luther's particular cultural background we are told little, aside from a reference to his father's military occupation and his own preference for books. In fact, in narrative terms he is defined only by his job, love for his (estranged, later deceased) wife Zoe, his temperament and admiration for David Bowie. Instead of the routine incidents by which returning TV detectives are often defined, *Luther* instead uses complex sub-plotting to develop character, interwoven with both series and serial narratives. In the first series, a favourite strategy is to run a highly sensational primary plot alongside parallel storylines, one of which documents John's disintegrating marriage. A more complex sub-plot traces his engaging conflict with the brilliant physicist, Alice Morgan (Ruth Wilson), who with her fair skin, blue eyes and red hair offers a striking visual opposition to Elba. Alice begins the first episode under suspicion of killing her own parents, but is developed into Luther's nemesis, aide and adversary in successive scenes that brim over with sexual tension. The idea, clearly, is to suggest Luther's vulnerability to temptation, but as the whole narrative is built around his particular brand of maverick justice, his ideological distance from his 'other' must ultimately be enforced. A notable example of this comes in the fourth episode, after Alice suffocates Madsen in his hospital bed. This is a convenient outcome for Luther, who looked set to be accused by him of attempted murder, but the rage of his response affirms a man indisputably more concerned with moral justice than expedience. On receipt of her call he leaves his work station, threatens arrest and finally screams for her to 'stay away' whilst he vents his fury by smashing up office equipment. These gestures are liable to further misunderstanding by fellow officers, obliging him to attribute the call to Zoe, a deceit that later rebounds.

John's personal ethics are further carved out in opposition to his trusted colleague Ian Reed (Steven Mackintosh) who in episode 5 is revealed as an inside party to a diamond robbery. Reed's moral collapse offers a comparator for Luther's violent behaviour in the same episode, providing an example of truly corrupt policing against which Luther's ever rightfully intended misdemeanours must be judged. Ironically, it is for Reed that Luther compromises himself by covering up the other officer's assault on a suspect, although little is made of this grossly misplaced trust in the unravelling of the episode plot that follows, which culminates in Reed murdering Zoe to protect himself. Luther's own code of practice is instinctive, primal, retaliatory; but unlike Reed his disrespect for procedure is always distinguished from self-interest. As later observed by the character Frank Hodge, an ex-copper turned racketeer: 'He's not a dirty copper. He's a man over a barrel and that's a completely different thing' (series 2, episode 3). Indeed, it is only by becoming an outlaw, remaining at large and deploying unorthodox methods, that John is able to both do good *and* survive, proving DS Ripley's maxim that there is 'a difference between getting your hands dirty and being dirty'.

Fittingly, at the close of series 1, it is to Alice that Luther must turn, and she who fires the shot that finally kills Reed, thus breaking the very rules that even Luther will not break. Alice takes a delicious pleasure in transgressing moral codes, becoming a figurable representation of Luther's own 'Devil's side', but against which his ethics are sharpened by comparison. Within the series structure of moral allegiance, Alice also symbolises the seductive lure of evil, despite John's insistence that he believes only in the redeeming pre-eminence of love. Although the character returns in series 2 (this time incarcerated in a secure hospital), Alice's appearances are increasingly intermittent until she flees the country, leaving John to adopt a new 'muse' in Jenny, a young girl he rescues from a vice gang who had coerced her into appearing in hard-core pornographic movies. Jenny's kinky Venetian harlequin style costume is typical of the occasional stylish spectacle enjoyed by the series, and reinforces her as different, awkward within this world, and in need of his protection. Her youth and vulnerability thus open up paternal possibilities for Luther now his romantic opportunities have been curtailed. In the third episode of this second series, he shelters Jenny in the decrepit tower block flat that substitutes for the elegant town house he once shared with Zoe, making her a cooked breakfast, and nagging her to get a job. The scene brings an interesting depth to his characterisation, for once 'normal' and sweat-panted amongst the strips of peeling wallpaper, endearingly reliant on what Jenny calls a 'minging' kettle, and it offers a confident interlude in an altogether more nuanced narrative than any seen in the first series.

With Alice in a minor role, the structure of moral allegiance in the second series is sustained through the use of different narrative devices to those favoured by the first. In the second of the four episodes, John finds himself blackmailed by a criminal vice gang for which girls are procured and 'owned' by Baba (Pam Ferris), and put into a predicament that is demonstrated visually by a shocking sequence in which his hand is literally nailed to the table. Thereafter he is between a rock and a hard place, obliged to work for the enemy in order to 'do good', so affirming the claim of the series to moral ambiguity and complexity, made explicit by its tagline: 'What if you were on the Devil's side without knowing it'. However, there is not much here to seriously offend, trouble or test the viewer, as Luther's essential integrity is, at heart, also customary: fully aware that he should follow professional procedure and keep his distance from Jenny, he knows what will happen to her if he does. Like all the dissenting detectives, his humanity is of greater significance than his authority, and he manages the problem with methods that are conventionally unorthodox, albeit extreme by the standards of TV policemen, cleverly framing Frank Hodge for the murder of

Baba's odious grandson, killed in self-defence by Jenny whilst in John's own flat.

Beyond these displays of maverick expedience it is Luther's volatile temperament that most distinguishes him from other TV detectives. In place of the weariness and the exasperation of Kurt Wallander, John bellows, throws over tables, smashes the glass of his office windows. Such demonstrations give him some of the fury of Fitz, save that the objects of his spleen are more likely to be individuals who breach his moral code – villains who pick on the vulnerable, police who cross the line – than the social injustices with which *Cracker* was preoccupied. That his character should be fleshed out in narrative terms primarily as angry, intelligent, romantic and principled is to say little, for these are all common tropes of the detective in any guise, and where Luther exceeds the character prototype is primarily through performance. Elba exceeds his place in the narrative more than any actor discussed so far, dominating and stealing every scene, prompting his character's creator to acknowledge:

> He's not just an exceptional actor, he's got a once-in-generation screen presence – so we knew he'd be good. What we could never have guessed was how good. He brought whole new levels of complexity to Luther, not least of them a startling vulnerability.[10]

Elba's demonstration of Luther's charisma exploits his volatility. A half-frown when smiling, an ironic raised eyebrow just before losing (and quickly regaining) control, a simple adjustment to the expected intonation of a well-worn phrase, the clenching of hands to suggest repressed emotion: his gestures play constantly with expectations. The performance is carefully layered, at its most mannered on those occasions when Luther the character must be seen as the able performer, whether stalling for time when the clock is against them or toying with the norms of police–suspect discourse, inviting admiration for his virtuoso play rather than sympathy. Although his trauma is occasionally glimpsed (like Kurt Wallander he begins an episode on sick leave), his experience is more likely to be expressed through rage than disintegration, acting as a model of vicarious activity rather than an object of pity. Amidst a cycle of TV detectives in which the protagonist is increasingly and chronically fallible, *Luther* preserves a more obviously mythological dimension of heroism for the role.

Relatively unusual hitherto is *Luther*'s marriage of a cinematic with a more parochial televisual tradition of crime fiction, through the incorporation of overblown serial killers, psychopathic 'slashers' and menacing gangland leaders ostensibly within the precinct-based 'routine' of the police drama. In a rare self-reflexive gesture, John commiserates with a duty officer, 'all very soul destroying isn't it? Actual police work' (series 2, episode 1), although for him, perpetrators are a far cry from the usual villains of British TV crime. The killers that Luther stalks are not motivated to murder in order to avenge loan sharks or drug peddlers, to conceal guilty secrets or escape tortuous personal constraints, they are sadistic, obsessive, sinister and need a detective willing to play 'mind hunter'. The depiction of the criminal *act* (and not just the corpse as evidence of its occurrence) is also highly graphic and full of lurid, bloody detail. On one occasion, John pursues Burgess (Paul Rhys), an accomplished occultist 'blood-letter', occasioning graphic sequences of torture and blood drinking (series 1, episode 3). On others he must rescue a prostitute who has locked herself into a bathroom with a bloody corpse to escape a crazed killer (series 1, episode 4), or race against the clock to collect the body parts of a kidnapped woman, dismembered before he could get there (series 1, episode 5). Such extended and graphic representations of the crime *in action* are rare in television detective fiction, which more usually foregrounds the process of investigation rather than aligning the viewer in any sustained way with the fear-stricken, present victim.

Also ostensibly cinematic in its mode of representation is the topography, which makes heavy use of narratively gratuitous skyline shots to conjure up a panoramic vista of the metropolis, and yet makes none of the narrative references to actual locations that facilitated the everyday operational realism of *Prime Suspect*. London in the first series is a city of extremes, exportable postcard views of the Thames counterbalanced by backdrops of suspiciously underpopulated council estates, tower blocks and seedy back alleys, but with little topographical orientation provided to connect the two. However, part of *Luther*'s attraction as a detective series was the relative unpredictability of a show that did not appear to have been through quite the same rigours of editorial interference and control as, say, *Lewis*. Never a show that suggested production-line uniformity, the direction, like the narrative of *Luther*, shows an interesting shift from first to second series,[11] cultivating a more holistic relationship between character and cityscape to reveal a London less signified by its landmarks and more likely to encompass the generic national places in which crime may ever occur. When a disturbed assassin smashes up a parked car at a petrol station or starts a massacre in a London railway station, it evokes the capital city as routinely lived in and worked in, without appearing to brand it as an internationally recognisable metropolis. London in the first series is a 'global city', but also one relatively untouched by everyday fear or routine policing; the second series presents a city that is both British and international, and of which Luther the policeman actually seems to be a part, whether that means eating ice cream from a street vendor or parking in a council car park.

The suspense, bloodshed and sensational narratives by which *Luther* differentiates itself also become all the more terrifying and possible in this second series, a strategy which meshes nicely with its more subtle use of space and fewer

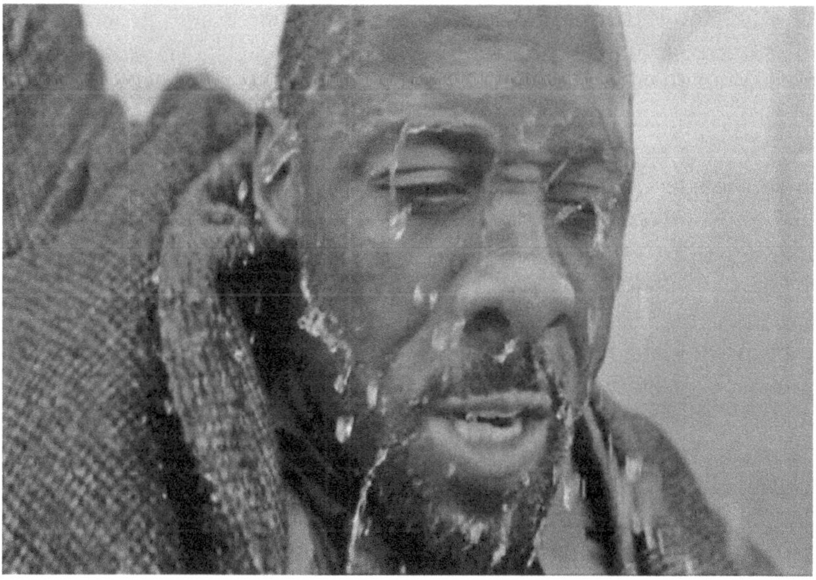

Figure 7.1 *Luther* – series 2, episode 4 (2012)

reiterations of the iconic 'tourist' view of London. The ultimate denouement of its second series exemplifies this, as the last builds to a climax in which central streets are evacuated whilst Millberry, an assassin wired up as a human bomb with a 'dead man's trigger', walks through the city, looked on by helpless police marksmen. As the head of the armed response unit weighs up the alternatives in terms of however many hundreds of casualties will result, it becomes clear that only someone as able at brinkmanship, as reckless with his own safety, and as ingenuous as Luther could save the day without any collateral damage at all. Of course he pulls it off – dousing himself with petrol (Figure 7.1), luring Millberry into a lorry, orchestrating that he be shot by exact sniper fire – but it is still an extraordinarily tense scenario, located squarely in the middle of one of the densest business and residential districts in the world, bringing the cinematic and utopian possibility of near superhuman prowess to the resolution of large-scale disaster whilst remaining (just) within the conventions of the domestic TV police series.

Scott & Bailey

Taking a swipe at the machismo of the heroic TV detective was *Scott & Bailey*, a series centred on two female police officers, Janet Scott (Lesley Sharp) and

Rachel Bailey (Suranne Jones) who somewhat refreshingly work under the supervision of another female, the acerbic DCI Gill Murray (Amelia Bullmore), who is in charge of a Greater Manchester metropolitan Major Incident Team (MIT). In marked contrast to the metropolis of dramatic extremes constructed for *Luther*, the exterior sequences in *Scott & Bailey* are mostly limited to establishing shots of Oldham police station, crime scenes in industrial wastelands and tightly framed exchanges conducted outside 1960s council estates or Victorian back-to-back terraces.

Janet Scott and Rachel Bailey work primarily as a pair, prompting popular comparison with the American female prototype *Cagney & Lacey* (1981–8), although the similarities will not be explored here. Like *Vera*, *Scott & Bailey* also boasted an unusually high quota of women on its development/production team, and all series to date have been executive produced by Nicola Shindler through her own Red Production Company for ITV.[12] The original idea for the show is credited in part to Suranne Jones herself, who professed herself frustrated by the uninteresting parts she was being offered, and almost all episodes to date have been written by Sally Wainwright, who insists: 'I like writing women and watching women. For me, *Scott & Bailey* is the antithesis of something macho like *Luther*. I feel I've seen it all before. It doesn't appeal at all to me and procedurally is rubbish'.[13]

As we have already seen, the 'mean streets', violence and psychotic murderers featured in *Luther* are strongly reminiscent of cinematic 'tough crime' genres in which acts of male power and sadism serve as visceral 'reminders' of the brutal 'reality' of the criminal netherworld. *Scott & Bailey*'s realist counter-claim is staked, first, on its alternative authenticity of everyday procedural detail, and secondly, on its rejection as fantasy the possibility that such procedures can ever be disregarded by the (usually male) maverick cop. Importantly, the series was also developed with the assistance of Diane Taylor, an ex-detective with Greater Manchester police.[14] Remarkably, in tele-land at least, Janet and Rachel each hold the more ordinary rank of detective constable, wear ID cards or name badges whilst interviewing witnesses and suspects, carry clipboards, make notes, fill in forms and endure successive witnesses who say nothing other than 'no comment'. All this they juggle with another sort of existence that involves managing homes, meal times and familial strife.

In place of the lonely detective occasionally brought low by a neglected private life, *Scott & Bailey* dramatises the very process by which female police officers are obliged to compromise their careers. Although she is 46 and has long since passed her sergeant exams, Janet is reluctant to climb the career ladder, reminding her mother 'if I was Gill, I wouldn't get home until after midnight, every night'. Rachel is younger, more hedonistic and allegedly aggressive, and professes herself more ambitious ('In ten years' time I'm going to be a DCI in charge of my own syndicate'), but she is no Tennison, refusing to go through with a termination when she is pregnant, and showing herself a little too eager to accept a proposal of marriage (series 1, episode 6). Indeed, the progress of Rachel's sexual relationship with Nick Savage, a married barrister, dominates both series. Rachel is evicted from Savage's flat, suffers an attempt on her life by a hit man he commissioned, miscarries his baby and nearly ends up 'back in uniform' after she misuses the PNC (Police National Computer) to find his family address, a disciplinary offence. No less sensationally, Janet's assistance in resurrecting the cold-case murder of a childhood schoolfriend leads to her being stabbed in her own kitchen by Geoff Hastings, brother of the original victim (series 1, episode 5). When she eventually returns to work she is newly wedded to the philosophy that 'life is short', and before long resumes a former fling with colleague DS Andy Roper, a storyline that is further developed in the second series.

Scott & Bailey thus fashions a hybrid, serialised series narrative where some ongoing cases and long-running personal storylines exist in some tension with the shorter investigations that are resolved over one or two weeks. Typically, these cases will involve characters such as Kenny Benedict (series 2, episode 6), introduced with a distorting close-up by an upwards tilted camera, as a representative of 'the Great British public' of which Rachel repeatedly despairs. Such characters are largely mediated through Janet and Rachel's unspoken reactions and demonstrate the sometimes vulnerable 'underclass' with which they have daily contact. Although the weekly crimes are given a degree of narrative prominence in each series, the personal progressively overshadows them as serial storylines build to climax and resolution. In the final episode of series 1, only minimal screen time (five minutes, seven seconds) is allotted to the episodic investigation of a shooting, the sole narrative purpose of which is to reveal Janet's prowess as an interrogator when she questions a young witness who quickly confesses. Nevertheless, if the emphasis on intimate relationships pushes the series ever closer to the soap opera form, it also enables it to resonate with identifiable tensions around the contemporary workplace, using the private/public opposition itself to rhetorically endorse its claim to authenticity by presenting the messiness of 'real life'. Challenging the more facile female stereotypes, care is taken to emphasise the women's ability to maintain professional standards. Typically, when the duo arrive to interview a suspect, Nadia Hicks, they hold a conversation that seamlessly shifts between discussing their own rather too full personal lives and deliberating her whereabouts (series 2, episode 1). Crucially, personal conversations, even gossip, are fitted around the job and have nothing of the lascivious idle tone that marks the dialogue and curtails the characterisation of series such as *Mistresses* (BBC 2008–10). On another occasion, Rachel and Gill drive to Bristol, using a break in a service station café to quickly make calls and resolve their respective domestic crises, but switching gear immediately afterwards to discuss the case in hand (series 2, episode 3). At work they demonstrate prowess through painstaking attention to detail and incisive deductions (Rachel is nicknamed 'Sherlock') and bury its emotional impact on them in gallows humour, delivered with a pithy northern vernacular.

Unlike most other male detective characters – for whom female partners and relations are either neglected, dead or absent – the husbands and lovers of the women in *Scott & Bailey* are an active, constant source of trouble and frustration. In series 2, Janet's husband Adrian leaves the family home, forcing her to rely on her mother's help with childcare, whilst the new problem in Rachel's life is the arrival of her brother, a formerly convicted armed robber who, much as she fears, is soon again on the wrong side of the law. In the face of such obstacles, the women share the same resilience that enables them to survive their jobs ('did you think I was a knobhead?') and invariably manage, as Janet puts it, to 'move on'. Although men outnumber women in the MIT team, opportunities to sympathise with them are restricted by a textual structure of moral allegiance which offers no spatial access to the male officers without the mediating presence of the central characters, and they are frequently even marginalised even within the frame (Figure 7.2). DS Roper is the more prominent figure but even he is of narrative interest primarily as Janet's lover, and he relinquishes any claim to sympathy when he abuses his supervisory powers after she ends the relationship. Minor, often unspeaking, procedural functions are

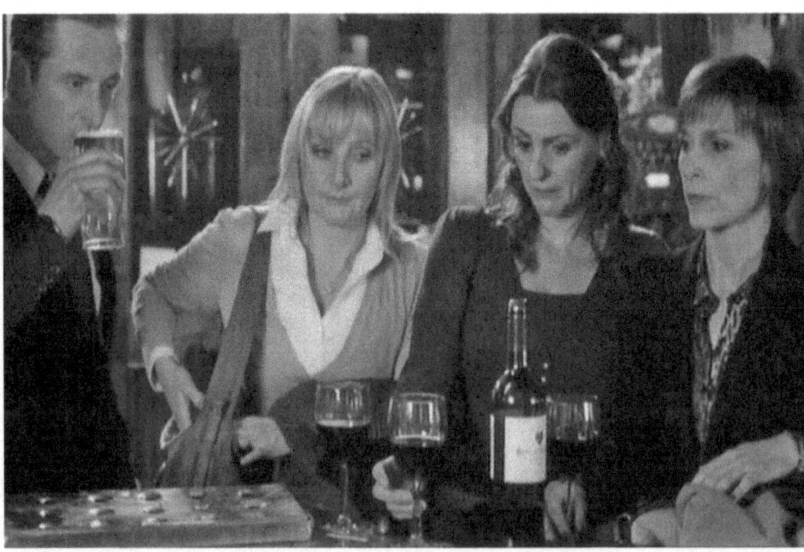

Figure 7.2 *Scott & Bailey* – series 1, episode 6 (2011)

undertaken by a number of others such as DC Broadhurst, a requisite black officer who has barely a handful of lines throughout the first series.

The broader ensemble is developed somewhat in series 2, including the hapless Kevin, transferred to MIT by another female DCI only too pleased to see the back of him, whose single act of professional competence is to rescue Rachel from an assault, much to her amazement. Yet the women remain emphatically centre stage, frequently debating cases in the gendered, cloistered space of the ladies' lavatories, and revealing themselves to be consistently more adroit in their judgements than any of the men around them. If the broader context of the Manchester police force is significant, it is for reasons of verisimilitude, to reinforce a lived sense of routine team work. To this end, Rachel and Janet share an open plan office with colleagues, attend rather than lead briefings around crowded tables, always call for back-up when pursuing a lead and participate in regular office life: making 'brews', organising celebrations and getting 'bollocked' for leaving mouldy food in the communal fridge. This is a drama as much about women in the workplace as it is about crime, which is perhaps to its credit, as such narratives are exceptional.

As the more senior 'career officer', it is Gill Murray who would seem most indebted to Jane Tennison, liking to get close to the gruesome detail of a case, peering intimately at the corpses on the mortician's slab and frequently 'seeing' what others do not. The presence of her errant ex-husband, DCS Dave Murray, is used to create a masculine/feminine opposition that is professional as much as domestic, as he is the senior officer, but demonstrably less competent. When he attempts to resurrect their relationship, she is quick to pull him down to size, quipping: 'you had your car repossessed, you're living with your mother, everyone in MIT knows you rely on those beneath you to make you look good in the job, and you're a shag bandit. It's just not attractive, is it?' Moreover, when Gill later has to leave an important briefing to attend to a domestic crisis, it is one that he has caused.

Journalistic response to either run of the series was not uniformly positive, although one suspects a degree of prejudice, even misogyny, at work in many of the critiques. In the *Independent*, Tom Sutcliffe lamented the 'less-than-courageous' decision to produce another police drama in spite of 'the ocean of narrative possibilities spread wide' before it,[15] although this was not a complaint he extended to the 'stylishly incredible' *Luther* less than a month later.[16] It is also difficult to see the possible justification for Wollaston's dismissal of *Scott & Bailey* as 'Lewis with skirts on',[17] or for the critic at the *Mirror* to show his hand and declare baldly that *all* female TV detectives are 'ultimately, inferior' and these two 'couldn't be more mundane'.[18] Notwithstanding the inference of all this hostility ('why can a woman not be more like a man?'), the series was a popular success, sustaining regular, returning audiences in excess of 5.8 million across its first two runs.

Line of Duty

I would like to round off this chapter with something of a coda giving a revealing example from another police drama, *Line of Duty* (2012). This was originally broadcast as a discrete serial yet quickly recommissioned in response to the high ratings it brought to BBC2 and the excited public debate around its transmission, for example via the social website Twitter. The first incarnation of this drama is most relevant here for its meta-commentary on the police genre, its relation to the realities of crime prevention and the dramatised fallibility of its central detective character. Produced for BBC2 by World Productions and written by Jed Mercurio, *Line of Duty* starred Lennie James[19] as DCI Gates, a black officer at the peak of his career, first seen heroically apprehending a mugger whilst off duty and later collecting the award of 'Officer of the Year'. What follows is a classically Shakespearian tragic trajectory that sees Gates's life unravel in the course of the five episodes, a high-status figure brought down by professional and personal desire. His essential flaws are revealed by his implausibly high crime figures (which make him the subject of an internal inquiry into 'laddering'), and by his adulterous relationship with Jacky Laverty, a businesswoman linked to the underworld through illegal money laundering activity, and whose subsequent murder is then used by a mysterious gang leader ('Tommy') to frame and blackmail Gates into further corrupt activity.

Distinctive to the serial (and complicating the possibilities for its renewal as a returning format) is a structure of allegiance that is divided and underpinned by dual systems of spatial alignment with both Gates and DS Arnott (Martin Compston), the very officer investigating him on behalf of AC-12, a police anti-corruption unit. As a character, Arnott had been introduced prior to Gates as an officer with the integrity to resist peer and senior management pressure to cover up the fatal shooting by police of Karim Ali, a man mistakenly under suspicion of terrorist activity. Arnott is an idealistic figure, a target of institutional bullying and political pressure, but the opposition he presents to Gates is repeatedly undermined and confounded in an extremely complex moral framework. Running parallel with the stories of both Gates and Arnott is a murder investigation located on a virtually unpoliceable estate (Greek Lane, also known as 'The Bog') from which vulnerable young boys are recruited by gangs and drug cartels.

Line of Duty weaves together multiple plotlines, all too intricate to rehearse here, but coming as it does at the end of the period in question – at a point in which the detective genre appears to be moving in different visual and narrative directions – it acts as an important reminder of the potential of the genre for incisive and topical critique, much as *The Cops* had done over a decade before.[20] Of particular interest here is the drama's exposé, not of 'bad cops' and corruption, but of broader political and institutional pressures as key corrupting forces. Moreover, the unravelling of Gates's career is an allegory that implicitly questions the legitimacy of the popular television detective, and the possibility of remaining in, yet not of, an official system of surveillant and political power – the very premise of the detective's articulation of dissent.

Both Gates and Arnott fit the heroic model in different ways, yet Gates ends up dead, committing suicide when he knows he cannot resolve his predicament in any other way, although he disguises it as an act in 'the line of duty' in order to ensure the financial well-being of his surviving family. He dies leaving evidence against Tommy, the orchestrator of the murders of Laverty and others on the Greek Lane Estate, but the closing sequence shows how this evidence is suppressed by one of Gates's own team, an officer corrupted by the desire to save his own reputation. Arnott eschews Gates's 'rogue cop' methods and courageously gives evidence against those responsible for the shooting of Ali, but the closing on-screen legends reveal that this evidence nevertheless failed to lead to the prosecution of any of those responsible. It is on all counts a bleak, deliberately unsatisfying closure to a sometimes shocking story, one that is essentially a parable of a good man brought down by hubris and desire, countered by a truth-teller whose courage is futile against a system that conspires to protect itself at all costs. Indeed, in the final episode there is only one identifiable and brief gesture of hope, still tinged with pessimism but which reveals some of the emotional expectation that continues to be invested dramatically in the individuated police officer. Around 30 minutes before the end, two community officers for Greek Lane return to their car, apparently resigned to the likely fate of Ryan, a young boy neglected by his mother, recruited by Tommy and already versed in organised crime. One of the officers, Bannerjee, suddenly has a change of heart, and shrugging off the cynicism of his colleague, returns to Ryan's house to give the boy his card and phone number, just in case he ever wants someone just to buy him a burger. Rather than rejecting the offer as expected, Ryan's face softens slightly, he shrugs 'Okay' and takes the card. 'Promise?' says Bannerjee, to which he nods his assent. It is a straw to clutch at but an optimistic moment nevertheless. In the wake of all the cynicism of the series round frustrated community initiatives, it tantalises that possibility may exist, not from institutional initiatives or the ingrained habitus of the senior decision-makers, but as something local, unconditional and outside of procedure. The setting is unlikely but it is a kindly gesture, simply made and received as paternal, unorthodox and altruistic. Much the sort of invitation, in fact, that Jack Frost might once have made.

8

The Resonance of the Detective

For much of its history, the British police detective series has belonged to what John Corner has noted as a 'strong tradition of entertainment with a marked "public" character to it'.[1] From the foregoing case studies it should have become apparent that the genre itself is ideally placed to address collective, often national, preoccupations, particularly those to do with social breakdown and governance, and has perhaps moved into the gap made vacant by the demise of the topical single play, emerging as the televisual form most likely to express the mood of public anxiety. Indeed, it is precisely this capability that prompted Charlotte Brunsdon in the 1990s to describe it as a 'privileged site for the staging of the trauma of the breakup of the post-war settlement'.[2] Following Richard Sparks, who also suggests that TV crime series are 'phenomena which bear the imprint of their times',[3] Brunsdon engages with them as neither spectacle of fear nor narrative puzzle, but as important reflexive 'state of the nation' pieces.

Claims as to the social, and perhaps political, significance of television crime drama rest on a number of other assumptions which may need to be acknowledged briefly, not least the premise that broadcast TV continues to enjoy discursive centrality within British popular culture. Whereas this could once be taken for granted – particularly if a single television drama could cause questions to be raised in Parliament, or attract some two-thirds of the viewing public in one sitting – it may now need reaffirmation. The new orthodoxy that British television is 'just another' consumer product provider has a political counterpart in American 'postnetwork thinking', the inference of which is that questions of hegemony have been obviated. This is well demonstrated by Elana Levine's example of students who refuse to engage in questions of representational politics under the assumption that choice – if pleasurable and freely made – effectively stands outside of power relations, as if the 'diversity of available perspectives' somehow removes the need to critique any particular one.[4] Levine aligns the implicit logic of this with the late rejection of once cherished ideals of feminism, race or class politics, as manifest in the 'posting' of them (as 'post-feminist', 'post-race', 'post-class') in what has become 'the new, hegemonic common sense of our time'.[5]

The logic inherent in 'posting' is problematic in any guise, but in the context of television prompts Levine to retrieve Fiske's dictum that '[t]elevision-as-culture is a crucial part of the social dynamics by which the social structure maintains itself'.[6] Broadcast television is both informed by and contributes to the discourses of the public sphere, supplies a plethora of potentially influential 'usable stories'[7] and, for an astonishing 44 per cent of the population, watching television is still the main leisure activity.[8] As neither the social nor ideological possibility of a TV text depends upon the medium having exclusive, monopolistic powers of mass persuasion, we must continue to recognise what Georgina Born describes as 'the necessary and inescapable representational and cultural power in the moment of cultural production'.[9]

The broad social significance of crime drama as a key television genre is further encouraged by its particular narrative and visual strategies, and facilitated in part by the relationship its diegetic worlds tend to bear to the world we inhabit. This relationship may be analogous rather than referential, for although the social world in which we live has a knowable material presence it also, like the text, exists as a form of imaginary that may be shared. As Arjun Appadurai suggests, in late modernity imagination has 'broken out of the special expressive space of art, myth and ritual' to inform the logic of everyday life and 'become a collective, social fact'.[10] The British police-detective genre is exemplary in this regard, emerging as an 'everyday cultural practice through which the work of the imagination is transformed'.[11] Historical shifts in the collective imagination might be further understood using Raymond Williams's concept of 'structures of feeling', the aptness of which to contemporary crime drama has been demonstrated by Brunsdon.[12] The value of Williams's concept is that it foregrounds the embryonic processes of social thinking and experience that develop prior to their articulation (as, say, discourse or art) enabling cultural products to be understood as indirectly expressive of 'a particular quality of social experience and relationship, historically distinct from other particular qualities, which gives the sense of a generation or period'.[13] The term 'feeling' is used in preference to 'experience' to avoid inferring a past tense, but it is 'feeling as thought' rather than as something opposed to it, and it is particularly useful for understanding the affective dimensions of some art and literature as integral with belief systems, but not reducible to them. Semantic forms and conventions 'are often among the very first indications that such a new structure is forming'.[14] By extension, it may be supposed that texts can reveal, as well as contribute to the formation of collective concerns and climates of opinion.

Although I would recognise Georgina Born's concern that ideas such as 'structure of feeling' may be 'overly agnostic' for a sociology of television, they will be useful here to underpin 'the simple proposition that media and cultural production have broader effects on the collective imagination and resonate with social-historical experiences and wider discursive practices'.[15] To suggest that a particular text may resonate is to imply that it reverberates across cultures by evoking particular images, sentiments and ideas about contemporary phenomena. Ultimately, resonance will be unpredictable, but as Mills observes in the light of fan discussion around *Life on Mars*: 'The place where television is made, as well as what it is seen to say about that place, continue to be central to the meanings and pleasures on offer from broadcasting, and viewers appear to define themselves in relation to this'.[16]

Strictly speaking, it is not necessary for a text to be made in Britain in order for it to be understood to say something *about* 'Britain', but it is more likely that home-grown product will be received as such. Although broadcasting institutions often encourage a sense of Britishness through branding and presentation strategies, audience recognition of diegetic faces, voices and places will be instrumental to its acknowledgement that a given text is, in important ways, a national product. The intention of this final chapter is to reflect upon the ways in which police-detective series thereby address collective anxieties around everyday life, law enforcement, crime and deviance in contemporary Britain.

Place and Nation

The significance of place in the contemporary detective series has been the subject of a number of projects clustering at the interstices of geography, sociology, tourist and cultural studies.[17] Stijn Reijinders argues, a little vaguely, that the landscapes of detective drama often become 'injected' with narrative meaning, as in *Inspector Morse* for which the 'local atmosphere is intensified by the representation of stereotypical weather conditions' of blue skies and an 'occasional English shower'.[18] The viewer who identifies him or herself with 'the fortunes of the detectives' generates a personal involvement that 'radiates onto the locations where the programmes take place – even more so because the *couleur locale* appears to be so important to the plot, episode after episode'.[19] Analytically more precise than 'radiates' is Jeff Hopkins's 'mapping' of screen place, which provides a semiotic explanation for how film encourages in the viewer a state of mind in which 'temporalities and spatialities may collapse into one schizophrenic, albeit pleasurable, present where the boundaries of past, present, and future, of here and there, are distorted into one heterotopic "now" and "everywhere"'.[20]

The positioning of the spectator in dramatic screen narratives depends upon conventions which enable the creation of dynamic space *and* coherency of place, bridging the tension between the two and allowing distinctions between the real and the imaginary to become blurred. This 'blurring' is crucial to the significance of the television detective series which manages to function at both a symbolic and literal level by representing the empirical world at the same time as it transforms and reflects upon it.

In Chapter 2 I argued that these dramas may function as both mythological/melodramatic *and* as social realist texts, a duality that is mirrored by the construction of *misé-en-scène* and landscape as interchangeably generic *and* geographically specific, metaphorical *and* literal. On the one hand, place as active landscape can 'become spectacle, a signifier of the film's subject, a metaphor for the state of mind of the protagonist';[21] on the other, texts make an indexical connection to the material world, by reference to places which may be encountered independently of the television series in which they are featured. Indeed, Reijinders gives the amusing example of a legal dispute over the alcohol-drenched 'Wallander' cake in Ystad, covered in police-blue icing and served by Kurt's favourite *konditori* to visitors on the (literary) Wallander Tour. It is an emblematic instance of tourists being 'invited to consume their own imagination'.[22] Elsewhere he observes that 'the liminality between fiction and reality appears to be precisely part of the attraction of these locations' to visitors on 'detective tours' in Oxford, Ystad and Amsterdam.[23] To the armchair viewer the liminal is also crucial, because what detective drama so often provides is a selective version of a topographical landscape that very carefully blends the recognisable and the feared: this may require that the grim or anxious spaces of banal contemporary life are excluded (as in the idealised versions of historic Hastings in *Foyle's War*, or heritage Oxford in *Lewis*), or perhaps exaggerated to create a territory of almost apocalyptic extremes (as with London in *Luther*). In short, real landscapes may become interchangeable with diegetic spaces, creating an ambiguity that mirrors the mutable division between the real and the imaginary in the representation and resolution of crime.

That place should be important to the dramatic representation of crime is inevitable given that it also figures heavily in experiences, fears, and perceptions of criminal activity. Although 'crime' may also be acknowledged and deployed as an abstraction (particularly by politicians), in everyday discourse it tends to be referred to as a set of location-specific events. Research conducted by Girling, Loader and Sparks anticipates, correctly, that:

> 'Crime-talk' and 'place-talk' are unlikely to prove to be clearly separable and both are likely to bear in some way on the experiences of change ... that confront[s] people both in the immediate circumstances of their daily

> routines and through the larger relays of media and political culture. Crime resonates in *both* terms of the local/global dialectic.[24]

Although the discourses documented by the authors tend to reference the specific streets, neighbourhoods and communities of Macclesfield, the 'common places of crime' that they disclose are also generic (estates, high-rise blocks, shopping precincts, patches of woodland, suburban avenues). These generic spaces are manifestly 'national' and common to most British towns; when they are recognised in TV drama as crime scenes, they may remind that violence *may ever yet occur* in any similar public space.

The duality of the geographically specific/generic is operationally crucial to television's role in connecting domestic space with national space, in bridging smaller and larger imaginaries of 'home'. 'Home' can be aligned with nation in opposition to 'abroad' but it is also the domestic context in which television is usually viewed and which, as Roger Silverstone notes, bears a 'transactional relationship to the world of public goods and meanings'.[25] His argument is that television has a dialectical relationship to 'the moral economy of the household' which determines how it is used and 'mobilised', but television may in turn 'transform a household's reach... affecting or reinforcing the household's links with neighbourhood and community; and locking the household ever more firmly into an increasingly privatised and commodified domestic world'.[26] In such ways television both structures *and* represents the everyday; watching television is an integral part of everyday activity, and a crucial source of information about 'home' (in both registers). As Corner also notes, '[t]elevision, by the very nature of its depictive flows, is involved in the constitution and maintenance of the contemporary public'.[27] It supplies some of the raw materials for the construction of national, social and personal identity often in relation to a cultural understanding of others, also mediated by televisual representation. As we shall see, the broader sense of home as nation is a persistent 'structuring absence' in almost all British television drama, particularly the favoured institutional genres of police and hospital series. If, as Silverstone argues, television has 'been a principal factor' in the shift from public to private that has been experienced during capitalist modernity, it has also tended to present itself as the solution to these very alienations, much as the World Wide Web is today perceived as a form of cultural 'correction' to the dislocations of economic globalisation.

In other contexts, 'nation' is regarded as a problematic empirical and political category: 'dependent upon an extensive appeal to ethnicity, frequently constructed against the threat of the "alien"',[28] and demonstrated by Benedict Anderson to be a by-product of print capitalism, a work of 'imagination' born of linguistic convenience.[29] However, the abstract and the imaginary can manifest themselves in tangible ways, and the *cultural* importance of the nation state does not rest or fall on its claim to ethnic authenticity or historical legitimacy. At any time, various national imaginaries may compete and circulate, meaning that even if the nation-state is politically 'on its last legs',[30] it may persist as a cultural imaginary, legitimised by borders which secure a shared geographical space that accommodates fields of shared experience. It is something of a paradox that the number of official 'nation-states' should actually have increased over the past two decades at the same time as their autonomy has come under increasing pressure from globalising trends, perhaps because, as Edensor insists 'at a practical and imaginary level, national geographies continue to predominate over other forms of spatial entity'.[31] The lived quotidian is still fundamental to a sense of (national) spatial belonging, not least because familiar British signifiers, such as road signs, street names, pillar boxes, styles of house-building, flora and fauna, public houses and so on, may be recognisable across the country despite minor differences. These amount to generic landscapes that 'stitch the local and the national together through their serial reproduction'.[32] In this fashion we 'make our home by the accretion of habitual enactions, by our familiar engagement with the physical space in which we live'[33] and with signifiers that are absent when we travel abroad.

Edensor's premise that recognisable signifiers might be cobbled together to produce a mental map of nation is one that would clearly include the visual topography of the detective series, which both reflects and informs the country we both see and imagine to surround us. Landscapes may be bleak, remote, drab, familiar or even exotic, but in the context of terrestrial television's address to 'us', such places and places are also encoded as 'ours'. Some recent series, such as *Vera*, share elements of the 'spectacle of landscape', tradition and the 'strong heritage discourse' that Holdsworth associates with newer self-consciously British genres, such as the 'historical travelogue'.[34] However, even the relentlessly generic urban and suburban streets of the fictional town of Denton (*A Touch of Frost*) show how 'anywhere' can become an 'everywhere' that is nevertheless distinctively, unmistakably British. As Edensor goes on to argue, for 'national space to retain its power, it must be domesticated, replicated in local contexts and be understood as part of everyday life'.[35] Television's role in the process of replication and assimilation is played out in the development and reappropriation by the detective series of its own iconography.

Studies of screen crime narratives have paid considerable attention to the modern and post-modern city as a space of danger in these fictions. However, such discussion is usually dominated by American and/or cinematic examples – particularly of film noir, gangster movies and 'precinct' dramas – often cited in comparison to the western. The rationale for this, as Sparks notes, is that

> The frontier and the city are both open to being represented as situations of disorder, but the Western allegory of the foundation of the law

> in the process of nation building is supplanted by another notion of heroism whose main concern is with the maintenance of integrity in the face of urban anomie.[36]

In this allegorical context, the city is space for disorder and thus a crucial signifier of social breakdown that may be linked to anxieties about social authority more generally. However, the noir-ish cityscape is a far from typical setting for the British TV detective series which may equally display a preference for wild, heritage or suburban landscapes and of which it is no longer true to say that 'the representation of crime and law enforcement in Britain is fundamentally also the representation of metropolitan experience'.[37] For those series that do retain a contemporary urban setting, the city imaginary may be very different in appearance to the cinematic and/or American model.

The emphatically British (council) 'estate' as allegory first appeared on British television screens in the 1960s, most memorably in *Z Cars*, the premise of which was that a new type of police car squad was necessary to patrol the newly built housing estates of the fictive 'Newtown', likened in turn by one officer to the 'Wild West' and compared by another to 'a jungle' ('Four of a Kind', BBC 1962): deliberate allusions to a cinematic tradition. However, the shift from bobby on the beat to car patrol was decisive, feeding popular perceptions of policing as increasingly remote, and of domestic space as similarly removed, 'only reachable through technical and heavily mediated forms of communication'.[38] The representation of the urban conurbation pulled away from the 'urban jungle' motif and became compounded with a sense of domestic fear and isolation.

Characteristically, in the one-off mini-series *Butterfly Collectors* (Granada/ ITV 1999), the Prozac-popping, lethargic Inspector McKeown (Pete Postlethwaite) is obliged to drive with a colleague to the notoriously 'sink' Rushton estate on the fringes of the city, replete with burnt-out pubs and boarded-up houses. Lads stop kicking around a football to stare at the car, young mothers glare as they hurry past with push chairs; all is grey and derelict, punctured only by green, untended post-apocalyptic wastelands. A similarly hopeless tone pervades the Skeetsmoor Estate in *The Cops* (BBC 1998–2001), which in series 2 provides the setting for the story of Debbie Sharpe ('just another' 14-year-old smack addict who died after an overdose) which is sustained across several weeks, punctuated weekly by the shockingly routine neighbourhood spats, petty crimes and burglaries that characterise estate life. Unusually, this serial explored in some depth the aftermath of the crime by showing the insensitivity of the police to local feeling and the attempts of community groups to exact their own justice when the police fail to arrest the primary drug supplier. By the end of the twentieth century, the estate seemed to have been cast adrift from the city, and served as TV shorthand for banal criminality and drugs culture, supplying both reason and metaphor for despair.

Whereas sites of deprivation may be among the most common locations in detective series, middle-class experience of crime is also addressed – something that could happen, so the character Jack Frost points out, even 'in leafy suburbia' (*A Touch of Frost*, 'Hidden Truth'). Again, this appeals to a quite different imaginary from that of the modern or postmodern city. Silverstone argues that television may itself be theorised as a fundamentally 'suburban' medium that has irreversibly domesticated public affairs to make them accessible and recognisable, contributing to a form of late modernist public culture typified by the connotations of 'conformity, self-interest and exclusion'.[39] In this context, the representation of suburbia itself becomes a metaphor or model of citizenship, although its use as crime scene has a further resonance. Under the chapter title 'anxieties of affluence' Girling et al. record how suburban villages such as Prestbury become emotionally invested as a sanctuary from some aspects of modern life, and this further shapes expectations of policing. The residents interviewed express a strong 'sense of the kind of place Prestbury ought to be, and the kinds of behaviour and social interaction that are expected to flow from this'.[40] Crime (except for motoring offences) and particular types of anti-social behaviour (intimidating groups of youths) are perceived as a threat not just to the individual, but also to *consensual cultural norms* and ideals, and attract intensely emotional reactions. Thus, it is not only city dwellers that are likely to associate living and other shared generic public spaces with anxiety. Fear is not just a literal expectation that everyday places may provide the setting for crime, but a more generalised trepidation about the very fabric of society breaking down. From this common perspective, every occurrence of crime in a recognisable space is regarded as yet another symptom of social deterioration.

Space and place are thus pivotal in the imaginative stitching together of local knowledge with national experience, and so also to the interpretative process by which a representation of a single event may be read as symptomatic of a broader, endemic, social malaise. Widely reported during the English city riots of August 2011 were the number of youths referring to the police as 'The feds': a popular (mis)appropriation of American slang that was read either as the pernicious influence of rap music and US film/television representations of crime, or as ironical and exclusive, a linguistic strategy for self-definition by an alienated group. In either reading, the spatial inferences of using the language of American inner cities evokes a particular topographical imaginary that is clearly, if reflexively, liminal. Crucially, the mutability between perceptions (of space, crime and policing) and media representation is two-way, indeed as one lexicographer commented at the time, many journalists also redeployed 'gangsta' language to describe the riots 'because it distils the mood and the type of person perceived to be behind the past few days'.[41] What was clearly at work in this instance was the invocation of a different national imaginary that seemed more appropriate to the social experience of the riots than any available English imaginary.

The self-images of a nation are often constructed in opposition to what lies beyond its borders, and the spectre of American 'influence' has enjoyed a rather interesting history in the context both of British social behaviour *and* of television 'quality', with connections often being assumed between the two. Since the 1920s when it first loomed large as a model of free-market 'chaos', American television has typically been cited as a cautionary tale of mass-market vulgarity, the example of which was deployed as a 'containment device' against commercialisation in Britain.[42] Nevertheless, and although suspicious of audience research, the alternative Reithian model of public service did result in a system of terrestrial broadcasting that 'attempted to supply its isolated listeners with a sense of the community they had lost, translated from a local to a national and even global level'.[43] British broadcasting produced, as well as addressed, the national audience it required, and provided a sense of collective engagement that continues today to inform many of the discourses that circulate around 'UK content' and even to underpin aspirational models of *global* television along the lines of the BBC motto 'Nation shall speak peace unto Nation'.

In recent years, as discussed in Chapter 1, British dramas have enjoyed worldwide distribution, although more significant worldwide sales have been achieved by (or with) the polished high-budget, high-volume series to have come out of America since the early 1990s. Jason Jacobs likens these to the establishment of an influential aesthetic tradition, arguing that their powerful claim to cultural value results from a 'serious engagement with cultural historical and political matters' which, although nationally specific in some ways, is marked by 'a deep introspection that tends to give the work a life beyond the time and place of its making'.[44] Leaving aside the vexed assumption that cultural value exceeds historical or cultural specificity – justified by his earlier rejection of the rather 'municipal sense of the medium'[45] in British television scholarship of the 1990s – it is telling that the profound strain of anxiety he traces from postwar American literature to contemporary American drama series appears to resonate internationally in a way that British television's preoccupation with typically 'British' anxieties may not.

By contrast to the US shows that Jacobs invokes for 'their ability to articulate as well as bear the burden of human significance',[46] one is returned to the proposition that British TV drama is not only more tied to spatial and cultural dimensions of the national everyday (in a contemporary imaginary that has less international currency) but is also bound up with a critical self-consciousness about 'our backyard', the sense that Britain is somehow (always) 'going to the dogs'. Indeed, international television buyers have been known to reject the '[d]istasteful characters and socio-political themes, down-market lifestyles and negative images, bleak and non-aspirational themes' of British television drama.[47] It is also telling, in this context, that the two postwar drama genres to have been most popular with UK domestic audiences have tended to revolve around similar recurrent and nationally contingent anxieties about healthcare (particularly the ever-jeopardised NHS) and law and order (including the accountability of the police). The NHS and the police force are regionally differentiated but essentially national institutions which, through size, importance and repetition, may become conflated in the collective imagination with the nation itself, allowing the narrative problems addressed in medical and crime genres to assume an emblematic significance.

Law and Order: Crime

The radical increase in reported crime since World War II is well-known, although the raw data can still make for alarming reading. Statistics mark a rise after 1954, when the number of recorded indictable offences in Britain was 9.7 per thousand of population, peaking in 1992 when it reached 109.4 per thousand.[48] Changed calculation methods make difficult a direct comparison with the present, although levels of recorded crime in the years since 1992 have certainly dropped and stabilised. The homicide rate, which in 1900 was 9.6 per million of population, dropped to a century low of 6.2 per million in the 1960s, before rising again to a high of 14.5 in the 1990s.[49] In spite of the high increases of recorded crime, successive government Home Office publications have sought to emphasis or even exaggerate the relatively low risk of an individual becoming a victim of crime.[50] The insistence that levels of fear are disproportionate to this risk has further generated a body of research into fear of crime so considerable that it now constitutes an entire subdiscipline of criminology.[51] Nevertheless, attempts to empirically measure public fear have lately been criticised for prioritising measurement over understanding and thus failing to properly consider whether fear may indeed be 'rational'.[52] Moreover, it is the assumption that fear is 'unwarranted' that has stoked interest in the media as its cause, with television in particular being singled out as an important factor. Influential ideas advanced by George Gerbner and Larry Gross in the 1970s and 1980s[53] suggested connections between television viewing, social withdrawal and fear of crime, although their reading of crime drama has itself since been criticised for lacking any 'systematic justification'.[54] Indeed, as Eamonn Carrabine also argues, 'the actual evidence on media coverage and public fear is decidedly mixed' and the particular claim that heavy television viewing encourages fear has been found to be unsustainable.[55] Criminology has moved lately towards an exploration of the psychological nature of fear rather than its measurement, and in studies such as Carrabine's this has begun to draw on ideas about spectatorship, and to belatedly work through some of the complications of the text–audience relationship that I discussed in Chapter 2. Rather than reading the television crime series text as *prima facie* evidence of ideological strategies around law and order, it is very much in the context of its expressive possibility that I locate this discussion of crime and policing.

Given the dominance of research into 'fear of crime' it is unsurprising that most criminological enquiries into television have tended to interrogate its causal relationship to that fear rather than exploring the aesthetic representation of 'crime' more flexibly, as metaphor for social well-being. Although media representations have a demonstrable relationship with moral panics and social anxiety, this is usually interpreted as party to (hegemonic, state) power, rather than as symptomatic or expressive of social discontent. An important exception here is the work of Richard Sparks, which raises the possibility that crime fiction may provide 'consolation for the messy inconclusiveness of the process of justice' and concludes that crime drama may:

> depict an orientation to law enforcement in which anxiety is endemic and the relation between public and private spheres chronically problematic. Within such a world crime fictions can only offer magical and contrived solutions... Yet the pleasure in seeing retribution exacted which they thereby offer serves to stave off a degree of cynicism about a dangerous and corrupt social world.[56]

Sparks's logic of anxiety-resolution is more nuanced than it is often taken to be in citation, not least because he positions it in relation to the very broad 'underlying set of preoccupations: order, community, integrity, masculinity, danger and the need for retribution'[57] suggested by crime drama series. In this his explanation differs from critiques of the police show as a 'limitation on our competence'[58] that may prevent a viewer from engaging critically with complex political dimensions of policing. It is my contention that, rather than constraining an audience's political understanding of law and order by contriving neat moral solutions, these texts may well express dissent from *other* social norms, such as increasing workplace regulation. From this perspective, empirical research into fear of crime may be problematic not just because it assumes that 'fear' is measurable, but because it may have mistaken its object.

Perceptions of crime are commonly interwoven with a range of complex anxieties around social behaviour and authority, and may be interpreted through analogies which infer provenance as well as effect, as with the monetary metaphor used in a report produced for Civitas: 'Crime and disorder lie in the loss column of the profit-and-loss account of the material and cultural changes experienced by the rich and free societies of the West.... They are part of the price that has been paid for its advantages'.[59] With such broad metaphors we are moving further towards collective abstraction and away from the location-specific events of crime with which the respondents interviewed by Girling et al. were most concerned. Crime is becoming inextricable from other symptoms of social change. What this movement might further suggest is a gap between the day-to-day experience of national life and wider ranging social imaginaries: a gap occupied by the embodied and figurative institution of the police.

Policing

The police force of a nation-state is in many respects the public face of its disciplinary system, a visible front for its operations of enforcement. Michel Foucault has argued that the formula for Western industrial disciplinary systems is typified by Bentham's nineteenth-century model of the all-seeing Panopticon.[60] Panopticism did not supplant other modes of power, he insists, but infiltrated them, providing the conditions for 'a whole technique of forces and bodies' in which 'the individual is carefully fabricated'.[61] Although criticism has since been levelled at the model, which arguably belies the more seductive modes of contemporary power, Roy Boyne insists that the panoptical impulse has not faded away, and with modification might remain useful as an analytical example of supposedly ideal social control through extreme visibility.[62] By extension one might suppose that the success of law enforcement in maintaining discipline will depend, crucially, on an ability to effectively 'see' all that is surveyed. The metaphor presented by the panopticon will be useful as it corroborates the very particular significance of 'seeing' to the TV detective. As demonstrated by the earlier discussion of *Prime Suspect*, the detective's ability to notice what others do not is often used to mark a character as emphatically superior to their surrounding teams.

The disciplinary role of the modern police force is no longer to demonstrate sovereign power but to ensure the implementation of normative behaviour, partly through the exposure of deviance, for as Gareth Palmer suggests, '[w]hat law enforcement has come to mean is the patrolling of human behaviour'.[63] This incursion into the private realm links directly to the levels of confidence enjoyed by the police, which are relative to their ability not just to keep violent disorder at bay, but to preserve the underlying fabric of contemporary society. If national crime levels are perceived with alarm as emblematic of social breakdown, then policing and punishment, the official 'solutions' to social deviance, will also become emotionally invested topics. An inability to maintain social boundaries will leave society itself in jeopardy.

It is for good reason then that the changing representation of the police has been one of the more well-attended concerns of television scholars, particularly in the context of television's broader ideological, hegemonic function.[64] What many analyses overlook is that it is precisely the instinctive judgement of the fictional police-detective that distinguishes them from official justice, and that the aforementioned 'fantasy' of heroic intervention actually rests on structures of moral alignment by which these figures are empowered for and by, yet not entirely *of*, the police. Policing might prioritise the state apparatus above the expectations of the public, but the television detective is very carefully aligned with the human recipients of its 'service' (witness, victim, occasionally even perpetrator), often in direct conflict with the forces of higher authority. Standing in as proxy for unseen institutional power may be the self-same senior officer with whom the detective is so often in conflict, such as Superintendent Mullett in *A Touch of Frost*, who is constantly obliged to 'cascade' to the ranks some new management idiocy or other. Senior officers may also be absent (*Vera*), or occasionally sympathetic (*Luther*) but they are invariably shackled by policy. Allegiance is actively discouraged for remote authority figures, usually sticklers for rules and wary of the press, and manifestly unable to match the insight into the criminal mind that the central detective character is able to provide.

Lead detectives may also be at odds with others amongst their peers, such as DS Beck in *Cracker*, who repeatedly demonstrates a comparative model of flawed policing against which the protagonist's judgement is idealised. The relative moral isolation of the individual detective can thus be an effective way of putting them at one remove from such colleagues and enables them to pass comment on the disciplinary regime. As Brunsdon notes of *Inspector Morse*, his may be 'a world in which he at least believes in responsibility, but also one in which there is considerable scepticism about the apparatuses of the criminal justice system'.[65] Scepticism distances these characters from the poor public esteem in which the real police force may be held, particularly in the wake of the miscarriages of justice, institutional racism, revelations of corruption and other scandals to have rocked policing since the late 1980s, and made 'responsibility' a key theme of early 1990s crime fiction, or as Brunsdon puts it '[w]hodunnit indeed, and who can be trusted to find out?'[66] By extension, the 'trust' and 'responsibility' elicited by and for the detective may appeal to a broader set of social expectations and concerns about power than might otherwise be suggested by the specific narrative crime in hand.

The breadth of expectations invested in the television detective is consistent with the emotional investment that citizens may wish to make in the actual British police. Key anxieties about crime and policing are documented by Girling et al. as 'narratives of attachment and loss', as their interviewees frequently elide talk of community authority figures with desire for an old-fashioned type of 'bobby on the beat', and express regret as to 'what in the post-war period has happened to "our police"'.[67] The respondents' concern is for a force 'increasingly and improperly remote from everyday life', with 'obscure' priorities beyond the local crime and routine incivility that mar the lives of residents. As I have already shown, anxieties about remote policing are encoded in the landscape of TV crime fiction, implicit to generic residential spaces. Changes in policing are regarded as symptomatic of the coming apart of social 'glue' that once bound, and the discourses of its loss indicate a powerful attachment to 'the service and guardianship roles traditionally attributed to the English police'.[68] Such sentiments are not exclusive to elderly residents – one does not need to remember the past in order to long for its apparent security – but anxieties about social cohesion nevertheless tend to play out rather differently amongst urban youth. Whereas the youths interviewed by Girling et al. 'often voiced irritation and bewilderment at what they see as a disproportionate amount of police attention', they were also quick to distinguish between 'good' and 'bad' forms of policing, and to wonder why they could not themselves be given greater protection from those who troubled them.[69] Similarly, the virulent hatred of the police expressed during the English riots of 2011 was attributed (in more liberal commentaries) to a generational sense of lost opportunity, hopelessness and a profound realisation that the police were not there for them: collective feelings that at first seem a world apart yet may still parallel the 'dismay, frustration and disenchantment' of the adult residents of Macclesfield.

Thus it is to a common desire for protective agency that TV detectives speak, and they often provide levels of community protection and interpersonal understanding that far exceed the job of law enforcement. Performance and narrative events may emphasise particular aspects of a detective character that appeal to more specific collective yearnings than this generalisation would suggest. For example, David Jason brings a fine populist blend of paternal warmth and worldly cynicism to the moral judgements made by Jack Frost when urging, say, tolerance of poverty or relationship breakdown, yet condemning perversion. Fitz in *Cracker* offers dazzling insights into the criminal mind of the perpetrator on the most scant of evidence, but he is also given to extending that insight to social injustice, giving way to tirades against, say, middle-class feminists who employ poor women to do their dirty work ('Mad Woman in the Attic'). When, during an interrogation, Fitz astonishes a suspect by appearing to better understand their motives than they do, he is also hazarding a diagnosis of the social causes of crime. *Cracker* repeatedly suggests that, whereas criminality may be a pathology, it is induced by society, inequality and familial dysfunction. The fantasy figure of the TV detective may thus be less of an apology for law and order than a critique of its inadequacies, as only the detective can exercise the sort of finely calibrated moral distinctions that the viewer is invited to see as necessary. Moreover, it is frequently inferred that to apprehend one culprit is always, and only ever, to attempt to stem the tide. In the case of both *Cracker* and *Wallander*, most murders occur after investigations have begun into the first: a repetitious structural trope that suggests the (near) impossibility of policing deviance in the face of a social system which produces it in the first place. More persuasive still is how in *Luther* and *Line of Duty* it is only by employing *criminal* tactics that the detective is able get 'off the hook' of a criminal gang which has easily outwitted rule-bound police operations.

Deviance and Criminality

Kirsten Thompson reminds us that criminal acts are defined by law in one of two precise ways, as *mala in se*/'against the laws of nature' or as *mala prohibita*/'against the laws of society'.[70] However, exactly what may or may not constitute a crime according to either definition will vary according to the regime or logic of power in place: for example, marriage between first cousins is prohibited in a number of US states, sodomy is regarded a crime in many Caribbean and African countries and Britain's blasphemy laws were repealed as recently as 2008. In spite of such variability, Foucault notes that 'the division between the permitted and the forbidden' is a constant, and he suggests – for the West at least – that displacements from one generation to another are less significant than the radically altered notion of 'crime' as 'the object with which penal practice is concerned'.[71] Societal interest in criminality and deviance is, in Foucault's theorisation, fundamentally enmeshed with its mechanisms of power, and he observes that over a relatively short period of European history (1760–1840), punishment as public torture and spectacle gave way to the administration of corrective penalties in closed institutions. Although this appeared to be a move towards 'humanism' and 'leniency', it actually masked a 'displacement in the very object of the punitive operation', to an altogether different economy of the body to hitherto.

Crucially, in Foucault's thesis, punishment was no longer exercised in judgement on the crime, but became relative to the culprit's psychology and circumstances. The sentence passed is not simply retributive, but 'bears within it an assessment of normality and a technical prescription for a possible normalization'.[72] From the comprehensive codification of all offences and illegalities emerged a modulation of the defendant himself, referring 'to his nature, to his way of life and his attitude of mind, to his past, to the "quality" and not to the intention of his will'.[73] Clearly, this process of individuation was intended not to delineate degrees of crime but to objectify criminality. The power relations that support the giving of punishment is duplicated by an object relation to the individual criminal, and enabled his nature to be carefully graded against normative behaviour. What results then is a 'normalizing gaze, a surveillance that makes it possible to qualify, to classify and to punish' and, somewhat paradoxically, it does not homogenize but makes differences 'useful'.[74]

It is significant to Foucault's model of panopticism that punishment itself has gradually become more and more hidden, and in so far as it continues to exist, the public spectacle of juridical power has shifted to the trial. Although extra-juridical elements, such as psychiatric assessment, have been increasingly absorbed by the juridical system it is precisely so that sentencing might appear to be something other than simply legal punishment, a form of power that is exercised rather than possessed. This retreat from view has left the trial, as a spectacle of moral correction, profoundly unsatisfying, perhaps, as Paul Mason suggests, stimulating an interest in television programmes about prison,[75] or encouraging the (TV) police to be invested with expectations that are moral and retributive in tone, but social in understanding. Within the strict limits of detective narratives, the desire for retribution must be at least partially sated during the process of detection, because unlike their real counterparts, the TV detective's interest in the criminal rarely extends beyond the moment when the culprit is arrested. Instead, moral judgement is exercised *in situ* by the fictional police who deliver what, arguably, amounts to a 'normalizing voice', presented as superior to judgements exercised in court, which it critiques for either being unduly lenient, or failing to recognise the nuanced context of social and emotional deprivation that may have led up to the criminal act.

Palmer's Foucauldian analysis of the 'truth effects' of television discourse emphasises a broader post-1980s context in which understanding criminality was increasingly rejected for a reinvigorated emphasis on punishment and community crime prevention. Certainly, programming such as *Crimewatch* (BBC 1984–) emphasises the victims of crime not the causes, and appeals directly for public assistance from the idealised, upstanding, 'active citizen'.[76] However, an interesting development of the 1990s is that crime fiction also began to deploy such media representations reflexively, showing the police detective participating in televised appeals (Tennison in *Prime Suspect*, Mullett in *A Touch of Frost*). In these fictional representations, the value of public engagement is often compromised, as on the occasion in *Cracker* when Fitz has a live conversation with a rapist on a radio phone-in show that is curtailed by the producer, leaving the rapist under the misunderstanding that he should in future kill his victims ('Men Should Weep'). Much later, in *Scott & Bailey*, a perpetrator himself gives himself away during a public appeal for information (series 2, episode 4), the vanity that prompted his appearance at odds with the reiteration of DCI Gill Murray's dislike of public speaking. Professional competence is thus distanced from media 'performance' by problematising the rhetoric of active citizenship for crime detection, other than to acknowledge its potential role in providing (very occasional) leads.

More significant to fictive crime-solving than any contribution made by the public is the innate understanding of human nature the detective is shown to possess. This may be much to the chagrin of professionals such as Katherine Ramsland, a forensic psychologist who is made to 'cringe' whenever Fitz is shown to 'listen to the facts of the case and then spin off a sophisticated character profile that wows everyone'.[77] The truth of the profession is of course more prosaic – as she notes, psychologists are not 'mental magicians' – but the fantasy of insight is a powerful one that responds to the anxiety generated by the objectification of criminality. Detective series differ widely on how they define and explain criminality, whether as monstrous 'Other'[78] or commonplace 'scum', or even in one memorable instance, as a 'misinformed dickhead with the IQ of a pork pie'.[79] However, a superior understanding of criminal motivation is a consistent trope, the radical possibilities of which are perhaps most fully exploited in *Cracker*, which constructs complex narrative parallels between Fitz's desires and those of the perpetrator. In this series, the resemblances are often so self-evident that it is the differences that become revealing, as in the contrast between Fitz's desire for excitement and the giddy murdering excess into which Sean and Tina are drawn ('To Say I Love You'). Although Fitz is an independent, academic, forensic psychologist, his understanding is as much instinctive (born of these parallels) as learnt. The conceit of *Cracker*, as with a number of other contemporary detective series, is not just that the investigator can crack the code and prove 'whodunnit', but that the detective is able to discover *why* apparently senseless or evil crimes are committed. Thus, criminality is not necessarily objectified in television crime fiction, nor is it simply enacted; it may also be rendered comprehensible, plausible and, through repetition, ultimately predictable.

Radicalism and Dissent

I would like now to return to the questions of power raised at the outset of this chapter when I emphasised the continuing cultural significance of television. The theorisation of television as hegemonic and ideologically influential has underpinned debate around the ideal of 'the progressive text', most frequently articulated through a modernist-influenced politics of form that, at best, has been essentially concerned with 'the kinds of readings and meanings and subjectivities which forms enable or prevent – enable *and* prevent'.[80] Within British television studies the debate has tended to play out through competing theories of realism and 'non-naturalism' that Caughie unpacks, effectively challenging both the formalist strains that dominated television theory in the 1960s and 1970s – reminding that '[t]exts do their work in contexts' and that neither form nor content can guarantee radicalism.[81] Crucially, Caughie also defends the 'capacity to bring into public discourse elements (the working class, social injustice, homelessness) which had previously been excluded', further suggesting that '[i]n an almost embarrassingly banal way, television's progressive function may indeed be to bring the world into the home in ways which sometimes escape the order of the institutional discourse – and sometimes don't'.[82]

It would be disingenuous and unnecessary for this study to stake a claim for the objective radicalism of any or all of the contemporary cycle of British detective series, although the orientation of the form towards anxiety, morality, criminality and the social order certainly predisposes it to 'bring the world into the home'. A more particular argument could be that television detectives have emerged as culturally significant characters whose participation in the diegetic public sphere allows them to express a degree of dissatisfaction about the way things are, and this may certainly chime with the experience and sentiments of viewers. In this respect, crime fiction differs crucially from other televisual discourses of law and order, including the police action documentaries such as *Police! Cameras! Action!* (ITV 1994–2010) that Gareth Palmer suggests have substituted sensationalism for any kind of political critique.[83] Of course, the critical documentary has not entirely disappeared from British schedules, and it is problematic that Palmer's argument should rely on such obviously shallow depictions of criminality, but the factual 'crimefighter' genre does sit uneasily alongside the more complex and ambivalent fictional detective genre. Reminded of Dennis Potter's claim that drama can provide 'one of the last remaining acres of possible truth-telling left to us in our over-manipulated and news-stuffed world',[84] I would suggest that the complex polysemic possibilities of television fiction can transcend the moral simplicity that 'cooperation with the police' may necessitate, and permit the expression of altogether more critical, even dissenting, attitudes.

Although a genealogy of the term 'dissent' would emphasise its meaning of religious non-conformity, I use it here in its broadest sense to allude to an expression of disagreement, to the withholding of express consent. Whereas official representatives of law and order may be restricted in their public utterances, the television detective's private grumbles have the ear of a national audience, enabling them to call into question some of the social and ideological doxa of the contemporary order, even though they may also reiterate others. The tendency of critics to laud individual, favoured texts that chime with their own views may simply distract from the fact that complex societal and ethical critique is characteristic of rather than exceptional to the detective genre. In this sense, the dissenting 'voice', whatever its political affiliations, may be seen to actively define the post-*Morse* cycle of serious British crime fiction.

If dissent is a trope then it is one that renders problematic the case made by American criminologists Cavender and Jurik for singling out an edition of *Prime Suspect* as a 'progressive moral fiction'.[85] Avoiding the debates about revolutionary form and content that have characterised the idea of the progressive text in television studies, the authors attempt to combine two ideals: Joan Aiken's concept of a 'provocateur for justice' who 'uses' the law in spite of its limitations in order to attain ideals of justice, and John Gardner's notion of a 'moral fiction' that presents 'a vision of what is possible, a vision that can inspire and encourage people toward virtue'.[86] The argument is that, in *Prime Suspect* 6, Jane Tennison is a positive feminist role model whose alignment with disempowered female victims enables her to emerge as a 'champion', a 'justice provocateur', and concludes with the observation that '[i]t is the mark of a progressive moral fiction that even a fictional character can inspire others to act in ways that may produce social transformation'.[87]

Although, as demonstrated previously, *Prime Suspect*'s strategy of moral allegiance does indeed rely upon Tennison's alignment with the powerless rather than the police squad, the progressiveness of any text does not rest on its correspondence to a liberal perspective (assumed as unassailable). Indeed, by singling out a number of the show's apparent propositions for approval, Cavender and Jurik's argument would seem to be symptomatic of 'a politics which sought to effect change by unveiling "the cause of social evil" but left the viewer secure in a position of superior knowledge'.[88] Their position further suggests that this particular text is exceptional, both to a US-centric model of 'conservative' police/crime drama, and to conventions of gender positioning unchanged since 1940s film noir, and dangerously decontextualises *Prime Suspect* from its generic peers and the mood in British society of the time of its production. By contrast, I would remind the reader that societal critique is commonplace – perhaps even institutionalised – in the British detective fiction of the past two decades. New series seeking to differentiate themselves from the norms of the genre tend to do so by reclaiming authenticity and/or rejecting generic tropes, not necessarily because these are reactionary, but because they are stagnating.[89] Series such as *Prime Suspect*, although innovative, are not ideological aberrations; they do not exist in spite of their genre but because of it, and celebrating such texts by recourse to a negative comparative stereotype sheds little light on the role routinely played by the television detective.

The notion of dissent that I have deployed in relation to the detective's 'voice' is obviously quite different to the 'deviance' of criminality. For a character to uphold official order whilst drawing attention to other moral and social injustices is simply to affirm another Foucauldian proposition, namely that 'resistance is never in a position of exteriority in relation to power'.[90] Perhaps because Foucault himself was working within an intellectual "logic of dissent",[91] his articulation of power is precisely that it accommodates oppositions between autocracy and resistance: it is diffuse and, crucially, it 'produces' reality, domains of objects and rituals of truth. The individual and the knowledge that may be gained of him belong to this production.'[92] The disciplinary system creates a field of knowledge, and it is within not outside of this that dissenting voices will emerge.

As Nicole Rafter has noted, cinematic crime films offer paradoxical pleasures: they may be critical of 'some aspect of society – police brutality, prison violence, legal barriers to justice, or the menace of crime', yet they can also encourage identification 'with a character who restores order at the end, even if that means the punishment or death of the bad-guy hero'.[93] The maverick, discontented television detective may accommodate both oppositional functions, by being critical of the prevailing system of justice at the same time as working to maintain it. Although a narrative compromise, there to stave the anxiety of anarchy, this equivocation allows them to be selective as to which social values to reject and which to reinforce, reminding that normative behaviour is crucial not just for the state, but for the coexistence of those who must jostle for position at the bottom of the pile. Television detectives are often morally ambiguous figures who have emerged amidst ambivalent feelings towards the police and yearnings for benevolent, community authority, whether lost or never really there for 'the likes of us'. For those who 'live in communities which have long been abandoned by the police',[94] as well as those enjoying 'anxieties of affluence', the prospect of protection and order remains a psychic, as much as a governmental necessity.

Notes

Introduction

1 Alan Plater, 'Speaking to nations', in T. Elsaesser *et al.* (eds), *Writing for the Medium* (Amsterdam, 1994).
2 Jason Mittell, 'A cultural approach to television genre theory', *Cinema Journal* 40/3 (Spring 2001), p. 5.
3 Glen Creeber, *Serial Television: Big Drama on the Small Screen* (London, 2004), p. 80.

1 Broadcasting the Detective, 1992–2012

1 John Caughie, 'Mourning television: the other screen', *Screen* 51/4 (2010), pp. 410–21.
2 Elana Levine, 'Teaching the politics of television culture in a "post-television" era', *Cinema Journal*, 50/4 (Summer 2011), pp. 177–82.
3 Charlotte Brunsdon, 'Is television studies history?', *Cinema Journal* 47/3 (Spring 2008), p. 134.
4 Georgina Born, 'Inside television: television studies and the sociology of culture', *Screen* 41/4 (Winter 2000), p. 406.
5 Derek Johnson, 'Inviting audiences in: the spatial reorganization of production and consumption in "TV III"', *New Review of Film and Television Studies* 5/1 (2007), p. 73.
6 John Ellis, *Seeing Things: Television in the Age of Uncertainty* (London 2002), p. 169.
7 Helen Piper, 'Vintage entertainment: nostalgia, the archive, and the disappearing pleasures of collective television viewing', *Journal of British Cinema and Television* 8/3 (Winter 2011), pp. 411–29.
8 Roger Silverstone, *Television and Everyday Life* (London, 1994), p. 21.
9 Ellis, *Seeing Things*.
10 Lyn Thomas, 'In love with Inspector Morse: feminist subculture and quality television', in C. Brunsdon *et al.* (eds), *Feminist Television Criticism* (Oxford, 1997), p. 187.

11 Helen Davis, 'Inspector Morse and the business of crime', *Television and New Media* 2/2 (May 2001), p. 147.
12 Thomas, 'In love with Morse', p. 185.
13 Mark Lawson, 'Watching the detective', *Guardian*, 13 November 2000.
14 *Broadcast*, 'Ratings analysis: BBC outgunned in drama battle', 8 December 2000.
15 Broadcasters Audience Research Board (BARB): http://www.barb.co.uk/viewing (accessed September 2012).
16 Early series episodes of *Frost* peaked in 1997 when the episode 'House Calls' achieved some 18.2 million viewers, according to data from BFI National Library, *The Stats: An Overview of the Film, Television, Video and DVD Industries in the UK 1990–2003* (London, 2004), p. 159.
17 Ibid., pp. 46–50.
18 Michael Jackson cited by Georgina Born, *Uncertain Vision: Birt, Dyke and the Reinvention of the BBC* (London, 2005), p. 291.
19 Some early reports were published in Duncan Petrie and Janet Willis (eds), *Television and the Household* (London, 1995); and the completed study forms the basis of David Gauntlett and Annette Hill *TV Living: Television Culture and Everyday Life* (London, 1999).
20 Gauntlett and Hill, *TV Living*, p. 50.
21 Ibid., p. 49.
22 Ibid., p. 141.
23 BFI, *The Stats*, p. 52.
24 Gauntlett and Hill, *TV Living*, p. 23.
25 Ibid., p. 146.
26 Ibid., p. 168.
27 Roberto Pace, 'Broadcasting trends', in Julian Friedmann and Pere Roca (eds), *Writing Long-Running Television Series* (Madrid, 1994), p. 170.
28 BFI, *The Stats*, p. 69.
29 John Birt, interviewed in *Television: The Journal of the Royal Television Society*, June 1999, p. 13.
30 Charles Denton, cited by Michael Leapman, 'BBC drama chief looks to swim in the mainstream', *Independent*, 21 July 1993.
31 Born, *Uncertain Vision*, p. 275.
32 Ibid., pp. 300–1.
33 'He who prides himself on giving what he thinks the public wants is often creating a fictitious demand for lower standards which he himself will then satisfy' (Reith in 1925, cited by Paddy Scannell, 'Public service broadcasting: the history of a concept', in A. Goodwin and G. Whannel (eds), *Understanding Television* (London, 1990), p. 13).
34 Dorothy Hobson, 'Making a crisis out of a drama', *Television*, June 1999, p. 15.
35 Ibid., p. 14.
36 Born, *Uncertain Vision*, p. 55.
37 Reported in *Broadcast*, 25 September 1998, p. 6.
38 Steven Barnett and Emily Seymour, '*A Shrinking Iceberg Travelling South* …', *Changing Trends in British Television* (London, 1999).

39 Ibid., p. 5.
40 Ibid., p. 43.
41 Ibid., p. 45.
42 Reported in *Broadcast*, 26 March 1999, p. 5.
43 Lawson, 'Watching the detective'.
44 Barry Cox, 'In my view', *Broadcast*, 24 November 2000.
45 Ellis, *Seeing Things*, p. 162.
46 Robin Nelson, *State of Play: Contemporary 'High-End' TV Drama* (Manchester 2007), p. 8.
47 Glen Creeber, 'It's not TV, it's online drama: the return of the intimate screen', *International Journal of Cultural Studies* 14/6 (2011), p. 595.
48 Deborah Jermyn, *Prime Suspect* (London, 2010), p. 87.
49 Nelson, *State of Play*, p. 66.
50 Ibid., p. 67.
51 BARB, average weekly viewing figures available at: http://www.barb.co.uk/viewing/weekly-total-viewing-summary (accessed 28 February 2013).
52 William Phillips, 'Tales of take up', *Television*, July 1999, p. 25.
53 Chris Smith, reported in *Television*, October 1999, p. 7.
54 Whereas these two channels had reliably achieved a combined average of 20 per cent or more of the audience since the late 1980s, by 2012 they were responsible for an average joint share of just over 12 per cent.
55 Many of the series discussed in this study have been remade overseas. For example, *Cracker* quickly became *Fitz* (1996–7) in a US version starring Robert Pastorelli as a tame, slim, moderate drinker with a penchant for unlit cigarettes; there have been both American and Spanish versions of *Life on Mars*, each providing a nationally specific recreation of 1973; and some 20 years after its British debut a much altered version of *Prime Suspect* was produced for the USA with Maria Bello cast as Detective Jane Timoney (NBC 2011–).
56 Joost De Bruin, 'Young people and police series: a multicultural television audience study', *Crime Media Culture* 6/3 (2010), pp. 309–28.
57 OFCOM *Communications Market Report 2012*, p. 117. Available at: http://stakeholders.ofcom.org.uk/binaries/research/cmr/cmr12/CMR_UK2012.pdf (accessed November 2012).
58 In 1999 ITV replaced *The News at Ten* with *The Nightly News*, a variable late evening programme that did not interrupt the screening of films and other drama/entertainment programming, but in 2001 it was obliged by the Independent Television Commission to reinstate a news programme in the 10pm slot on weeknights. There have been various compromises, moves, and restorations since then.
59 Andy Harries, cited by Maggie Brown, 'She's back: and not a moment too soon for ITV', *Guardian*, 21 August 2006.
60 Andrew Billen, 'We shall not see her like again', *New Statesman*, 23 October 2006, p. 44.
61 Jonathan Meades, 'The genius of gesture', *The Times*, 16 November 2002.
62 Reported by Kate McMahon, 'Bragg: restrictions are killing ITV', *Broadcast*, 7 May 2009.

63 Reported by Neil Midgley, 'ITV to slash drama as profits plunge', *Daily Telegraph*, 4 March 2009.
64 David Jason, cited by Daphne Lockyer, 'Sir David Jason: "Maybe David Cameron will make me Minister of Laughs"', *Daily Telegraph*, 28 March 2010.
65 An argument I develop elsewhere, see Helen Piper, 'Lost in participation', *Screen* 52/4 (Winter 2011), pp. 512–21.
66 Will Hutton, 'Money, or the lack of it, is the root of all the BBC's evils', *Guardian*, 21 March 1999.
67 Will Hutton, 'Creativity under threat', *Guardian*, 1 August 2005.
68 This statement was made during Murdoch's 'Worldview Address' to the Edinburgh International Television Festival, 29 August 1998. Similar 'free market' ideals were expressed by Peter Bazalgette in the MacTaggart Lecture the previous day, and by Richard Eyre in his MacTaggart Lecture the following year, 27 August 1999.
69 Nelson, *State of Play*, p. 74.
70 OFCOM's *Second Public Service Broadcasting Review: Putting Audiences First* (Final Statement), 21 January 2009, p. 4. Available at: http://stakeholders.ofcom.org.uk/binaries/consultations/psb2_phase2/statement/psb2statement.pdf (accessed May 2012).
71 Thomas Frank, 'The big con', *Guardian* (Review), 6 January 2001.
72 Lord Chris Patten, 'Is the BBC as good as it could be?', Speech to the Oxford Media Convention, 25 January 2012. Full text available at: http://www.guardian.co.uk/oxfordmediaconvention/lord-patten-of-barnes-is-the-bbc-as-good-as-it-could-be (accessed May 2012).
73 Jay Hunt cited by Stephen Armstrong, 'Under the wire', *Guardian*, 6 April 2009.
74 OFCOM *Second Review*, p. 22.
75 Reported in Tara Conlan, 'Too much crime on TV, says BBC1 chief', *Guardian*, 27 April 2011.
76 Maggie Brown, 'ITV shows renewed faith in drama for 2013', *The Stage*, 19 August 2011.
77 Damien Timmer, cited by Jake Kanter, 'Morse prequel goes to series', *Broadcast*, 12 March 2012.
78 ITV, 'The Morse legacy' (catalogue for MIPTV 2012). Available at: http://mip.itvstudios.com/programmes/drama-comedy/893/the-morse-legacy (accessed May 2012).
79 Barnett and Seymour, *Shrinking Iceberg*.
80 Christopher Hogg, 'Interview. "Gub Neal: cracking the business of TV drama production"', *Journal of British Cinema and Television* 8/1 (April 2011), p. 121.

2 Engaging with the Detective Character

1 John Tulloch, *Watching Television Audiences: Cultural Theories and Methods* (London, 2000), p. 35.

2 Several structural analyses of character functions in popular narrative were written following the publication in English of Vladimir Propp's *Morphology of the Folktale* in 1968. See for example Peter Wollen '*North by North-West*: a morphological analysis', *Film Form* 1/1 (1976), pp. 19–34.
3 Richard Dyer, *Stars* (London, 1979), p. 114.
4 Stuart Hall, cited by Tulloch, *Watching Television Audiences*, p. 36.
5 Murray Smith, *Engaging Characters: Fiction, Emotion, and the Cinema* (Oxford, 1995), p. 18.
6 *Raymond Williams on Television: Selected Writings*, ed. Alan O'Connor (London and New York, 1989), p. 71.
7 Sarah Crompton, 'The arts column: why we love the best TV "tecs"', *Daily Telegraph*, 13 November 2002.
8 Colin MacCabe, 'Realism in the cinema: notes on Brechtian theses', *Screen* 15/2 (Summer 1974), pp. 7–27.
9 Jonathan Bignell, 'Seeing and knowing: reflexivity and quality', in J. McCabe and K. Akass (eds), *Quality TV: Contemporary American Television and Beyond* (London and New York, 2007), p. 160.
10 Kirsten Moana Thompson, *Crime Films: Investigating the Scene* (London, 2007), p. 7.
11 Susan Sydney-Smith, *Beyond Dixon of Dock Green: Early British Police Series* (London, 2002), p. 11.
12 Marion Jordan, 'Realism and convention', in R. Dyer et al. (eds), *Coronation Street* (London, 1981) , p. 28.
13 Paul Cobley, 'The reactionary art of murder: contemporary crime fiction, criticism and verisimilitude', *Language and Literature* 21/3 (2012), pp. 286–7.
14 Cobley bases his argument on a schema developed by Jakobson in his 1921 essay 'On realism in art'.
15 Cobley, 'Reactionary art', p. 290.
16 Ibid., p. 293. By 'doxa' he refers primarily to a form of ideological consensus, marked by 'shifting expectations and understandings of the world' (p. 292).
17 Northrop Frye, *Anatomy of Criticism* (London, 1957), p. 136.
18 John Izod, *Myth, Mind and the Screen: Understanding the Heroes of Our Time* (Cambridge, 2001), p. 24.
19 Christine Gledhill, 'Pleasurable negotiations', in E. D. Pribram (ed.), *Female Spectators: Looking at Film and Television* (London, 1988), p. 75.
20 *Raymond Williams on Television*, p. 70.
21 A phrase used by Robert Audley, the amateur investigator and protagonist of *Lady Audley's Secret* by Mary Elizabeth Braddon, first serialised in 1862.
22 *Raymond Williams on Television*, p. 71.
23 See Janet Thumim (ed.), *Small Screens, Big Ideas: Television in the 1950s* (London, 2002), pp. 207–22.
24 Georg Lukács, 'Narrate or describe', in Arthur Kahn (ed. and tr.), *Writer and Critic* (London, 1970), p. 142.
25 Georg Lukács, 'The sociology of modern drama', tr. Lee Baxandall, *Tulane Drama Review*, 9/4 (Summer 1965), p. 154.
26 Dyer, *Stars*, p. 117.

27 Graeme Burton, *Talking Television: An Introduction to the Study of Television* (London, 2000), p. 208.
28 Alan Clarke, '"You're nicked!" Television police series and the fictional representation of law and order', in D. Strinati, and S. Wagg (eds), *Come On Down? Popular Media Culture in Post-War Britain* (London and New York, 1992), p. 250.
29 Lukács, 'Sociology of modern drama', p. 155.
30 Smith, *Engaging Characters*, p. 82.
31 Sonia Livingstone, *Making Sense of Television: The Psychology of Audience Interpretation* (2nd edn, London, 1988), p. 140.
32 Ibid., p. 150.
33 Umberto Eco, *The Role of the Reader: Explorations in the Semiotics of Texts* (Bloomington, IN, and London, 1979), p. 160.
34 Nicholas Abercrombie and Brian Longhurst, *Audiences: A Sociological Theory of Performance and Imagination* (London, 1998), p. 4.
35 Brian Massumi, *Parables for the Virtual: Movement, Affect, Sensation* (Durham, NC, and London, 2002), p. 3.
36 Ibid., p. 9.
37 Ibid., p. 10.
38 Terry Eagleton, *Literary Theory: An Introduction* (Oxford, 1983), p. 87.
39 Hans Robert Jauss, 'Levels of identification of hero and audience', *New Literary History* 5/2 (Winter 1974), pp. 283–317.
40 Ibid., p. 298.
41 Ibid., p. 297.
42 John Frow, 'Spectacle binding: on character', *Poetics Today*, 7/2 (1986), p. 233.
43 Ibid., p. 234.
44 Rhona Jackson, 'The skilled viewer', in S. Davin and R. Jackson (eds), *Television and Criticism* (Bristol and Chicago, 2008), pp. 82–3.
45 Abercrombie and Longhurst, *Audiences*, p. 65.
46 Noel Carroll, *The Philosophy of Horror: Or Paradoxes of the Heart* (New York and London, 1990), p. 94.
47 Murray Smith, '(Dis)engaging characters: a response to Lynne Pearce', *Screen* 40/3 (1999), p. 358.
48 Murray Smith, 'Altered states: character and emotional response in the cinema', *Cinema Journal* 33/4 (1994), p. 39.
49 Ibid., p. 36.
50 Ibid., p. 35.
51 Smith, *Engaging Characters*, p. 82.
52 Ibid., p. 153.
53 Ibid., p. 160.
54 Ibid., p. 168.
55 John Caughie, 'What do actors do when they act?', in J. Bignell et al. (eds), *British Television Drama: Past, Present and Future* (Basingstoke, 2000), pp. 162–74.
56 Smith, *Engaging Characters*, p. 189.
57 Ibid., p. 191.
58 Lynn Pearce, review of *Engaging Characters* for *Screen* 37/4 (1996), p. 416.

59 Smith, *Engaging Characters*, p. 110.
60 Karen Lury, 'A response to John Corner', *Screen* 48/3 (2007), p. 373.
61 Umberto Eco, 'Innovation and repetition: between modern and post-modern aesthetics', *Daedalus* 114 (Fall 1985), p. 178.
62 Ibid., pp. 174–5.
63 Milly Buonanno, *The Age of Television: Experiences and Theories* (Bristol, 2008), p. 121.
64 Paul Ricoeur, *Time and Narrative*, vol. 1, tr. K. McLaughlin and D. Pellauer (Chicago, 1984).
65 Buonanno, *Age of Television*, p. 125.
66 Ibid., p. 121.
67 Ibid., pp. 131–2.
68 Nancy Banks-Smith, '*Doctor Who* and *A Touch of Frost*', *Guardian*, 5 April 2010.
69 Eco, *Role of the Reader*, p. 162.

3 Residual Voices: *A Touch of Frost* and *Lewis*

1 Evi Girling et al., *Crime and Social Change in Middle England: Questions of Order in an English Town* (London, 2000), p. 115.
2 John Caughie, *Television Drama: Realism, Modernism, and British Culture* (Oxford, 2000), p. 110.
3 Erich Auerbach, *Mimesis: The Representation of Reality in Western Literature* (Princeton, 1968), p. 322.
4 Charlotte Brunsdon, 'Structure of anxiety: recent British television crime fiction', *Screen* 39/3 (Autumn 1998), p. 223.
5 Liz Thomas, 'Jack Frost hangs up his hat as David Jason bids emotional farewell to one of TV's most beloved detectives', *Daily Mail*, 6 April 2010.
6 For example, Granville in *Open All Hours* (BBC 1976–85) and 'Del Boy' in *Only Fools and Horses* (BBC 1981–2003).
7 Colin Dunne, 'The Jason files', *Radio Times*, 5–11 December 1992, p. 33.
8 Mike Ripley, 'Obituary: R. D. Wingfield', *Guardian*, 4 August 2007.
9 Lyn Thomas, 'In love with Inspector Morse: feminist subculture and quality television', in C. Brunsdon *et al.* (eds), *Feminist Television Criticism: A Reader* (Oxford, 1997), p. 188.
10 Nancy Banks-Smith, '*Doctor Who* and *A Touch of Frost*', *Guardian*, 5 April 2010.
11 Cited by Andrew Ffrench, 'Lewis actor finds it's "take your dad to work day"!', *Oxford Mail*, 20 March 2009.
12 Nevertheless, at the time of writing, ITV was refusing to rule out the possibility of a further special or series in 2014–15, see 'News: Lewis will return to small screen, ITV confirms', *Oxford Times*, 13 February 2013.
13 *Broadcast*, 'Tough opposition leaves Mayo trailing', 16 March 2006.
14 Brunsdon, 'Structure of anxiety', p. 231.

15 See Will Wright, *Six Guns and Society: A Structural Study of the Western* (Berkeley, CA, and London, 1975), p. 6.
16 Richard Dyer, *Only Entertainment* (London and New York, 1992), p. 26.
17 Thomas, 'In love with Inspector Morse'.
18 Joost De Bruin, 'Young people and police series: a multicultural television audience study', *Crime Media Culture* 6/3(2010), p. 312.
19 Reported by Naomi West, 'Kevin Whately and Laurence Fox on the new series of Lewis', *Daily Telegraph*, 23 April 2010.
20 Tina Vaz, 'The Masterpiece Mystery interview' (2009). Available at: http://www.pbs.org/wgbh/masterpiece/lewis/whatelyandfox.html (accessed May 2012)
21 The actual screenplay is credited to Helen Jenkins.
22 Sam Wollaston, 'The weekend's TV: Lewis', *Guardian*, 25 February 2008.

4 Ambivalent Voices: Moral Allegiance in *Prime Suspect* and *Cracker*

1 *Independent*, 'No-go Britain: where, what, why', 17 April 1994.
2 Charlotte Brunsdon, 'Structure of anxiety: recent British television crime fiction', *Screen* 39/3 (Autumn 1998), p. 242.
3 Linda Mizejewski, *Hardboiled and High Heeled: The Woman Detective in Popular Culture* (London and New York, 2004), p. 89.
4 Deborah Jermyn, *Prime Suspect* (London, 2010), p. 13.
5 Ibid., p. 14.
6 Conversation between the characters DCS Kernan and Commander Trayner in *Prime Suspect* 1(1991).
7 Sean O'Sullivan, 'UK policing and its television portrayal: "law and order" ideology or modernising agenda?', *Howard Journal* 44/5 (2005), p. 515.
8 Alison Halford was Assistant Chief Constable of Merseyside from 1983, but in 1990 made a formal complaint to the Equal Opportunities Commission about being repeatedly passed over for promotion. Coverage of the discrimination case had to contend with reports of a heavy drinking culture in the local police force when disciplinary proceedings were also brought against Halford for misconduct. She settled out of court and took early retirement in 1992 after which the disciplinary charges were also dropped. In a conscious echo of this case, Tennison is seen in *Prime Suspect 4: The Scent of Darkness* (1995) to speak up on behalf of a junior female officer who has been overlooked for promotion because, so Jane is told, 'she can't take a joke, and if you can't take a joke you shouldn't work in a team'.
9 Mary Eaton, 'A fair cop? Viewing the effects of the canteen culture in *Prime Suspect* and *Between the Lines*', in D Kidd-Hewitt and R. Osborne (eds), *Crime and the Media: the Postmodern Spectacle* (London, 1995), p. 164.
10 Jermyn, *Prime Suspect*, p. 47.
11 Ibid., *Prime Suspect*, p. 61.

12 Gray Cavender, and Nancy Jurik, 'Scene composition and justice for women: an analysis of the portrayal of Detective Tennison in the British television program *Prime Suspect*', *Feminist Criminology* 2/4 (2007), pp. 277–303.
13 Ibid., p. 283.
14 Deborah Jermyn, 'Women with a mission: Lynda La Plante, DCI Jane Tennison and the reinvention of British TV crime drama', *International Journal of Cultural Studies*, 6/1 (2003), p. 57.
15 Ibid., p. 55.
16 Jermyn, *Prime Suspect*, p. 44.
17 Glen Creeber, *Serial Television: Big Drama on the Small Screen* (London, 2004), pp. 82–5.
18 Jermyn, 'Women with a mission', p. 51.
19 Jermyn, *Prime Suspect*, p. 55.
20 'The 100 greatest sex symbols'. Available at: http://www.channel4.com/programmes/the-100-greatest-sex-symbols/articles/the-results (accessed February 2013).
21 Andrew Billen, 'We shall not see her like again', *New Statesman*, 23 October 2006, p. 44.
22 Libby Brooks, 'Struck down in her prime', *Guardian*, 24 October 2006.
23 Annette Kuhn, 'Women's genres: melodrama, soap opera, and theory', in C. Brunsdon *et al.* (eds), *Feminist Television Criticism: A Reader* (Oxford, 1997), p. 162.
24 Murray Smith, '(Dis)engaging characters: a response to Lynne Pearce', *Screen* 40/3 (1999), p. 359.
25 Brooks, 'Struck down in her prime'.
26 During a press conference, September 2006. Tennison's imminent onscreen death was thereafter widely reported as fact, even by television reviewers such as Billen, much to their later embarrassment.
27 Steve Blandford, paper given at the 'Performance and Television Spaces' symposium at the University of Glamorgan, 20 April 2012.
28 Christopher Hogg, 'Interview. "Gub Neal: cracking the business of TV drama production', *Journal of British Cinema and Television* 8/1 (April 2011), p. 121.
29 Ibid.
30 McGovern cited by John Crace, *Cracker: The Truth Behind the Fiction* (London, 1994), p. 22.
31 Mark Duguid, *Cracker* (London, 2009), p. 39.
32 Jimmy McGovern cited by Sean Day-Lewis, *Talk of Drama: Views of the Television Dramatist Now and Then* (Luton, 1998), p. 68.
33 The decision to make a serving police officer a rape victim was carefully calculated. Jimmy McGovern has observed that he had wanted to write an episode of *Prime Suspect* in which Tennison was raped, but used his idea in *Cracker* instead (see http://www.crackertv.co.uk/jimmymcgovernoncracker.htm accessed September 2012).
34 Jimmy McGovern has since said he was unhappy with this denouement, see Duguid, *Cracker*, p. 58.
35 Stefan Kiszko served a 16-year sentence for the sexually motivated murder of Lesley Molseed, an 11-year-old schoolgirl after confessing without a solicitor

present. He was cleared and released on appeal in 1992 but died of a heart attack the following year before receiving full compensation.

36 Although unlikely, the return of *Cracker* has never been categorically ruled out by Jimmy McGovern; see Duguid, *Cracker*, p. 138.

37 Jimmy McGovern, cited by Hannah Pool, 'Question time: scriptwriter Jimmy McGovern', *Guardian*, 1 November 2007.

38 Hogg, 'Interview Gub Neal', p. 124.

39 Duguid, *Cracker*, p. 116.

40 The occasion of 15 April 1989 on which 96 Liverpool football supporters lost their lives, trapped by inadequate police management of the crowd and high cage fences around the stadium. Senior police figures blamed the fans, claiming they had been drinking and had forced a gate, a story taken up without reservation by the *Sun* newspaper which claimed the fans had also robbed and urinated on the dead. The struggle for justice was the subject of Jimmy McGovern's later award-winning drama on the subject, *Hillsborough* (ITV 1996), finally vindicated by an independent report published in September 2012.

41 Duguid, *Cracker*, p. 68.

42 A. D. Nuttall, *Why Does Tragedy Give Pleasure?* (Oxford, 1996), p. 77.

43 Duguid, *Cracker*, p. 46.

5 The Reactionary Voice: *Life on Mars* and 'The Gene Genie'

1 Brian Cathcart, 'The newspapers on Mars', *New Statesman*, 26 February 2007, p. 24.

2 Deborah Jermyn, *Prime Suspect* (London, 2010), p. 26.

3 For example, see Stephen Lacey and Ruth McElroy (eds), *Life on Mars: From Manchester to New York* (Cardiff, 2012).

4 The series' creator reportedly described The Railway Arms as 'a site that became part of the LOM/ASHES story, not simply an adjunct to it', Ashley Pharoah (April 2010). Available at www.domeofstars.com/forum (accessed October 2012).

5 From a selection of newspaper reviews reprinted in 'Life on Mars', *Guardian* (Media), 10 January 2006.

6 Ibid.

7 Andrew Billen, 'Space oddity', *New Statesman*, 16 January 2006, p. 48.

8 Tim Edensor, *National Identity, Popular Culture and Everyday Life* (Oxford and New York, 2002), p. 104.

9 John Curzon, 'Sam Tyler and the "New North"', in Lacey and McElroy, *Life on Mars*, p. 70.

10 Ibid.

11 Filmed at the large red Victorian structure of Queen Street Mill, Burnley.

12 Susan Sydney-Smith, 'Changing places: touring the British crime film', *Tourist Studies* 6/1 (2006), p. 92.

13 Charlotte Brunsdon, 'Space in the British crime film', in S. Chibnall and R. Murphy (eds), *British Crime Cinema* (London and New York, 1999), p. 148.
14 Lez Cooke, 'The police series', in G. Creeber (ed.), *The Television Genre Book* (London, 2001), p. 22.
15 Leon Hunt, 'Dog eat dog: *The Squeeze* and the *Sweeney* films', in Chibnall and Murphy, *British Crime Cinema*, p. 137.
16 Ibid., p. 146.
17 Jon Garland and Charlotte Bilby, 'What next, dwarves? Images of police culture in *Life on Mars*', *Crime Media Culture* 7/2 (2011), p. 117.
18 Matt Hills, 'The medium is the monster… or the world?', in Lacey and McElroy, *Life on Mars*, p. 105.
19 Ibid., p. 106.
20 Richard Sparks, *Television and the Drama of Crime: Moral Tales and the Place of Crime in Public Life* (Buckingham, 1992), p. 25.
21 Cited by Richard Garner, 'Teachers blame "Life on Mars" for rise of homophobia in schools', *Belfast Telegraph*, 13 April 2007, www.belfasttelegraph.co.uk/news/education/teachers-blame-life-on-mars-for-rise-of-homophobia-in-schools (accessed July 2011). Chris Keates (General Secretary of the National Association of Schoolmasters Union of Women Teachers) had argued that Hunt's use of terminology such as 'fairy boy' in *Life on Mars* could incite homophobic bullying.
22 Amy Holdsworth, *Television, Memory and Nostalgia* (Basingstoke, 2011), p. 105.
23 Holdsworth, *Television, Memory and Nostalgia*, p. 107.
24 Julianne Pidduck, 'Of windows and country walks: frames of space and movement in 1990s Austen adaptations', *Screen* 39/4 (Winter 1998), pp. 381–400.
25 Svetlana Boym, *The Future of Nostalgia* (New York, 2001), p. xiv.
26 Michael Pickering and Emily Keightley, 'The modalities of nostalgia', *Current Sociology* 54/6 (November 2006), p. 921.
27 Andreas Huyssen, *Present Pasts: Urban Palimpsests and the Politics of Memory* (Stanford, CA, 2003), p. 21.
28 James Chapman, 'Not "another bloody cop show": *Life on Mars* and British television drama', *Film International* 38/7/2 (2009), p. 8.
29 James Donaghy, 'Is there life after *Life on Mars?*', *Guardian*, 11 April 2007.
30 Given examples drawn from 'Life on Mars: general discussion threads' posted between April 2006 and May 2011, The Railway Arms (all retrieved October 2012).
31 Brett Mills, '"American remake – shudder", online debates about *Life on Mars* and "British-ness"', in Lacey and McElroy, *Life on Mars*, pp. 133–44.
32 Paul Vize, '*Life on Mars*: your questions', BBC Online, 2007. Available at http://www.bbc.co.uk/lifeonmars/backstage/questions_inspiration.shtml (accessed January 2011).
33 Glenda Cooper, 'Why women love DCI Hunt', *Daily Telegraph*, 13 April 2007.
34 Cited in BBC press release: *Ashes to Ashes*, 2007. Available at: http://www.bbc.co.uk/pressoffice/pressreleases/stories/2007/04_april/11/ashes.shtml (accessed October 2012).
35 Laura Mulvey, 'Visual pleasure and narrative cinema', *Screen* 16/3 (Autumn 1975), p. 12.

36 gavin.1001, 'A2A: Episode One' (2008), The Railway Arms: http://www.domeofstars.com/forum/index.php?topic=3231.105 (accessed October 2012).
37 Ruth McElroy, 'Consuming retrosexualities', in Lacey and McElroy, *Life on Mars*, pp. 117–29.

6 Emergent Voices I: *Wallander* and *Vera*

1 Jonathan Bignell, 'Seeing and knowing: reflexivity and quality', in J. McCabe and K. Akass (eds), *Quality TV: Contemporary American Television and Beyond* (London and New York, 2007), p. 159.
2 The first two series were all written or co-written by Richard Cottan, the third by Peter Harness. Eight different directors were responsible for the nine episodes discussed in this chapter.
3 Cleeves's Vera novels include *Silent Voices*, *The Glass Room*, *The Crow Trap*, *Telling Tales* and *Hidden Depths*. A number of different television writers have worked on the first three series, the most prolific of which has been Paul Rutman, whose previous credits included writing for *Lewis*. Similarly, six different directors were responsible for the eight episodes shown in 2011 and 2012. Executive producer and producer credits suggest a predominantly female team, most notably Kate Bartlett, Kate Lewis and Elaine Collins.
4 These were distributed rather erratically, some had a Swedish cinematic release and others went straight to DVD. All were later broadcast by the Swedish channel TV4, as two separate series, each of 13 stand-alone episodes in 2005/6 and 2009/10 (and in the UK, on BBC4, between 2009 and 2011).
5 Will Strauss, 'Anthony Dod Mantle interview', *Broadcast*, 13 May 2009.
6 Paul Cobley, 'The reactionary art of murder: contemporary crime fiction, criticism and verisimilitude', *Language and Literature* 21/3 (2012), p. 291.
7 Michael Tapper, 'More than ABBA and skinny-dipping in mountain lakes: Swedish dystopia, Henning Mankell and the British Wallander series', *Film International* 38/7/2 (2009), p. 63.
8 Philip Martin, 'On location: *Wallander*', *Broadcast*, 26 November 2008.
9 OFCOM's *Second Public Service Broadcasting Review: Putting Audiences First* (Final Statement), 21 January 2009.
10 Rachel Cooke, 'Hard-boiled Swede', *New Statesman*, 28 January 2010.
11 The tune was specially composed for the production, as later discovered by the readers of the 'Material Witness' crime fiction blog, see: http://materialwitness.typepad.com/material_witness/2010/01/the-unsolved-mystery-of-the-wallander-ringtone.html (accessed October 2012).
12 Neil Midgley, 'Partners in crime', *Radio Times*, 7–13 July 2012, p. 17.
13 See Henning Mankell, *The Dogs of Riga*, tr. Laurie Thompson (London, 2009), p. 341.
14 Ibid., p. 36.
15 Tom Sutcliffe, 'The weekend's viewing', *Independent*, 9 July 2012.

16 Jane Feuer, 'Narrative form in American network television', in C. MacCabe (ed.), *High Theory/Low Culture* (Manchester, 1986), p. 112.
17 Esther May Campbell (director of 'Dogs of Riga'), interview with the author, 30 January 2012.
18 *Raymond Williams on Television: Selected Writings*, ed. Alan O'Connor (London and New York, 1989), p. 71.
19 James Rampton, 'Kenneth Branagh: the stunning, troubled world of the "Norse Morse"', *Daily Telegraph*, 1 November 2008.
20 Interviewed by Anna Blundy, 'Five books interviews: Ann Cleeves on Nordic crime fiction'. Available at: http://thebrowser.com/interviews/ann-cleeves-on-nordic-crime-fiction (accessed October 2012).
21 Lyn Thomas, 'In love with Inspector Morse: feminist subculture and quality television', in C. Brunsdon *et al.* (eds), *Feminist Television Criticism: A Reader* (Oxford, 1997), pp. 184–204.
22 Benji Wilson, 'Review', *Daily Telegraph*, 4 January 2010.
23 Georg Lukács, 'The sociology of modern drama', tr. Lee Baxandall, *Tulane Drama Review*, 9/4 (Summer 1965), p. 155.

7 Emergent Voices II: *Luther, Scott & Bailey* and *Line of Duty*

1 Although the series was designed for television, since broadcast Cross has also published a novel featuring the central character: *Luther: The Calling* (Simon & Schuster, 2011).
2 The first two series of *Luther* were executive produced by Phillippa Giles. Idris Elba also received an associate producer credit.
3 Glen Creeber, 'Hideously white: British television, globalisation and national identity', *Television and New Media Journal*, 5/1 (February 2004), pp. 27–39.
4 Jim Pines, 'Black cops and black villains in film and TV crime fiction', in D. Kidd Hewitt and R. Osborne (eds), *Crime and the Media: The Post-Modern Spectacle* (London, 1995), p. 70.
5 Ibid., p. 76.
6 Ibid.
7 An accusation first made by the MacPherson report into the failed investigation of Stephen Lawrence's murder in 1993. It has been repeated many times since, for example by Sgt Alfred John, Chairman of the Metropolitan Black Police Association, during one of a number of black officer boycotts of recruitment drives aimed at ethnic minorities. See Vikram Dodd, 'Black officers to begin recruitment boycott at Met', *Guardian*, 5 October 2008.
8 Charlotte Brunsdon, 'Structure of anxiety: recent British television crime fiction', *Screen* 39/3 (1998), pp. 234–5.
9 Pines, 'Black cops', p. 74.

10 Interviewed by Gareth McLean, 'Back to Blighty', *Radio Times*, 1–7 May 2010, p. 13.
11 Given the continuities of writer and producer, the shift in direction to which I refer may well be attributed to the increased involvement of Sam Miller, who directed only two episodes of the first series, but all four of the second.
12 Series 1 (2011) comprised six episodes, and series 2 (2012) consisted of eight. A third series of eight episodes was scheduled for broadcast in 2013.
13 Interviewed by Gareth McLean, 'The No 1 ladies' detective agency', *Radio Times*, 10–16 March 2012, p. 11.
14 See Taylor's interview with Helen Tither, 'TV cop dramas irritated me, so I made my own, says the former Detective Inspector behind Scott And Bailey', *Manchester Evening News*, 22 June 2011.
15 Tom Sutcliffe, 'The weekend's TV', *Guardian*, 30 May 2011.
16 Tom Sutcliffe, 'It isn't a crime to laugh at the police', *Guardian*, 17 June 2011.
17 Sam Wollaston, 'TV review', *Guardian*, 29 May 2011.
18 Jim Shelley, 'Scott & Bailey review', *Mirror*, 12 March 2012.
19 Ironically, James had played DC Tanner in *A Touch of Frost: A Minority of One* (1994) who, on arrival at Frost's office, declared himself a grateful but undeserving beneficiary of positive discrimination.
20 *The Cops* (1999–2001) was also made for the BBC by World Productions, for a brief discussion of this see Chapter 8.

8 The Resonance of the Detective

1 John Corner, *Television Form and Public Address* (London, 1995), p. 7.
2 Charlotte Brunsdon, 'Structure of anxiety: recent British television crime fiction', *Screen* 39/3 (Autumn 1998), p. 223.
3 Richard Sparks, 'Inspector Morse: the last enemy', in G. Brandt (ed.), *British Television Drama in the 1980s* (Cambridge, 1993), p. 99.
4 Elana Levine, 'Teaching the politics of television culture in a "post-television" era', *Cinema Journal* 50/4 (Summer 2011), p. 179.
5 Ibid., p. 180.
6 Cited ibid., p. 182.
7 John Mepham, 'The ethics of quality in television', in G. Mulgan (ed.), *The Question of Quality* (London, 1990), pp. 56–72.
8 BARB, 'Lifestyle insights survey' (2010). The average time spent watching television has also remained stable over the past two decades, varying between 28 and 34 hours per week. Available at http://www.barb.co.uk/graph/weekly-viewing?_s=4 (accessed June 2012).
9 Georgina Born, 'Inside television: television studies and the sociology of culture', *Screen* 41/4 (Winter 2000), pp. 405–6.
10 Arjun Appadurai, *Modernity at Large: Cultural Dimensions of Globalization* (Minneapolis, 1996), p. 5.
11 Ibid., p. 9.

12 Brunsdon, 'Structure of anxiety', pp. 223–43.
13 Raymond Williams, *Marxism and Literature* (Oxford, 1977), p. 131.
14 Ibid., p. 133.
15 Born, 'Inside television', p. 412.
16 Brett Mills, '"American remake – shudder", online debates about *Life on Mars* and "British-ness"', in S. Lacey and R. McElroy (eds), *Life on Mars: From Manchester to New York* (Cardiff, 2012), p. 142.
17 For example, see Stijn Reijnders, 'Watching the detectives: inside the guilty landscapes of *Inspector Morse*, *Baantjer* and *Wallander*', *European Journal of Communication* 24/2 (2009), pp. 165–81; and Susan Sydney-Smith, 'Changing places: touring the British crime film', *Tourist Studies* 6/1 (2006), pp. 79–94.
18 Reijnders, 'Watching the detectives', p. 171.
19 Ibid., p. 172.
20 Jeff Hopkins, 'Mapping of cinematic places: icons, ideology, and the power of (mis)representation', in S. C. Aitken and L. E. Zonn (eds), *Place, Power, Situation, and Spectacle: A Geography of Film* (Lanham, MD, and London, 1994), pp. 47–68.
21 Stuart Aitken and Leo Zonn, 'Re-presenting the place pastiche', in Aitken and Zonn (eds), *Place, Power, Situation*, p. 17.
22 Stijn Reijnders, 'Places of the imagination: an ethnography of the TV detective tour', *Cultural Geographies* 17/1 (2010), p. 43.
23 Reijnders, 'Watching the detectives', p. 176.
24 Evi Girling et al., *Crime and Social Change in Middle England: Questions of Order in an English Town* (London, 2000), p. 9. The research was conducted in Macclesfield, an 'unremarkable' town that is used to avoid the polarising tendency in much criminology and urban sociology, 'by turns mesmerized and appalled by the drama, romance, glamour and degradation of the city' (p. 1).
25 Roger Silverstone, *Television and Everyday Life* (London, 1994), p. 50.
26 Ibid.
27 John Corner, *Critical Ideas in Television Studies* (Oxford, 1999), p. 21.
28 Iain Chambers, 'Narratives of nationalism: being "British"', in E. Carter et al. (eds), *Space and Place: Theories of Identity and Location* (London, 1993), p. 153.
29 Benedict Anderson, *Imagined Communities: Reflections on the Origin and Spread of Nationalism* (revised edn, London and New York, 2006).
30 Appadurai, *Modernity at Large*, p. 19.
31 Tim Edensor, *National Identity, Popular Culture and Everyday Life* (Oxford and New York, 2002), p. 39.
32 Ibid., p. 53.
33 Ibid., p. 51.
34 Amy Holdsworth, *Television, Memory and Nostalgia* (Basingstoke, 2011), pp. 84–5.
35 Edensor, *National Identity*, p. 65.
36 Richard Sparks, *Television and the Drama of Crime: Moral Tales and the Place of Crime in Public Life* (Buckingham, 1992), p. 32.
37 Ibid., p. 125.
38 Silverstone, *Television and Everyday Life*, pp. 50–1.

39 Ibid., p. 69.
40 Girling et al., *Crime and Social Change in Middle England*, p. 108.
41 Susie Dent cited by Jon Kelly, 'England riots: what's the meaning of the words behind the chaos?' BBC Online, 12 August 2011. Available at: http://www.bbc.co.uk/news/magazine-14506159 (accessed July 2012).
42 Michele Hilmes, 'Who we are, who we are not: battle of the global paradigms', in L. Parks and S. Kumar (eds), *Planet TV: A Global Television Reader* (London and New York, 2003), p. 69.
43 David Cardiff and Paddy Scannell, 'Broadcasting and national unity', in J. Curran et al. (eds), *Impacts and Influences: Essays on Media Power in the Twentieth Century* (London and New York, 1987), p. 162.
44 Jason Jacobs, 'The medium in crisis: Caughie, Brunsdon and the problem of US television', *Screen* 52/4 (Winter 2011), p. 509.
45 Ibid., p. 506.
46 Ibid., 'Medium in crisis', p. 510.
47 Tim Colwell and David Price, *Rights of Passage: British Television in the Global Market* (London, 2004), p. 30.
48 Joe Hicks and Grahame Allen, *A Century of Change: Trends in UK Statistics since 1900*, House of Commons research paper 99/111 (21 December 1999), p. 14.
49 Ibid., p. 14.
50 Norman Dennis and George Erdos, *Cultures and Crimes: Policing in Four Nations* (London, 2005), p. 58.
51 Eamonn Carrabine, *Crime, Culture and the Media* (Cambridge, 2008), p. 40.
52 Sparks, *Television and the Drama of Crime*, p. 7.
53 George Gerbner and Larry Gross, 'The scary world of TV's heavy viewer', *Psychology Today* (April 1976), pp. 89–91.
54 Sparks, *Television and the Drama of Crime*, p. 96.
55 Carrabine, *Crime, Culture and the Media*, pp. 44–5.
56 Sparks, *Television and the Drama of Crime*, p. 160.
57 Ibid., p. 30.
58 Ibid., p. 53.
59 Dennis and Erdos, *Cultures and Crimes*, p. 201.
60 The Panopticon that features in Bentham's eighteenth-century designs for a model prison is an inspection tower surrounded by a circular periphery building in which prisoners would be incarcerated. The periphery is divided into cells from each of which one window opens to the inside of the centre ring and one to the outside to admit light. The tower is windowed so the supervisor may look out. Foucault was fascinated by the shift it heralded, not least in how it reversed three functions of the dungeon: 'to enclose, to deprive of light and to hide'. See Michel Foucault, *Discipline and Punish: The Birth of the Prison* (London, 1991), p. 200.
61 Ibid., p. 217.
62 Roy Boyne, 'Post-panopticism', *Economy and Society* 29/2 (2000), pp. 285–307.
63 Gareth Palmer, *Discipline and Liberty* (Manchester, 2003), p. 16.
64 See John Tulloch's useful overview in *Watching Television Audiences: Cultural Theories and Methods* (London, 2000), pp. 33–55.
65 Brunsdon, 'Structure of anxiety', pp. 230–1.

66 Ibid., p. 228.
67 Girling et al., *Crime and Social Change in Middle England*, p. 119.
68 Ibid., p. 124.
69 Ibid., p. 126.
70 Kirsten Moana Thompson, *Crime Films: Investigating the Scene* (London, 2007), pp. 1–2.
71 Foucault, *Discipline and Punish*, p. 17.
72 Ibid., p. 21.
73 Ibid., p. 99.
74 Ibid., p. 184.
75 Paul Mason, 'Prime time punishment: the British prison and television', in D. Kidd-Hewitt and R. Osborn (eds), *Crime and the Media* (London, 1995), pp. 185–205.
76 Palmer, *Discipline and Liberty*, p. 75.
77 Katherine Ramsland, *The Criminal Mind: A Writer's Guide to Forensic Psychology* (Cincinnati, OH, 2002), p. 19.
78 A concept much used in the study of the horror film, notably by Robin Wood, *Hollywood from Vietnam to Reagan* (New York, 1986), pp. 73–5.
79 Spoken by the character Rachel Bailey in *Scott & Bailey* (series 2, episode 5).
80 John Caughie, *Television Drama: Realism, Modernism, and British Culture* (Oxford, 2000), p. 91.
81 Ibid., p. 108.
82 Ibid., p. 109.
83 Palmer, *Discipline and Liberty*, p. 8.
84 Dennis Potter, MacTaggart Lecture, Edinburgh International Television Festival 1993.
85 Gray Cavender and Nancy Jurik, 'Scene composition and justice for women: an analysis of the portrayal of Detective Tennison in the British television program Prime Suspect', *Feminist Criminology* 2/4 (2007), pp. 277–303.
86 Ibid., p. 283.
87 Ibid., p. 301.
88 Caughie, *Television Drama*, p. 106.
89 Paul Cobley, 'The reactionary art of murder: contemporary crime fiction, criticism and verisimilitude', *Language and Literature* 21/3 (2012), p. 293.
90 Michel Foucault, *The History of Sexuality*, vol. 1, tr. Robert Hurley (London, 1998), p. 95.
91 Eve Tavor Bannet, *Structuralism and the Logic of Dissent: Barthes, Derrida, Foucault, Lacan* (Basingstoke 1989), pp. 3–4.
92 Foucault, *Discipline and Punish*, p. 194.
93 Nicole Rafter, *Shots in the Mirror: Crime Films and Society* (Oxford, 2006), p. 3.
94 Palmer, *Discipline and Liberty*, p. 88.

Bibliography

Abercrombie, Nicholas, and Longhurst, Brian, *Audiences: A Sociological Theory of Performance and Imagination* (London: Sage, 1998).

Aitken, Stuart C., and Zonn, Leo E., 'Re-presenting the place pastiche', in S. C. Aitken and L. E. Zonn (eds), *Place, Power, Situation, and Spectacle: A Geography of Film* (Lanham, MD, and London: Rowman & Littlefield, 1994), pp. 3–25.

Anderson, Benedict, *Imagined Communities: Reflections on the Origin and Spread of Nationalism* (revised edn, London and New York: Verso, 2006).

Appadurai, Arjun, *Modernity at Large: Cultural Dimensions of Globalization* (Minneapolis and London: University of Minnesota Press, 1996).

Armstrong, Stephen, 'Under the wire', *Guardian*, 6 April 2009. Available at: http://www.guardian.co.uk/media/2009/apr/06/television-ratings-viewing-habits (accessed May 2012).

Auerbach, Erich, *Mimesis: The Representation of Reality in Western Literature* (Princeton: Princeton University Press, 1968).

Banks-Smith, Nancy, '*Doctor Who* and *A Touch of Frost*', *Guardian*, 5 April 2010. Available at: http://www.guardian.co.uk/tv-and-radio/2010/apr/05/doctor-who-touch-of-frost (accessed May 2012).

Barnett, Steven, and Seymour, Emily, *'A Shrinking Iceberg Travelling South …': Changing Trends in British Television. A Case Study of Drama and Current Affairs*, A Report for the Campaign for Quality Television Ltd (London: University of Westminster, Sept. 1999).

BBC, 'Press release: Ashes to Ashes', BBC Press Office, 2007. Available at: http://www.bbc.co.uk/pressoffice/pressreleases/stories/2007/04_april/11/ashes.shtml (accessed October 2012).

BFI National Library, *The Stats: An Overview of the Film, Television, Video and DVD Industries in the UK 1990–2003* (London: BFI, 2004).

Bignell, Jonathan, 'Seeing and knowing: reflexivity and quality', in J. McCabe and K. Akass (eds), *Quality TV: Contemporary American Television and Beyond* (London and New York: I.B.Tauris, 2007), pp. 158–70.

Billen, Andrew, 'Space oddity', *New Statesman*, 16 January 2006, p. 48.
—— 'We shall not see her like again', *New Statesman*, 23 October 2006, p. 44.
Blundy, Anna, 'Five books interviews: Ann Cleeves on Nordic crime fiction', http://thebrowser.com/interviews/ann-cleeves-on-nordic-crime-fiction (accessed October 2012).
Born, Georgina, 'Inside television: television studies and the sociology of culture', *Screen* 41/4 (Winter 2000), pp. 404–24.
—— *Uncertain Vision: Birt, Dyke and the Reinvention of the BBC* (London: Secker & Warburg. 2004).
Boym, Svetlana, *The Future of Nostalgia* (New York: Basic Books, 2001).
Boyne, Roy, 'Post-panopticism', *Economy and Society* 29/2 (2000), pp. 285–307.
Broadcast, 'Ratings analysis: BBC outgunned in drama battle', 8 December 2000. Available at http://www.broadcastnow.co.uk/news/multi-platform/news/ratings-analysis-bbc-outgunned-in-drama-battle/1206372.article (accessed November 2011).
—— 'Tough opposition leaves Mayo trailing', 16 March 2006. Available at http://www.broadcastnow.co.uk/news/multi-platform/news/tough-opposition-leaves-mayo-trailing/155713.article (accessed May 2012).
Broadcasters Audience Research Board (BARB): http://www.barb.co.uk/viewing.
Brooks, Libby, 'Struck down in her prime', *Guardian*, 24 October 2006. Available at: http://www.guardian.co.uk/commentisfree/2006/oct/24/comment.gender?INTCMP=SRCH (accessed September 2012).
Brown, Maggie, 'ITV shows renewed faith in drama for 2013', *The Stage*, 19 August 2011. Available at: http://www.thestage.co.uk/news/newsstory.php/33253/itv-shows-renewed-faith-in-drama-for-2013 (accessed February 2012).
—— 'She's back: and not a moment too soon for ITV', *Guardian*, 21 August 2006. Available at: http://www.guardian.co.uk/media/2006/aug/21/broadcasting.mondaymediasection1?INTCMP=SRCH (accessed September 2012).
Brunsdon, Charlotte, 'Structure of anxiety: recent British television crime fiction', *Screen* 39/3 (Autumn 1998), pp. 223–43.
—— 'Space in the British crime film', in S. Chibnall and R. Murphy (eds), *British Crime Cinema* (London and New York: Routledge, 1999), pp. 148–59.
—— 'Is television studies history?', *Cinema Journal* 47/3 (Spring 2008), pp. 127–37.
Buonanno, Milly, *The Age of Television: Experiences and Theories* (Bristol: Intellect, 2008).
Burton, Graeme, *Talking Television: An Introduction to the Study of Television* (London: Arnold, 2000).

Cardiff, David, and Scannell, Paddy, 'Broadcasting and national unity', in J. Curran, A. Smith and P. Wingate (eds), *Impacts and Influences: Essays on Media Power in the Twentieth Century* (London and New York: Methuen, 1987), pp. 157–73.

Carrabine, Eamonn, *Crime, Culture and the Media* (Cambridge: Polity Press, 2008).

Carroll, Noel, *The Philosophy of Horror: Or Paradoxes of the Heart* (New York and London: Routledge, 1990).

Cathcart, Brian, 'The newspapers on Mars', *New Statesman*, 26 February 2007, p. 24.

Caughie, John 'What do actors do when they act?', in J. Bignell, S. Lacey and M. Macmurraugh-Kavanagh (eds), *British Television Drama: Past, Present and Future* (Basingstoke and New York: Palgrave, 2000), pp. 162–74.

—— *Television Drama: Realism, Modernism, and British Culture* (Oxford: Oxford University Press, 2000).

—— 'Mourning television: the other screen', *Screen* 51/4 (Winter 2010), pp. 410–21.

Cavender, Gray, and Jurik, Nancy, 'Scene composition and justice for women: an analysis of the portrayal of Detective Tennison in the British television program Prime Suspect', *Feminist Criminology* 2/4 (2007), pp. 277–303.

Chambers, Iain, 'Narratives of nationalism: being "British"', in E. Carter, J. Donald and J. Squires (eds), *Space and Place: Theories of Identity and Location* (London: Lawrence & Wishart, 1993), pp. 145–64.

Chapman, James, 'Not "another bloody cop show": *Life on Mars* and British television drama', *Film International* 38/7/2 (2009), pp. 6–18.

Chibnall, Steve, and Murphy, Robert (eds), *British Crime Cinema* (London and New York: Routledge, 1999).

Clarke, Alan, '"You're nicked!" Television police series and the fictional representation of law and order', in D. Strinati and S. Wagg (eds), *Come On Down? Popular Media Culture in Post-War Britain* (London and New York: Routledge, 1992), pp. 232–53.

Cobley, Paul, 'The reactionary art of murder: contemporary crime fiction, criticism and verisimilitude', *Language and Literature* 21/3 (2012), pp. 286–98.

Colwell, Tim, and Price, David, *Rights of Passage: British Television in the Global Market: A Report by Television Research Partnership* (London: Commissioned by British Television Distributors' Association and UK Trade & Investment, 2004).

Conlan, Tara, 'Too much crime on TV, says BBC1 chief', *Guardian*, 27 April 2011. Available at: http://www.guardian.co.uk/media/2011/apr/27/tv-crime-drama-bbc1-chief (accessed September 2012).

Cooke, Lez, 'The police series', in G. Creeber (ed.), *The Television Genre Book* (London: BFI, 2001).

Cooke, Rachel, 'Hard-boiled Swede', *New Statesman*, 28 January 2010. Available at: http://www.newstatesman.com/television/2010/02/mankell-wallander-sweden-bbc (accessed October 2012).

Cooper, Glenda, 'Why women love DCI Hunt', *Daily Telegraph*, 13 April 2007.

Corner, John, *Television Form and Public Address* (London: Edward Arnold, 1995).

—— *Critical Ideas in Television Studies* (Oxford: Clarendon Press, 1999).

Cox, Barry, 'In my view: Barry Cox', *Broadcast*, 24 November 2000. Available at: http://www.broadcastnow.co.uk/news/multi-platform/news/in-my-view-barry-cox/1205770.article (accessed March 2012).

Crace, John, *Cracker: The Truth Behind the Fiction* (London: Boxtree, 1994).

Creeber, Glen, 'Hideously white: British television, globalisation and national identity', *Television and New Media Journal* 5/1 (February 2004), pp. 27–39.

—— *Serial Television: Big Drama on the Small Screen* (London: BFI, 2004).

—— 'It's not TV, it's online drama: the return of the intimate screen', *International Journal of Cultural Studies* 14/6 (2011), pp. 591–606.

Crompton, Sarah, 'The arts column: why we love the best TV "tecs"', *Daily Telegraph*, 13 November 2002. Available at: http://www.telegraph.co.uk/culture/tvandradio/3585701/The-arts-column-why-we-love-the-best-TV-tecs.html (accessed May 2012).

Curzon, John, 'Sam Tyler and the "New North"', in S. Lacey and R. McElroy (eds), *Life on Mars: From Manchester to New York* (Cardiff: University of Wales Press, 2012), pp. 69–78.

Davis, Helen, 'Inspector Morse and the business of crime', *Television and New Media* 2/2 (May 2001), pp. 133–48.

Day-Lewis, Sean, *Talk of Drama: Views of the Television Dramatist Now and Then* (Luton: University of Luton Press, 1998).

De Bruin, Joost, 'Young people and police series: a multicultural television audience study', *Crime Media Culture* 6/3 (2010), pp. 309–28.

Dennis, Norman, and Erdos, George, *Cultures and Crimes: Policing in Four Nations* (London: Institute for the Study of Civil Society, 2005).

Dodd, Vikram. 'Black officers to begin recruitment boycott at Met', *Guardian*, 5 October 2008. Available at: http://www.guardian.co.uk/uk/2008/oct/05/police (accessed November 2012).

Donaghy, James, 'Is there life after Life on Mars?', *Guardian*, 11 April 2007. Available at: http://www.guardian.co.uk/media/2007/apr/11/broadcasting.g2 (accessed January 2011).

Duguid, Mark, *Cracker* (London: BFI, 2009).

Dunne, Colin, 'The Jason files', *Radio Times*, 5–11 December 1992, pp. 33–4.

Dyer, Richard, *Stars* (London: BFI, 1979).

—— *Only Entertainment* (London and New York: Routledge, 1992).
Eagleton, Terry, *Literary Theory: An Introduction* (Oxford: Blackwell, 1983).
Eaton, Mary, 'A fair cop? Viewing the effects of the canteen culture in *Prime Suspect* and *Between the Lines*', in D. Kidd-Hewitt and R. Osborne (eds), *Crime and the Media: the Postmodern Spectacle* (London: Pluto, 1995), pp. 164–84.
Eco, Umberto, *The Role of the Reader: Explorations in the Semiotics of Texts* (Bloomington, IN, and London: Indiana University Press, 1979).
—— 'Innovation and repetition: between modern and post-modern aesthetics', *Daedalus* 114 (Fall 1985), pp. 161–84.
Edensor, Tim, *National Identity, Popular Culture and Everyday Life* (Oxford and New York: Berg, 2002).
Ellis, John, *Seeing Things: Television in the Age of Uncertainty* (London and New York: I.B.Tauris, 2002).
Feuer, Jane, 'Narrative form in American network television', in C. MacCabe (ed.), *High Theory/Low Culture* (Manchester: Manchester University Press, 1986), pp. 101–14.
Ffrench, Andrew, 'Lewis actor finds it's "take your dad to work day"!', *Oxford Mail*, 20 March 2009. Available at: http://www.oxfordmail.co.uk/news/4220190.Lewis_actor_finds_it_s__take_your_dad_to_work_day (accessed May 2012).
Foucault, Michel, *Discipline and Punish: The Birth of the Prison*, tr. Alan Sheridan (London: Penguin Books, 1991).
—— *The History of Sexuality*, vol. 1, tr. Robert Hurley (London: Penguin Books, 1998).
Frank, Thomas, 'The big con', *Guardian* (Review), 6 January 2001, p. 1.
Frow, John, 'Spectacle binding: on character', *Poetics Today* 7/2 (1986), pp. 227–50.
Frye, Northrop, *Anatomy of Criticism* (London: Penguin, 1957).
Garland, Jon, and Bilby, Charlotte, 'What next, dwarves? Images of police culture in *Life on Mars*', *Crime Media Culture*, 7/2 (2011), pp. 115–32.
Garner, Richard, 'Teachers blame "Life on Mars" for rise of homophobia in schools', *Belfast Telegraph*, 13 April 2007. Available at: www.belfasttelegraph.co.uk/news/education/teachers-blame-life-on-mars-for-rise-of-homophobia-in-schools (accessed July 2011).
Gauntlett, David, and Hill, Annette, *TV Living: Television Culture and Everyday Life* (London: Routledge, 1999).
Gerbner, George, and Gross, Larry, 'The scary world of TV's heavy viewer', *Psychology Today* (April 1976), pp. 89–91.
Girling, Evi, Loader, Ian, and Sparks, Richard, *Crime and Social Change in Middle England: Questions of Order in an English Town* (London: Routledge, 2000).

Gledhill, Christine, 'Pleasurable negotiations', in E. D. Pribram (ed.), *Female Spectators: Looking at Film and Television* (London: Verso, 1988), pp. 64–89.

Guardian, '*Life on Mars*', Media section, 10 January 2006. Available at: http://www.guardian.co.uk/media/2006/jan/10/firstnight.broadcasting (accessed January 2011).

Hicks, Joe, and Allen, Grahame, *A Century of Change: Trends in UK Statistics since 1900*, House of Commons research paper, 99/111 (21 December 1999). Available at: http://www.parliament.uk/documents/commons/lib/research/rp99/rp99-111.pdf (accessed March 2012).

Hills, Matt, 'The medium is the monster … or the world?', in S. Lacey and R. McElroy (eds), *Life on Mars: From Manchester to New York* (Cardiff: University of Wales Press, 2012), pp. 105–16.

Hilmes, Michele, 'Who we are, who we are not: battle of the global paradigms', in L. Parks and S. Kumar (eds), *Planet TV: A Global Television Reader* (London and New York: New York University Press, 2003), pp. 53–73.

Hobson, Dorothy, 'Making a crisis out of a drama', *Television: The Journal of the Royal Television Society*, June 1999, pp. 15–16.

Hogg, Christopher, 'Interview. Gub Neal: cracking the business of TV drama production', *Journal of British Cinema and Television* 8/1 (April 2011), pp. 118–32.

Holdsworth, Amy, *Television, Memory and Nostalgia* (Basingstoke: Palgrave Macmillan, 2011).

Hopkins, Jeff, 'Mapping of cinematic places: icons, ideology, and the power of (mis)representation', in S. C. Aitken and L. E. Zonn (eds), *Place, Power, Situation, and Spectacle: A Geography of Film* (Lanham, MD, and London: Rowman & Littlefield, 1994), pp. 47–68.

Hunt, Leon, 'Dog eat dog: *The Squeeze* and the *Sweeney* films', in Steve Chibnall and Robert Murphy (eds), *British Crime Cinema* (London and New York: Routledge, 1999), pp. 134–47.

Hutton, Will, 'Money, or the lack of it, is the root of all the BBC's evils', *Guardian*, 21 March 1999. Available at: http://www.guardian.co.uk/media/1999/mar/21/bbc (accessed September 2012).

—— 'Creativity under threat', *Guardian*, 1 August 2005. Available at: http://www.guardian.co.uk/media/2005/aug/01/broadcastng.comment (accessed September 2012).

Huyssen, Andreas, *Present Pasts: Urban Palimpsests and the Politics of Memory* (Stanford, CA: Stanford University Press, 2003).

Independent, 'No-go Britain: where, what, why', 17 April 1994. Available at: http://www.independent.co.uk/news/uk/nogo-britain-where-what-why-1370749.html (accessed February 2013).

ITV, 'The Morse legacy', http://mip.itvstudios.com/programmes/drama-comedy/893/the-morse-legacy (accessed May 2012).

Izod, John, *Myth, Mind and the Screen: Understanding the Heroes of Our Time* (Cambridge: Cambridge University Press, 2001).

Jackson, Rhona, 'The skilled viewer', in Solange Davin and Rhona Jackson (eds), *Television and Criticism* (Bristol and Chicago: Intellect Books, 2008), pp. 75–88.

Jacobs, Jason, 'The medium in crisis: Caughie, Brunsdon and the problem of US television', *Screen* 52/4 (Winter 2011), pp. 503–11.

Jauss, Hans Robert, 'Levels of identification of hero and audience', *New Literary History* 5/2 (Winter 1974), pp. 283–317.

Jermyn, Deborah, 'Women with a mission: Lynda La Plante, DCI Jane Tennison and the reinvention of British TV crime drama', *International Journal of Cultural Studies* 6/1 (2003), pp. 46–63.

—— *Prime Suspect* (London: BFI, 2010).

Johnson, Derek, 'Inviting audiences in: the spatial reorganization of production and consumption in "TV III"', *New Review of Film and Television Studies* 5/1 (2007), pp. 61–80.

Jordan, Marion, 'Realism and convention', in R. Dyer, C. Geraghty, M. Jordan, T. Lovell, R. Paterson and J. Stewart, *Coronation Street* (London: BFI, 1981).

Kanter, Jake, 'Morse prequel goes to series', *Broadcast*, 12 March 2012. Available at: http://www.broadcastnow.co.uk/news/commissioning/morse-prequel-goes-to-series/5039154.article (accessed June 2012).

Kelly, Jon, 'England riots: what's the meaning of the words behind the chaos?', BBC Online, 12 August 2011. Available at: http://www.bbc.co.uk/news/magazine-14506159 (accessed July 2012).

Kuhn, Annette, 'Women's genres', *Screen* 25/1 (Spring 1984), pp. 18–29.

—— 'Women's genres: melodrama, soap opera, and theory', in C. Brunsdon, J. D'Acci and L. Spigel (eds), *Feminist Television Criticism: A Reader* (Oxford: Oxford University Press, 1997), pp. 145–54.

Lacey, Stephen, and McElroy, Ruth (eds), *Life on Mars: From Manchester to New York* (Cardiff: University of Wales Press, 2012).

Lawson, Mark, 'Watching the detective', *Guardian*, 13 November 2000. Available at: http://www.guardian.co.uk/media/2000/nov/13/tvandradio.television3 (accessed February 2012).

Leapman, Michael, 'BBC drama chief looks to swim in the mainstream', *Independent*, 21 July 1993. Available at: http://www.independent.co.uk/news/uk/bbc-drama-chief-looks-to-swim-in-the-mainstream-michael-leapman-finds-that-the-corporations-winter-tv-schedule-hints-at-division-among-its-executives-1486116.html (accessed February 2012).

Levine, Elana, 'Teaching the politics of television culture in a "post-television" era', *Cinema Journal* 50/4 (Summer 2011), pp. 177–82.

Livingstone, Sonia, *Making Sense of Television: The Psychology of Audience Interpretation* (2nd edn, London: Routledge, 1998).

Lockyer, Daphne, 'Sir David Jason: "Maybe David Cameron will make me Minister of Laughs"', *Daily Telegraph*, 28 March 2010. Available at: http://www.telegraph.co.uk/culture/tvandradio/7531194/Sir-David-Jason-Maybe-David-Cameron-will-make-me-Minister-of-Laughs.html (accessed May 2012).

Lukács, Georg, 'The sociology of modern drama', tr. Lee Baxandall, *Tulane Drama Review* 9/4 (Summer 1965), pp. 146–70.

—— 'Narrate or describe', in Arthur Kahn (ed. and tr.), *Writer and Critic, and Other Essays* (London: Merlin Press, 1970), pp. 110–48.

Lury, Karen, 'A response to John Corner', *Screen* 48/3 (Autumn 2007), pp. 371–6.

MacCabe, Colin, 'Realism in the cinema: notes on Brechtian theses', *Screen* 15/2 (Summer 1974), pp. 7–27.

McElroy, Ruth, 'Consuming retrosexualities', in S. Lacey and R. McElroy (eds), *Life on Mars: From Manchester to New York* (Cardiff: University of Wales Press, 2012), pp. 117–29.

McLean, Gareth, 'Back to Blighty', *Radio Times*, 1–7 May 2010, pp. 10–13.

—— 'The No 1 ladies' detective agency', *Radio Times*, 10–16 March 2012, pp. 10–13.

McMahon, Kate, 'Bragg: restrictions are killing ITV', *Broadcast*, 7 May 2009. Available at http://www.broadcastnow.co.uk/news/multi-platform/news/bragg-restrictions-are-killing-itv/2027206.article (accessed February 2012).

Mankell, Henning, *The Dogs of Riga*, tr. Laurie Thompson (London: Vintage, 2009).

Martin, Philip, 'On location: *Wallander*', *Broadcast*, 26 November 2008. Available at: http://www.broadcastnow.co.uk/on-location-wallander/1935374.article (accessed October 2012).

Mason, Paul, 'Prime time punishment: the British prison and television', in D. Kidd-Hewitt and R. Osborn (eds), *Crime and the Media* (London: Pluto Press, 1995), pp. 185–205.

Massumi, Brian, *Parables for the Virtual: Movement, Affect, Sensation* (Durham, NC, and London: Duke University Press, 2002).

Meades, Jonathan, 'The genius of gesture', *The Times*, 16 November 2002.

Mepham, John, 'The ethics of quality in television', in G. Mulgan (ed.), *The Question of Quality* (London: BFI, 1990), pp. 56–72.

Midgley, Neil, 'ITV to slash drama as profits plunge', *Daily Telegraph*, 4 March 2009. Available at: http://www.telegraph.co.uk/culture (accessed February 2012).

—— 'Partners in crime', *Radio Times*, 7–13 July 2012, pp. 16–19.

Mills, Brett, '"American remake – shudder", online debates about *Life on Mars* and "British-ness"', in S. Lacey and R. McElroy (eds), *Life on Mars: From*

Manchester to New York (Cardiff: University of Wales Press, 2012), pp. 133–44.

Mittell, Jason, 'A cultural approach to television genre theory', *Cinema Journal* 40/3 (Spring 2001), pp. 3–24.

Mizejewski, Linda, *Hardboiled and High Heeled: The Woman Detective in Popular Culture* (London and New York: Routledge, 2004).

Mulvey, Laura, 'Visual pleasure and narrative cinema', *Screen* 16/3 (Autumn 1975), pp. 6–18.

Nelson, Robin, *State of Play: Contemporary 'High-End' TV Drama* (Manchester: Manchester University Press, 2007).

Nuttall, A. D., *Why Does Tragedy Give Pleasure?* (Oxford: Clarendon Press, 1996).

OFCOM, *OFCOM's Second Public Service Broadcasting Review: Putting Audiences First* (Final Statement, 21 January 2009). Available at: http://stakeholders.ofcom.org.uk/binaries/consultations/psb2_phase2/statement/psb2statement.pdf (accessed May 2012).

—— *OFCOM Communications Market Report*. Available at: http://stakeholders.ofcom.org.uk/binaries/research/cmr/cmr12/CMR_UK2012.pdf (accessed November 2012).

O'Sullivan, Sean, 'UK policing and its television portrayal: "law and order" ideology or modernising agenda?', *Howard Journal* 44/5 (2005), pp. 504–26.

Pace, Roberto, 'Broadcasting trends', in Julian Friedmann and Pere Roca (eds), *Writing Long-Running Television Series* (Madrid: Media Business School Publication, 1994), pp. 167–74.

Palmer, Gareth, *Discipline and Liberty* (Manchester: Manchester University Press. 2003).

Patten, Lord Chris, 'Is the BBC as good as it could be?' (Speech to the Oxford Media Convention), 25 January 2012. Available at: http://www.guardian.co.uk/oxfordmediaconvention/lord-patten-of-barnes-is-the-bbc-as-good-as-it-could-be (accessed May 2012).

Pearce, Lynn, 'Review of *Engaging Characters*', *Screen* 37/4 (Winter, 1996), pp. 415–18.

Petrie, Duncan, and Willis, Janet (eds), *Television and the Household* (London: BFI, 1995).

Phillips, William, 'Tales of take up', *Television: The Journal of the Royal Television Society*, July 1999, pp. 24–5.

Pickering, Michael, and Keightley, Emily, 'The modalities of nostalgia', *Current Sociology* 54/6 (November 2006), pp. 919–41.

Pidduck, Julianne, 'Of windows and country walks: frames of space and movement in 1990s Austen adaptations', *Screen* 39/4 (Winter 1998), pp. 381–400.

Pines, Jim, 'Black cops and black villains in film and TV crime fiction', in D. Kidd Hewitt and R. Osborne (eds), *Crime and the Media: The Post-Modern Spectacle* (London: Pluto Press, 1995), pp. 67–77.

Piper, Helen, '"How long since you were last alive?": Fitz and Tennison ten years on', *Screen* 50/2 (Spring 2009), pp. 233–50.

—— 'Vintage entertainment: nostalgia, the archive, and the disappearing pleasures of collective television viewing', *Journal of British Cinema and Television* 8/3 (2011), pp. 411–29.

—— 'Lost in participation', *Screen* 52/4 (Winter 2011), pp. 512–21.

Plater, Alan, 'Speaking to nations', in T. Elsaesser, J. Simons and L. Bronk (eds), *Writing for the Medium* (Amsterdam: Amsterdam University Press, 1994), pp. 118–30.

Pool, Hannah, 'Question time: scriptwriter Jimmy McGovern', *Guardian*, 1 November 2007. Available at: http://www.guardian.co.uk/media/2007/nov/01/culture.itv?INTCMP=SRCH (accessed September 2012).

Potter, Dennis, MacTaggart Lecture, Edinburgh International Television Festival, 1993.

Propp, Vladimir, *Morphology of the Folktale*, tr. Laurence Scott (Austin, TX, and London: University of Texas Press, 1968).

Rafter, Nicole, *Shots in the Mirror: Crime Films and Society* (Oxford: Oxford University Press, 2006).

Rampton, James, 'Kenneth Branagh: the stunning, troubled world of the "Norse Morse"', *Daily Telegraph*, 1 November 2008. Available at: http://www.telegraph.co.uk/culture/3562765/Kenneth-Branagh-The-stunning-troubled-world-of-the-Norse-Morse.html (accessed November 2012).

Ramsland, Katherine, *The Criminal Mind: A Writer's Guide to Forensic Psychology* (Cincinnati, OH: Writer's Digest Books, 2002).

Reijnders, Stijn, 'Watching the detectives: inside the guilty landscapes of Inspector Morse, Baantjer and Wallander', *European Journal of Communication* 24/2 (2009), pp. 165–81.

—— 'Places of the imagination: an ethnography of the TV detective tour', *Cultural Geographies* 17/1 (2010), pp. 37–52.

Ricoeur, Paul, *Time and Narrative*, vol. 1, tr. K. McLaughlin and D. Pellauer (Chicago: University of Chicago Press, 1984).

Ripley, Mike, 'Obituary: R. D. Wingfield', *Guardian*, 4 August 2007. Available at: http://www.guardian.co.uk/news/2007/aug/04/guardianobituaries.obituaries (accessed March 2012).

Scannell, Paddy, 'Public service broadcasting: the history of a concept', in A. Goodwin and G. Whannel (eds), *Understanding Television* (London: Routledge, 1990), pp. 11–29.

Screenwatch, http://www.attentional.com/screenwatch/viewings (accessed January 2013).

Shelley, Jim, '*Scott & Bailey* review', *Mirror*, 12 March 2012. Available at: http://www.mirror.co.uk/tv/tv-previews/scott-and-bailey-review-women-detectives-759325 (accessed January 2013).
Silverstone, Roger, *Television and Everyday Life* (London: Routledge, 1994).
Smith, Chris, 'The big switch', *Television: The Journal of the Royal Television Society*, October 1999, pp. 7–12.
Smith, Murray, 'Altered states: character and emotional response in the cinema', *Cinema Journal* 33/4 (1994), pp. 34–56.
—— *Engaging Characters: Fiction, Emotion, and the Cinema* (Oxford: Oxford University Press, 1995).
—— '(Dis)engaging characters: a response to Lynne Pearce', *Screen* 40/3 (1999), pp. 358–62.
Sparks, Richard F., *Television and the Drama of Crime: Moral Tales and the Place of Crime in Public Life* (Buckingham: Open University Press, 1992).
—— 'Inspector Morse: the last enemy', in George Brandt (ed.), *British Television Drama in the 1980s* (Cambridge: Cambridge University Press, 1993), pp. 86–102.
Strauss, Will, 'Anthony Dod Mantle interview', *Broadcast*, 13 May 2009. Available at: http://www.broadcastnow.co.uk/anthony-dod-mantle-interview/1331315.article (accessed October 2012).
Sutcliffe, Tom, 'The weekend's TV', *Guardian*, 30 May 2011. Available at: http://www.independent.co.uk/arts-entertainment/tv/reviews/the-weekends-tv-scott-amp-bailey-sun-itv1brpaul-mertons-birth-of-hollywood-fri-bbc2-2290736.html (accessed January 2013).
—— 'It isn't a crime to laugh at the police', *Guardian*, 17 June 2011. Available at: http://www.independent.co.uk/voices/columnists/thomas-sutcliffe/tom-sutcliffe-it-isnt-a-crime-to-laugh-at-the-police-2298487.html?origin=internalSearch (accessed January 2013).
—— 'The weekend's viewing', *Independent*, 9 July 2012. Available at: http://www.independent.co.uk/arts-entertainment/tv/reviews/the-weekends-viewing (accessed October 2012).
Sydney-Smith, Susan, *Beyond Dixon of Dock Green: Early British Police Series* (London: I.B.Tauris, 2002).
—— 'Changing places: touring the British crime film', *Tourist Studies* 6/1 (2006), pp. 79–94.
Tapper, Michael, 'More than ABBA and skinny-dipping in mountain lakes: Swedish dystopia, Henning Mankell and the British Wallander series', *Film International* 38/7/2 (2009), pp. 60–9.
Tavor Bannet, Eve, *Structuralism and the Logic of Dissent: Barthes, Derrida, Foucault, Lacan* (Basingstoke: Macmillan Press, 1989).
Thomas, Liz, 'Jack Frost hangs up his hat as David Jason bids emotional farewell to one of TV's most beloved detectives', *Daily Mail*, 6 April 2010. Available

at: http://www.dailymail.co.uk/tvshowbiz/article-1263827/Jack-Frost-hangs-hat-David-Jason-bids-emotional-farewell-TVs-beloved-detectives.html (accessed November 2011).

Thomas, Lyn, 'In love with Inspector Morse: feminist subculture and quality television', in C. Brunsdon, J. D'Acci and L. Spigel (eds), *Feminist Television Criticism: A Reader* (Oxford: Oxford University Press, 1997), pp. 184–204.

Thompson, Kirsten Moana, *Crime Films: Investigating the Scene* (London: Wallflower Press, 2007).

Thumim, Janet, 'Women at work: popular drama on British television 1955–1960', in J. Thumim (ed.), *Small Screens, Big Ideas: Television in the 1950s* (London and New York: I.B.Tauris, 2002), pp. 207–22.

Tither, Helen, 'TV cop dramas irritated me, so I made my own, says the former Detective Inspector behind Scott and Bailey', *Manchester Evening News*, 22 June 2011. Available at: http://www.manchestereveningnews.co.uk/whats-on/film-and-tv/tv-cop-dramas-irritated-me-863725 (accessed January 2013).

Tulloch, John, *Watching Television Audiences: Cultural Theories and Methods* (London: Arnold, 2000).

Vaz, Tina, 'The Masterpiece Mystery! Interview' (2009). Available at: http://www.pbs.org/wgbh/masterpiece/lewis/whatelyandfox.html (accessed May 2012).

West, Naomi, 'Kevin Whately and Laurence Fox on the new series of Lewis', *Daily Telegraph*, 23 April 2010. Available at: http://www.telegraph.co.uk/culture/tvandradio/7625419/Kevin-Whately-and-Laurence-Fox-on-the-new-series-of-Lewis.html (accessed February 2012).

Williams, Raymond, *Marxism and Literature* (Oxford: Oxford University Press, 1977).

—— *Raymond Williams on Television: Selected Writings*, ed. Alan O'Connor (London and New York: Routledge, 1989).

Wilson, Benji, 'Review', *Daily Telegraph*, 4 Jan 2010. Available at: http://www.telegraph.co.uk/culture/tvandradio/6932711/Wallander-BBC-One-Poirot (accessed October 2012).

Wollaston, Sam, 'The weekend's TV: Lewis', *Guardian*, 25 February 2008. Available at: http://www.guardian.co.uk/culture/tvandradioblog/2008/feb/25/theweekendstv2?INTCMP=SRCH (accessed May 2012).

—— 'TV review', *Guardian*, 29 May 2011. Available at: http://www.guardian.co.uk/tv-and-radio/2011/may/29/scott-bailey-tv-review (accessed January 2013).

Wollen, Peter, '*North by North-West*: a morphological analysis', *Film Form* 1/1 (1976), pp. 19–34.

Wood, Robin, *Hollywood from Vietnam to Reagan* (New York: Columbia University Press, 1986).

Wright, Will, *Six Guns and Society: A Structural Study of the Western* (Berkeley, CA, and London: University of California Press, 1975).

Index

Note: excludes authors cited directly, for which see bibliography; bold type denotes chapter ranges and detailed analysis.

Aiken, Joan, 153
Alexander, Bruce, 52
alignment, 36, 39, 43, 48, 70, 74, 82, 114, 116, 118, 119, 128, 148
  optical, 36–37, 70, 75, 81, 83, 84, 94, 109
  spatial, 37, 62, 70, 75, 83, 84, 119, 132, 134
All3Media, 17
allegiance (moral), 31, 37–39, 43, 52, 66, 67, 72, 74, 75, 76, 79, 81, 82, 84, 116, 119, 126, 132, 134, 148, 154
American drama series, 16, 20, 21, 144
American influence, 143–145
Amuka-Bird, Nikki, 124
Andrew, Dean, 93
Angel of the North, 117
Arnott, DS (character), 134–135
Ashes to Ashes, 22, 25–26, 88, 103–106

Baantjer, 16
Bacon, Francis, 59–60
Bailey, Rachel (character), 130–133
Barker, Emily, 112
Bartlett, Kate, 167n
Battersby, Roy, 47
Bazalgette, Peter, 159n
Bentham, Jeremy, 147
Bill, The, 7, 23
Billing, Paul, 67
Bird, Antonia, 84
Birt, John, 10,
Blethyn, Brenda, 108
Bloody Sunday, 99
Bodies, 30
Bordwell, David, 36
Bowie, David, 125
Bradbury, Malcolm, 48
Brady, Orla, 114
Bragg, Melvyn, 18
Branagh, Kenneth, 107, 108, 111, 113, 116, 121
British Academy of Film & Television Awards (BAFTAs), 6, 88
British Audience Research Bureau (BARB), 8, 14
British Broadcasting Corporation (BBC), 5, 10, 16, 17, 19, 20, 98, 102, 108
  BBC1 (channel), 5, 7, 11, 14, 15, 21, 87
  BBC2 (channel), 7, 12, 15
  BBC4 (channel), 15
  BBC Scotland, 108
Brown, Warren, 125
Buchanan, Colin, 11
Buck, Michelle, 55
Bullmore, Amelia, 130
Burt, Chris, 55
Butterfly Collectors, 142

Cagney and Lacey, 76, 130
Callow, Simon, 55
Camberwick Green, 96

Cameron, David, 106, 159n
Campaign for Quality Television (CQTV), 12, 22
Campbell, Esther May, 116
Cardiac Arrest, 30
Carlton Television, 16, 55
Carlyle, Robert, 85
Case Sensitive, 108
Casualty, 9
Central Television, 6
Channel 4, 7, 15, 16, 20, 87
Chapman, John, 84
Chinese Detective, The, 123
Chipchase Castle, 117
Churchett, Stephen, 55, 57, 64
City Central, 23
City of Vice, 22
Civitas, 146
Clarke, Warren, 11
Cleeves, Ann, 108, 118
Cohen, Danny, 21
Cold War, 112
Collins, Elaine, 167n
Coltrane, Robbie, 67, 84
Communications Act (2003), 17
Compston, Martin, 134
Conservative Party, 68, 106
Cops, The, 134, 142, 169n
Cornwell, Patricia, 67
Cottan, Richard, 167n
council estates, 45, 110, 128, 130, 134, 135, 140, 142
Coyle, Richard, 83
Cracker, 2, 7, 10, 17, 22, 29, 31, 41, 42, 60, 66, 67, 72, **77–86**, 101, 127, 148, 149, 151, 152, 158n, 164n
  'Big Crunch, The', 77, 78, 80, 82
  'Brotherly Love, 77, 81
  'Mad Woman In The Attic, The', 78, 149
  'Men Should Weep', 80, 84, 151
  'Nine-Eleven', 77, 78, 83–84
  'One Day a Lemming Will Fly', 81
  'To Be A Somebody', 77, 80, 85
  'To Say I Love You', 77, 79, 152
  'White Ghost', 77
Cranitch, Lorcan, 80
crime
  as narrative event 113, 117, 127, 128, 130
  rates of, 145, 147
  as sign of social malaise, 66, 113, 116, 142, 143, 146
  spaces of 142, 143
  see also deviance
Crimewatch, 26, 151
Criminal Justice, 20
Cross, Neil, 122

Dalziel and Pascoe, 11
DCI Banks, 108
Deasy, Frank, 67
Denton (fictional town), 45, 46, 47, 56, 141
Denton, Charles, 10, 157n
deviance, 2, 43, 81, 85, 86, 138, 147, 149, 150, 154; *see also* crime
Dexter, 16
Dexter, Colin, 55
Digital Video Disc/Digital Versatile Disc (DVD), 9, 40
dissent, 43, 65, 67, 82, 85, 86, 121, 126, 135, 146, 153, 154
Dixon of Dock Green, 53
Dogme film movement, 108
Drake, Alex (character), 103–106
Dupin (character), 28
Duran Duran, 104
Duration, 41, 43

Eccleston, Christopher, 80
Elba, Idris, 123, 125, 127
Endeavour, 21, 22
Endemol, 17
engagement (of viewer), 4, 23–43, 119, 144
Equity, 11
everyday, 7, 28, 65, 85, 107, 137, 138, 141, 144, 148
  culture, 91, 95–96, 100, 137, 140
  discourse, 139
  experience of crime, 111, 128
  representation of, 89, 90, 100, 109, 110, 111, 130, 139, 140
Eyre, Richard, 159n

fear (of crime), 61, 128, 139, 142, 143, 145, 146, 148
Featherstone, Jane, 103

femininity, 69, 70–72, 76, 97, 105, 131, 133; *see also* gender; women
Ferris, Pam, 126,
Fincham, Peter, 18
Finlay, Frank, 74
Fitz/Fitzgerald, Dr (character), 29, 42, **77–86**, 101, 121, 127, 149, 151, 152
Five Days, 20
Flanagan, Anthony, 83
forensics, 54, 67, 77–78, 87, 89, 95, 151, 152
Fox, Laurence, 56, 62
Foyle, Inspector (character), 29
Foyle's War, 18, 21, 22, 89
Freemasonry, 68, 71, 124
Freeview, 14, 15
Front, Rebecca, 56
Frost, Jack (character), 29, 30, 42, 44–55, 65, 72, 111, 120, 135, 143, 149

Galloping Gourmet, The, 96
Gangsters, 123
Gardner, John, 153
Garrow's Law, 22
Gates, DCI (character), 134–135
gender, 32, 35, 68, 71, 72, 105, 124, 133, 154; *see also* femininity; masculinity; women
genre, 2, 3, 10, 65, 70, 71, 74, 94, 95, 116, 123, 124, 137, 140, 144, 153, 154
Gentle Touch, The, 68, 71, 93
Get Carter, 88
Glenister, Philip, 87, 97, 98
Glenister, Robert, 50
globalisation 140, 141
Good, the Bad and the Ugly, The, 98
Grade, Michael, 18
Graham, Matthew, 87, 102
Granada Television, 16, 66, 67

Halford, Alison, 68, 163n
Hardy, Robert, 55
Harness, Peter, 167n
Harries, Andy, 158n
Hathaway, James (character), 55–65, 120
Heartbeat, 99
Henriksson, Krister, 108
hero (detective as), 25–30, 34, 41, 52, 64, 72, 83, 86, 105, 113, 116, 120, 123, 127, 134, 135, 147, 154
Hill, Reginald, 11
Hillsborough stadium disaster, 85, 99
Hillsborough, 165n
Holman, Clare, 64
Home Box Office (HBO), 21
homophobia, 97, 98, 166n
Hunt, Gene (character), 25–26, 31, 72, 87–106, 119
Hunt, Jay, 159n

identification, 34–39, 72, 154
independent production companies, 17
individualism, 29, 30, 41, 92
Inspector George Gently, 101
Inspector Montalbano, 16
Inspector Morse, 6, 7, 10, 18, 21, 22, 23, 44, 45, 46, 48, 55, 56, 61, 63, 66, 67, 77, 138, 148, 153
  'Remorseful Day, The' 12
International Emmy Awards, 88
internet, 7, 54, 140
iPlayer, 19
IRA, The, 96, 99
ITV (institution), 5, 6, 9, 12, 16, 17, 20, 21, 22, 55, 66, 77
ITV (channel), 5, 6, 7, 10, 11, 13, 14, 15, 18, 21, 44, 48, 130
ITV3, 15, 44
ITV Studios, 16, 21

Jackson, Michael, 7, 157n
Jakobson, Roman, 27
James, Lennie, 49, 134, 169n
Jason, David, 44, 49, 52, 54, 149, 159n
Jones, Suranne, 130
Jowell, Tessa, 15
Juliet Bravo, 68

Kamakawiwo'ole, Israel, 101
Keitel, Harvey, 97
Killing, The, 15, 16, 111
Kiszko, Stefan, 82–83, 165n
Kitchen, Michael, 18
Kongos, John, 99
Kudos Productions, 17, 87

La Plante, Lynda, 67, 72
Labour Party, 15, 19, 106
Lady Audley's Secret, 28, 160n
Lancaster, Marshall, 93
landscape, 13, 77, 108, 110, 111, 113, 117, 118, 128, 138, 139, 141, 142, 148
Lassgård, Rolf, 108, 112
Latvia, 110–111
Lawrence, Stephen, 168n
Left Bank Pictures, 17, 108
Leon, David, 119
Lewis, 2, 21, 22, 44, 46, 55–65, 92, 111, 128, 133
  'Allegory of Love', 57, 61
  'And the Moonbeams Kiss the Sea', 57
  'Counter Culture Blues', 57, 60
  'Dark Matter', 56, 60
  'Dead of Winter, The', 57, 62, 63
  'Falling Darkness', 59, 60
  'Fearful Symmetry', 60, 65
  'Generation of Vipers', 64
  'Gift of Promise, The', 61
  'Indelible Stain, The', 60, 61
  'Intelligent Design', 64
  'Life Born of Fire', 56, 62, 63
  'Old, Unhappy, Far Off Things', 59, 64
  Pilot episode, 56, 57, 62
  'Point of Vanishing, The', 57, 60, 64
  'Quality of Mercy, The', 57
  'Soul of Genius, The', 57
  'Whom the Gods Would Destroy', 60, 61, 63
  'Wild Justice', 57–60, 61
  'Your Sudden Death Question', 62
Lewis, Kate, 167n
Lewis, Robbie (character), 29, 116, 55–65, 116
Lewis, Russell, 21, 55
Life on Mars, 2, 22, 25, 26, 36, 72, 87–106, 158n
  fans of, 102–103, 138
Lindisfarne, 117
Line of Duty, 2, 122, 124, 134–135, 149
Logan, Phyllis, 47, 111
London, 16, 68, 106, 122, 123, 124, 128, 129, 139
Luther, 2, 111, 122–129, 130, 133, 139, 148, 149
Luther, John (character), 29, 111, 122–129

Mackintosh, Steven, 125,
Malling, Søren, 111
Malton, Jackie, 67
Manchester, 16, 68, 77, 83, 87, 90, 91, 92, 93, 102, 106, 130, 133
Mankell, Henning, 107, 108, 113, 116,
Mantle, Anthony Dod, 108
masculinity, 64, 69, 71, 72, 88, 97, 103, 106, 129, 130, 133, 146; *see also* gender
McGovern, Jimmy, 78, 84, 164n, 165n
mediation, 24, 39, 43, 89, 100, 101, 107, 120, 130, 132, 140
Mercurio, Jed, 134
metalanguage, 24–25, 99
Metropolitan Police Force (London), 124
Miller, Sam, 169n
MIPTV, 21
Mirren, Helen, 67, 68, 72, 74, 76
Mistresses, 131
morality (of detective/crime fiction), 24, 25, 30, 31, 46, 49, 65, 67, 69, 70, 73, 75, 76, 80, 81, 83, 85, 86, 93, 96, 99, 125, 134, 149, 151, 152, 153, 155
Morecambe and Wise Show, The, 96
Morrison, Jon, 119
Morse, Inspector (character), 12, 17, 21, 29, 42, 54, 60, 62, 64, 77, 88, 116, 118, 119, 120
Mosaku, Wunmi, 119
Moses Jones, 123
Mullett, Superintendent (character), 30, 46, 48, 49, 50, 52–53, 55. 61, 148, 151
Murdoch, Elisabeth, 19
Murray, Gill (character), 130–133, 151
music (soundtrack), 99–100, 103, 113
music (theme), 112, 120
myth, 25, 27–28, 60, 61
mythology, 27, 60, 127, 139

nation, 1, 2, 140, 141, 144
  spaces of, 111, 128, 139, 140, 141
  state of the, 113, 136
nation state, 147
national audience, 111, 144, 153
National Health Service (NHS), The, 145
national identity, 89, 140, 144

National Television Awards, 6, 88
Neal, Gub, 77, 78, 84, 159n
News at Ten, The, 17, 158n
Nine o'Clock News, The, 7
Nordic noir, 110, 118; *see also* Scandinavian crime drama
Northern Film and Media, 117
nostalgia, 88, 95, 100–102

OFCOM, 17, 19, 20, 21
Oldham, 130
ONdigital, 14
Only Fools and Horses, 162n
Open All Hours, 162n
Oxford, 45, 55, 56, 57, 58, 59, 60, 61, 92, 139
Oxford University, 56, 57, 59

Panopticon/panopticism, 147, 150, 171n
Parkes, Shaun, 123
Patten, Lord Chris, 20
Patterson, James, 67
Perry Mason, 7
Pharaoh, Ashley, 87, 165n
Pitt, Nick, 11
Plater, Alan, 2
Poe, Edgar Allen, 28
police force, 6, 123, 148, 149
  corruption in, 125, 134–135, 148
  as national institution, 49, 145, 147
Police National Computer (PNC), 131
Police! Camera! Action!, 153
Postlethwaite, Pete, 142
Potter, Dennis, 153
Pride and Prejudice, 11
Prime Suspect, 2, 10, 13, 17, 31, 41, 60, **66–77**, 78, 79, 86, 88, 113, 120, 124, 128, 147, 151, 153, 154, 158n, 164n
  Prime Suspect 2, 68–69
  Prime Suspect 3, 71, 72
  Prime Suspect 4 – 'The Scent of Darkness', 68, 72, 73, 163n
  Prime Suspect 4 – The Lost Child, 72
  Prime Suspect 5 – Errors of Judgement, 68, 70
  Prime Suspect 6 – The Last Witness, 13, 70, 71, 74, 153
  Prime Suspect 7 – The Final Act, 17, **73–77**, 86
private/public conflict, 28–31, 72, 74, 110, 113–117, 119–121, 125–126, 130–133
Producer Choice, 10

quality television, 13, 14, 16, 17, 22, 107, 144

race/racism, 16, 32, 49, 66, 78, 85, 93, 113, 122–125, 137, 148
Railway Arms, The, (fictional location), 91, 94, 106
Railway Arms, The, (internet fan forum), 102, 103, 165n, 166n
realism, 25–30, 109, 128, 130, 152; *see also* social realism
recognition/re-recognition, 36, 39, 40–43, 50, 83, 104, 105
Red Productions, 17, 130
Reeves, Saskia, 111, 124
Reith, Lord John, 11, 144, 157n
Rhodes, 10
Rhys, Paul, 128
riots, 66, 143
Ritter, Paul, 120
Rizzoli & Isles, 16
romantic attraction, 54, 63–65, 72, 111, 119–120, 124, 126
Royal Television Society, 15
Ruth Rendell Mysteries, The, 7
Rutman, Paul, 167n

Scandinavian crime drama, 16, 108, 109, 110; *see also* Nordic Noir
Scott & Bailey, 2, 21, 29, 122, 129–133, 151
Scott, Janet (character), 129, 130–133
serial form/seriality, 9, 29, 39–43, 112, 119, 125, 131
serial killers, 67, 79, 127
Shankar, Ananda, 99
Shed Media, 17
Sherlock, 28
Shindler, Nicola, 130
Shine Group, 17
Silence of the Lambs, The, 67
Simm, John, 87, 100
Sky Television/BSkyB, 15, 16
Smart, Sarah, 115
Smith, Chris, 15

Smith, Murray, **35–39**; *see also* structure of sympathy
social anxiety, 2, 16, 96, 110, 111, 136, 142, 143, 146, 149, 151, 152, 155
social class, 32, 63, 65, 89, 90, 91, 98, 137, 152
social media, 19, 134
social realism, 2, 6, 66, 139; *see also* realism
Sopranos, The, 16
South Bank Show, The, 18
Spangen, 16
spectatorship, 32–43, 138–139, 145
Spielberg, Stephen, 78
Spiral, 16
Stanhope, Vera (character), 108, **117–121**
Stevenson, Juliet, 55
Stranglers, The, 25
Strong, Mark, 71
structure of feeling, 137–138
structure of sympathy, **34–39**, 74; *see also* Murray Smith
Sveriges Television (STV), 108
Sweeney! 95
Sweeney, The, 88, 124
Swinden, Katie, 122

Taylor, Diane, 130
Teletext, 15
television broadcasting, 136, 137, 144
  digital, 14, 15, 16, 111
  multiplatform 5
  public service, 11, 17, 19, 20, 144
  satellite/cable, 7, 8, 9, 14, 15
television licence fee, 11, 20
Tennison, Jane (character), 29, **67–77**, 83, 86, 93, 120, 121, 124, 130, 133, 151, 154, 164n
Thatcher, Margaret, 66
Thaw, Abigail, 21
Thaw, John, 21, 54
Tiger Aspect Productions, 17
Timmer, Damien, 55, 159n
Tomlinson, Ricky, 80
Touch of Frost, A, 2, 6, 7, 8, 12, 13, 14, 18, **44–55**, 66, 67, 70, 73, 111, 113, 120, 141, 148, 151
  'Appropriate Adults', 53
  'Benefit of the Doubt', 50, 54
  'Care and Protection', 46, 52
  'Close Encounters', 45, 50
  'Conclusions', 46
  'Dancing In the Dark', 45
  'Dead End', 49
  'Dead Male One', 45
  'Deep Waters', 45
  'Endangered Species', 46, 47
  'Fun Time for Swingers', 46
  'Held In Trust', 45, 46, 51, 53
  'Hidden Truth', 45, 47, 48, 51, 53, 143
  'House Calls', 157n
  'If Dogs Run Free', 46, 53, 111
  'Keys to the Car', 46
  'Line of Fire', 46
  'Minority of One', 45, 49, 52, 169n
  'Mistaken Identity', 53
  'No Other Love', 46
  'No Refuge', 46, 50
  'Not with Kindness', 29
  'Paying the Price', 47
  'Penny for the Guy', 46, 48
  'Private Lives', 46, 47
  'Unknown Soldiers', 46
  'Widows and Orphans', 46, 47, 50
Trier, Lars von, 108
Tutti Frutti, 84
TV3, 13, 14, 19
Tyler, Sam (character), 36, **87–106**
Tyne Tees Television, 16

Ultravox, 103
Uriah Heep, **99**

Vera, 2, 21, 29, 31, 37, 108, 117–121, 130, 141, 148
  'Ghost Position, The', 119, 120
  'Hidden Depths', 117
  'Little Lazarus', 119
  'Sandancers', 117
  'Silent Voices', 117, 119, 120
Video Cassette Recorder (VCR), 8, 15, 19

Wainwright, Sally, 130
Wallander, 2, 16, **107–121**, 122, 149
  'Before the Frost', 115
  'Dogs of Riga', 109, 112, 117
  'Event In Autumn, An', 111, 115
  'Faceless Killers', 109, 111, 112, 113, 114

Wallander – *Continued*
'Fifth Woman, The', 109, 114
'Firewall', 112, 114
'Man Who Smiled, The', 114, 120
'One Step Behind', 108, 114
'Sidetracked', 108, 113
Wallander, Kurt (character), 29, 35, 107–121, 127, 139
Walters, Minette, 67
West, Timothy, 55
westerns, 60, 61, 97, 104, 141–142
Whately, Kevin, 55, 63
White, Arthur, 54
White, Liz, 93
Wilson, Ruth, 125
Wingfield, R.D., 54
Wire, The, 16, 20, 123
Wire in the Blood, 17
Wives and Daughters, 11
Wolcott, 123
Wollheim, Richard, 35
women
as detective characters, 68–73, 76, 93, 103, 110, 124, 129–133
as production team, 130
in the workplace, 133
see also femininity; gender
Woodeson, Nicholas, 51–52
World Productions, 134
Writers' Guild, The, 11

Yellow Bird Productions, 108
Yentob, Alan, 12
Yorkshire Television, 16
YouTube, 19

Z Cars, 28, 142
Zenith Productions, 10